TALL TALES

TALL TALES

The Life of a Professional Hunter in the Zambezi Valley

by

Buzz Charlton

SAFARI PRESS

Charlton, Buzz

Second edition

Safari Press

2019, Long Beach, California

ISBN 978-1-57157-529-6

Library of Congress Catalog Card Number: 2018939126

10 9 8 7 6 5 4 3 2

Printed in China

This Book Is Dedicated to Zoe and Jessica, My Gorgeous Girls

Jesse having a bath, Charara, 2017.

Zoe and Jesse in the Manyemu River, Dande, 2015.

Zoe and her first catfish, Charara, 2017.

I worry that with rampant poaching, poor governmental management, and, sadly, a misunderstanding of the benefits of hunting, not only will our magnificent wildlife be destroyed, but the glorious wilderness where I have been so privileged to work and call home for the better part of my life will also disappear. I fear that in its place will one day be only maize and cotton fields.

I sincerely hope my daughters will be able to follow in my footsteps, not necessarily by hunting elephants and buffaloes, but by being able to walk through the wildness of the Zambezi Valley outside the parks and to enjoy nature at its finest. I also hope that they will be able to hold their heads high and say that their father was a hunter, and that he hunted, as do most hunters, not to destroy all forms of wildlife but to ensure that, through a system of selective and regulated culling, wildlife will thrive into the future.

My greatest wish, though, is that we will be able to walk in these wonderful wilderness places together.

Table of Contents

Foreword by Richard Harland vii
Preface ix
Acknowledgments and Thanks xi
Introduction xiii
Chapter 1 My First Buffalo 1
Chapter 2 Makoni, the Almost Complete Professional 5
Chapter 3 Practical 15
Chapter 4 Zambezi 18
Chapter 5 Buffalo Hunting 33
Chapter 6 The Tale of Bernard's Ankle 50
Chapter 7 Ovid 58
Chapter 8 Elephant Hunting 60
Chapter 9 Cliff Hanging 80
Chapter 10 Run Faster, Madam! 86
Chapter 11 The Luc Elephant Saga 90
Chapter 12 Smelly Affair 104
Chapter 13 Criton's Close Call 110
Chapter 14 Elephant Recoveries 123
Chapter 15 My Worst Safari 131
Chapter 16 Cat Hunting 139
Chapter 17 Never Pull a Leopard by Its Tail 155
Chapter 18 Protecting the Crown Jewels 161
Chapter 19 A Healthy Respect for Gravity 167
Chapter 20 Sven and Magnus, the Perfect Clients 177
Chapter 21 Race against a Dead Lion 186
Chapter 22 Crispen and the Hornbill 190
Chapter 23 Dangers on Land and Water 194
Chapter 24 Hippos and Crocs 205
Chapter 25 Michelle's Introduction to Africa 218
Chapter 26 Norbert Hansen 225
Chapter 27 Ike and Kate 234
Chapter 28 Mike Jines 244
Chapter 29 Kelly Gill 258
Chapter 30 Marty and Sue Vick 263
Chapter 31 Rob Jolly 275
Chapter 32 Family Hunts 286
Chapter 33 Tribute to My Trackers 306
Chapter 34 Conclusion 329

Foreword

As the frontiers of scientific discovery expand, they reveal the origins of the universe, galaxies, stars, and planets such as our own. Likewise, through an understanding of the origins of life and the randomness of selection—thank Charles Darwin for this—we can follow the fascinating evolution of our own species with greater accuracy as more and more evidence comes to light.

Thus far, it seems safe to say that somewhere, sometime, a prehominid species discovered the benefits of animal flesh in the diet as opposed to simply eating vegetation, and here began our hunt for other animals to eat. Vegetarian primates remained largely confined to forested and well-wooded habitats where food was abundant, while our meat-hungry ancestors became adventurous and hunted out of the forest and onto the savanna, where other animals were plentiful. Evolution, ever so slowly, found the early hunter/gatherer hominids using tools and developing into two-legged, large-brained, inventive creatures who, hundreds of thousands of years later, occupy much of their little planet today. No matter how far we have come, the inborn, natural desire or instinct to hunt other creatures remains embedded in most humans today . . .

Though it is underutilized and attacked by some who are totally ignorant of their own origins!

The standard-bearers of this proud heritage are today's modern hunters, and as a group they represent those long-lost Paleozoic hunter-leaders, the ones to whom we all owe our ancestry. Among those who carry the standard for modern-day hunting is James "Buzz" Charlton, a man who stands out as one of Africa's most experienced, talented, and acclaimed professional hunters active today. He is a specialist in the niche of hunting Africa's "dangerous game," a man respected and loved by hundreds of his safari clients, their wives, and their children for his quick sense of humour, natural charm, and deep sincerity. His total lack of ego puts one at ease immediately, and the confidence and calmness he exudes in tight spots with big game are a measure of his finely honed hunting skills.

Just like the safari clients who have shared campfires with him over the past twenty-five years, I, too, have had the huge pleasure of spending time in one of the Dande Safari Area hunting camps with Buzz and several of his clients mentioned in this book. What a fine bunch they are, gentlemen one and all. One measure of the quality of a safari operator and his hunting teams is the number of returning clients. CM Safaris (Buzz Charlton & Myles McCallum) sure have a top-rating in this department! As you read the captivating stories here, you will understand why.

In the mid-1960s I hunted elephants for their ivory in the Zambezi Valley, including in the Dande area. Then shortly after Zimbabwe gained independence in 1980, Dande was my safari concession. At the time there were reasonable numbers of game animals . . . as well as landmines on some of the bush tracks, leftover gifts from the Rhodesian Bush War! Visiting the same area fifty years after my first hunting trip, it was so apparent that the presence of CM Safaris in Dande, with its highly successful Dande Antipoaching Unit (DAPU) financed by the safari business, has resulted in far better numbers of most species and sustainable hunting quotas. It has not been an easy ride, and we can admire Buzz, Myles, and their professional hunters, trackers, and everyone on the team for their perseverance in spite of the many demands—physical, financial, and political—made on them. This is Africa, remember! The team at CM Safaris is a first-class example of "hunters are the best conservationists."

What you hold in your hands is a wonderful collection of stories and insights from Buzz's adventures over the last twenty-five years. As I read through the stories in this book, I relived the excitement of my own days as a hunter, and I laughed aloud at the stories of his humorous escapades. On turning the last page of this book, I resolved to force Buzz into writing Volume II. I *know* there are plenty more stories from this masterful hunter/raconteur!

Richard Harland
Harare, Zimbabwe
January 2018

Preface

After twenty-five years as a professional hunter in Zimbabwe, I have met a lot of remarkable people and experienced many unforgettable incidents. While I probably have more experience than most of today's professionals, especially when it comes to the pursuit of elephants, my amateurish literary efforts are not intended to compete with the great books written by early generations of adventurers, men who were fortunate enough to experience Africa as it was when great swathes of land were terra incognita. Those old-timers gained more experience in a single year than a present-day professional hunter gains in a lifetime. Instead, I'd prefer to think of this work as my "mile-high book" as it has been written over a fourteen-year period while traveling between Zimbabwe and the hunting conventions in the United States of America.

As I am not particularly partial to movies, I broke the monotony of those sixteen-hour flights by recording the numerous incidents in my life as a professional hunter. My writing style may have changed over time and possibly not for the better, so please bear with me in this regard as I have no wish to rewrite the older stories again. The narrative is intended to be lighthearted, encompassing some of the many dangerous and humorous incidents that I and my clients have experienced over a twenty-five-year period. Based on my own experiences, the work also covers the hunting of big-game species from my point of view. As you will see, I have also dedicated chapters to a selection of clients with whom I have hunted extensively and with whom I have come to regard as good friends rather than clients.

My ambition is to get this published so that my daughters, Zoe and Jessica, when they ultimately progress from Barney the Dinosaur and Bugs Bunny to reading adventures of a more realistic nature, they will understand what their father has proudly accomplished in his lifetime. It concerns me that by the time they become teenagers, hunting and a sporting life as I know it may very well be a thing of the past. When one combines Africa's dramatic population increase, rampant poaching, corruption, and questionable regulations set by foreign politicians, the future of hunting in

Africa looks bleak indeed. I speak of actions such as the one taken recently by the United States Fish and Wildlife Service when it banned the import of Zimbabwean lion and elephant trophies into the United States. This action was taken with no scientific facts to back up the regulation.

Such draconian regulations strip whatever value these animals might have had to local Africans who live, begrudgingly, side by side with them. Without value, be it meat or monetary, these magnificent animals are considered a problem because the predators kill the villagers' livestock while the bovines compete for grazing. At the end of the day, it's no wonder the locals take the law into their own hands by poaching elephants and poisoning lions.

Sadly, this may well herald the beginning of the end of these magnificent animals. It may also be the end of the wilderness where they roam and where I've been privileged to hunt. If hunting as we now know it comes to an end, the animals will surely disappear, and it will not be long before the wilderness vanishes in their wake.

Acknowledgments and Thanks

Doug Stoole

I initially requested via Facebook for someone to edit my book, and an old friend suggested her dad, Doug. Doug is an accomplished writer as well as a past English teacher who used to live in Zimbabwe. Not only is he well versed in English, he has also hunted in the areas that I have written about.

As a result, I was over the moon when he agreed. Having completed my book, I am absolutely certain he will never agree to edit a second book should I be foolish enough to write one! He had no idea how bad my spelling and grammar are and what a task he had unwittingly undertaken.

I am very grateful to Doug for turning what many might have thought was a book written in a foreign language—due to my terrible grasp of written English—into an easy, light read, which is exactly what my book is.

Kevin Robertson

Like any first-time authors, I had huge self-doubts concerning the quality of my book. After spending so many years writing it, I had totally lost a grasp on how readable my book might be, so I reached out to Kevin. Kev is not only a professional hunter, but he has also written several books. He, like Doug, has also spent a lot of his time hunting in the Zambezi Valley. Kev read my script and spiced it up when he felt it necessary. More importantly, he encouraged me to keep going when I hit one of my many "writers blocks!" Kev also supplied me with several stunning photographs of buffaloes that he has taken in Kruger Park. I am grateful for his help.

Richard Harland

Rich kindly wrote the foreword for my book, and for that I am greatly honored. I met Rich when I produced my first elephant hunting DVD. He graciously allowed me to interview him about his amazing hunting escapades during the tsetse-fly control days when he culled thousands of elephants and during his days as a professional hunter and operator. Coincidentally, Rich was the first operator in the Dande, the area where a lot of this book takes place.

Asking Rich to write the foreword obviously meant asking him to read the book from cover to cover. I must admit this was extremely hard for me because Rich is such an accomplished writer himself, having written several wonderful hunting-related books. I was concerned that because of Rich's beautiful writing style, his ability as a natural raconteur, and someone with amazing experiences of "old Africa," he would find my book mundane.

Over the years Rich and his wonderful wife, Brita, have become great friends. It is a friendship I value greatly, so, thank-you, Rich, for your help.

Dave Christensen

Dave is undoubtedly one of if not the best professional guides operating in Africa today. Dave and his wife, Carol, kindly spent numerous hours going through thousands of fantastic photos that Dave has taken over his many years of guiding. He allowed me to select as many as I wanted for my book, and for that I am very grateful. As a professional guide, Dave appreciates how important ethical hunting is in the big picture of conservation, a subject close to my heart. Dave has also been a loyal supporter of our DAPU (Dande Antipoaching Unit), and I thank him for his support.

Introduction

When I was only a year old, my father was tragically killed in a hang-glider accident in the Eastern Highlands of Rhodesia, as the country was then known. As a consequence, my introduction to and love of hunting can be traced back to the many hours I spent gazing at my late father's photograph albums in my childhood. These albums were full of pictures of the time he had spent in Kenya hunting for Ker & Downey Safaris under the well-known professional hunter John Kingsley-Heath.

I had very few hunting opportunities while growing up. On my own, however, I took it upon myself to provide our domestic worker with an unlimited supply of meat from the many birds, big or small, beautiful or drab, that had the misfortune to pass through our garden. I accomplished these acts of butchery with a Daisy pellet gun, which I loved dearly; in fact, if I were to be asked today which gun provided me with the most satisfaction in my life, I would have to say it was my Daisy!

That air rifle set me on the path of following in my father's footsteps, and I started my hunting career straight out of school. My first year was spent as an apprentice to Matetsi Wildlife Safaris under Lou Hallamore. From the Matetsi blocks I progressed to Dande North in the Zambezi Valley, where I was fortunate to become apprenticed to Dengesai Makoni. At the time, Makoni was the first African to become a fully licensed Zimbabwean professional hunter. As far as I'm concerned, he is one of the unsung heroes of the safari industry. I joined Makoni as his apprentice in 1993, and at the end of 1995, I qualified as a fully licensed professional. I then hunted full time for Zambezi Hunters until they lost their Dande concession. It was then that I decided to go out on my own.

I started my own company, Makorokoto Safaris, which in Shona means "congratulations." It was only after enduring three years of my clients' inability to pronounce the complicated name, let alone remembering what it meant, that I decided to change the name to Buzz Charlton Safaris, unimaginative perhaps, but far more practical. Buzz Charlton Safaris plodded along for a while, booking clients and taking them to various hunting concessions

My dad and John Kingsley-Heath in Kenya.

throughout Zimbabwe. Then fate played a positive hand in the direction of my future career.

I had recently broken up with a girlfriend by the name of Ashleigh. Consequently, I was feeling down in the dumps and sorry for myself, just why I'm not sure because she had every right to break off our relationship, having caught me misbehaving. To drown my sorrows,

I went to a local pub with a friend named Pete. We had already consumed a few beers when who should walk in but Ashleigh, hand in hand with a tall, blond young man. In my inebriated state, I asked Pete who the idiot was. Pete told me the man was a professional hunter by the name of Myles McCallum. Wanting nothing further to do with Ashleigh and even less with McCallum, I left with Pete to find happier drinking grounds.

On my way home in the early hours of that morning, I managed to skid in the rain and then roll over my Land Cruiser. Even though I was inebriated, I realized that I would be in all sorts of trouble if the police arrived. I was fortunate that someone was right behind me, and this young lady gave me a lift home. My intention was to report the accident in the morning, claiming I swerved to miss a dog and that I was in shock, hence the reason for not reporting it immediately. I hoped that the alcohol in my system would have worked itself out by then.

Little did I know that of all people, Ashleigh would be traveling along the same road shortly after the accident. Worst luck, she saw my Land Cruiser upside down with the police already there. When the accident occurred, I had a few bags of coarse salt in the back of the vehicle, which the police had kindly wrapped in black plastic to stop the salt from getting wet. Horror stricken, Ashleigh thought the black plastic was a body bag and gave the police my address.

I hadn't been home very long when much to my surprise there was a knock on the door. Standing there were two policemen with the apparatus for a Breathalyzer test. Trying to act sober, unsuccessfully I might add, I gave my version of the event. We discussed the state of my vehicle, and during the course of our conversation, I told the police I was meant to be going hunting the next day. This produced an immediate effect.

They inquired about game meat, a much-prized commodity in Zimbabwe. After a short negotiation, the Breathalyzer apparatus was conveniently put away, and the police left. The next day I managed to borrow a Land Cruiser, did a quick buffalo hunt, and as per our agreement, returned to Harare, reversed the vehicle into the back parking area of the police station, and left half the buffalo meat with the same policemen.

Snares recovered by DAPU in the Dande Safari Area.

Their comment was classic Africa: "Mr. Charlton," they said. "If you ever have a similar problem, please do not hesitate to contact us!"

Anyway, I digress, so back to my story. A couple of weeks after the Land Cruiser incident, I received a call from Myles McCallum who said he wanted to see me. Myles duly arrived, and straight off the cuff he mentioned that he, too, had broken up with Ashleigh, but that was not the real reason he had come by to see me. He was there to propose a joint business venture, and to this end his reasoning was sound: We were both professional hunters without a concession, we both attended the same overseas hunting shows, we both advertised in the same magazines, and we were both essentially competing for the same clients.

So it was, on that day, Charlton McCallum Safaris or CMS for short, was formed. The partnership was very simple as the assets of the newly formed company consisted of two old Land Cruisers (mine had *really* seen better days) and a handful of faithful trackers. These meagre assets were complemented by loads of enthusiasm and energy, and the result has been a very successful and enjoyable partnership.

A lot of water has passed under the bridge since Myles and I joined forces. We have operated in Makuti and in the Dande North and East Safari Areas, considered some of Zimbabwe's prime big-game concessions. We have also had short stints in the Save, Kwekwe, and Hwange areas, Mozambique, and the Selous Game Reserve in Tanzania. Hundreds of clients have come and gone through CMS, and I am proud to say I can count the dissatisfied clients on one hand. We have forged great friendships with people from all parts of the world and are very proud of our 60 percent client return rate.

At the present time we are still operating in the Dande North Safari Area, and we are spending a lot of energy, time, and money on DAPU, our own effective Dande Antipoaching Unit. The unit has made huge inroads into the area's rampant poaching, and as a result I believe there's a glimmer of hope that hunting and exploring in the vast wildernesses of our country might just survive long enough for my girls to appreciate.

******

Recently we embarked on a new venture, cattle ranching. "Ranching" is probably an extravagant word to describe our diversification. It was actually more a case of the blind leading the blind when we purchased our first breeding stock.

After dedicated research on the Internet, Myles insisted the ideal stock to start the CMS's premier herd would be two-year-old cows that have two permanent lower front incisors. These young cows would, he insisted, bear many offspring for us! From the locals we proudly bought two, "two-toothed, two-year-old" heifers. Our ignorance in cattle breeding was quickly exploited. It didn't take us long to discover that we had been swindled, for the cows we purchased were old and barren, so old in fact that they only had two teeth left!

CMS's premier herd now consists of one hundred Mashona cows and a fine, imported South African, Boran bull. I'm sure our Boran bull

Herd of elephants eating the acacia pods at Mana Pools.

must question daily what he did wrong to deserve being moved from the lush highlands of Kwa Zulu Natal to the harsh, dusty, dry, and tsetse-fly infested Zambezi Valley . . . especially since he was given a few miserable old Mashona cows with which to mate.

******

Tall Tales is an account of twenty-five years of hunting in the Zambezi Valley. It is a light and amusing read comprising many entertaining stories. It follows my career from an apprentice hunter in the early 1990s to today. When a PH hunts twenty-five full seasons, he gets to meet some exceptional clients, and I am proud to say that many have become firm friends. Dangerous situations, trying times, and exhaustion have all lent to cement these friendships. I am honored to have shared many campfires with these people.

I do hope, you the reader, will enjoy this book. I would imagine you are either a hunter or a conservationist, someone who realizes and appreciates the vital role that hunting plays in conservation. It is folks like you who will ultimately contribute to the survival of my most favourite place, the Zambezi Valley. For this, I thank you.

My First Buffalo

Chapter One

After my first season as an apprentice in Matetsi, in the Victoria Falls area, I joined Zambezi Hunters to complete my apprenticeship. Zambezi Hunters, which operated in the Dande North Safari area of the Zambezi Valley, was at that time owned and run by Ian Piercy, a well-respected operator who was one of the first in the safari business; he was also known for being a real stickler for the rules. In the eyes of the hunting world, apprentices, who work from sunup to well after the last client has gone to bed while earning a pittance, are seen as the lowest form of life. My starting salary was a miserly Z$300 a month, the equivalent of about U.S. $60, which at the time was not even enough to buy a tank of diesel to fill my vehicle.

To be an apprentice meant being a jack-of-all-trades: mechanic, plumber, cook, and general dogsbody, to name but a few! I was sent to Pedza Pasi, Zambezi Hunters' main camp in the Dande, and since it was early in the season, I was initially assigned to the job of repairing the roads on the hunting concession. After the usual heavy rainy season, this job, which is done annually, is known to be extremely hard work. It would take me and my gang the better part of a month to complete, and the whole time we would be sleeping out in the bush wherever we'd finished the day's work, only to continue first thing the following morning. The only contact I had with the outside world was via radio communication with the main camp once a day around lunchtime.

It was during one of these daily, keep-in-contact-with-main-camp calls, that my boss, Ian, who had come down to see how the camp's renovations were progressing, asked me to shoot a buffalo cow for lion bait. Ian had a client for a lion hunt due to arrive in two days' time, and the client had requested pre-baiting before his arrival. I was duly instructed to get on with it.

Shooting a buffalo cow and hanging up two baits was a welcome break from the monotony of road repairing, so I jumped at the opportunity, especially since it offered me the chance to shoot my first buffalo. I enthusiastically set off with Fibion, one of the road crew who claimed to be a tracker.

Unfortunately, we saw little evidence of buffalo in the area where we were working, so we ventured farther afield and ended up on the road to Mururu, one of the other camps in the Dande. As we came around a bend in the road, we were confronted by the ugliest old *dagga* boy I had ever seen. This presented me with a quandary, especially since by that time it was already late afternoon.

I mulled over my options: *To be expected to find and track a herd of buffaloes at that late stage of the day in order to specifically carry out Ian's instructions would take a lot of time and effort, and even if we were successful in shooting a cow, it would more than likely entail cutting a road into the bush well into night in order to retrieve her.* These were the thoughts that raced through my mind as I stood looking at the old *dagga* boy standing next to the road right in front of me. After serious reflection and despite being instructed by Ian to shoot a cow only, I decided that this bull presented too good an opportunity to pass up.

That the bull was a pathetic trophy, an animal no self-respecting client would give a second glance to, let alone shoot at, convinced me of the rightness of my decision. The old *dagga* boy, with its miserable set of horns was just asking to be shot, so I obliged with my Ruger .416 Rigby and a 400-grain softnose bullet. The buffalo buckled at the impact of the heavy bullet and thundered off. A few minutes later—and much to my relief—we were greeted with his final death bellow. We found him stone dead not more than twenty yards off the road, which made his recovery a doodle. Everything had worked perfectly: my first buffalo, a quick and merciful one-shot kill, an easy recovery . . . and all done and dusted by nightfall. What could be better!

So we set about carefully taking care of the evidence. This entailed removing the bull's less-than-impressive head, his scrotum (commonly referred to as the "ball-bag"), his two impressively large testicles, and all four of his hoofs as they were considerably larger than those of any cow. I then

An ancient dagga *boy.*

instructed Fibion, my newfound tracker and confidant, to carry away all the evidence and hide it under a bush at least a kilometre from the road.

An hour or so later Fibion returned having successfully, or so he assured me, "hidden" all the evidence in a place the hyenas were sure to find and dispose of that night. We then cut the buffalo into two halves and loaded them onto the Land Cruiser. To the untrained eye, each half of the carcass could easily be mistaken for those of a large-bodied old cow. As requested, we hung half a carcass at each of the two lion baits.

Smugly happy with my first buffalo kill, I was on the radio as scheduled the following day to tell Ian that the mission had been accomplished and that the baits were hanging. To my horror I was instead lambasted by my furious boss, who told me in no uncertain terms to "get my skinny little arse back to the main camp ASAP." I knew immediately that our carefully laid plans had somehow gone awry and I was in deep trouble.

It transpired that shortly after we had loaded the two halves of the buffalo and driven away, Ian had taken a drive down to Mururu to inspect the camp. Coming around a corner he had seen hundreds of vultures landing about forty yards off the road, so he decided to stop and investigate. I can imagine his face and feel his anger when he found neatly hidden under a bush the remains of four buffalo feet, a ball-bag complete with testicles, and the head of an old *dagga* boy!

It was fairly obvious who the culprit was, and likewise it was painfully obvious that Fibion had only walked about sixty yards or so into the bush to hide the evidence instead of the instructed kilometre. Worse still, to make it appear he had walked a long way while hiding the evidence, Fibion had then taken a siesta under a shady tree for an hour! That I was in those long-ago days still naïve to the ways of the rural African was fairly obvious; in fact, I was extremely lucky not to have been be fired for insubordination. As for lazy old Fibion, his career as a tracker was very short lived.

MAKONI, THE ALMOST COMPLETE PROFESSIONAL

CHAPTER TWO

Zambezi Hunters operated in the Dande North Safari Area of the Zambezi Valley, and despite a few villages scattered about in the area, a more pristine track of wilderness would be hard to find anywhere south of the Zambezi River. At the time, Ian Piercy employed a full-time professional hunter by the name of Dengesai Makoni. Dengesai became my mentor, and under his tutorship I completed my three-year training to become a professional hunter.

Makoni was a truly remarkable professional hunter. Initially he had been employed by Ian as a general camp hand, but after a year or two he was promoted to the respected position of skinner. Ian took a real liking to Makoni, who eventually graduated to become Ian's tracker and right-hand man. Several years after proving his capabilities, Ian decided that Makoni should be given the opportunity of obtaining a Zimbabwean professional hunters license.

Apart from the practical examination, which all aspiring professional hunters must pass, Makoni was obliged to complete an oral exam instead of the usual written one. This was because he was illiterate. But he succeeded and went on to become the first fully qualified African professional hunter in Zimbabwe. This was the start of a long and successful professional hunting career that spanned no less than twenty years. Due to his all-round hunting skills, he became very popular with the clients, which resulted in him achieving the highest client return rate in the company.

I regarded Makoni as the almost perfect professional hunter. To achieve a high standard in this difficult profession one needs to be a jack-of-all-trades, and Makoni certainly was. It would not concern him in the slightest if his trackers failed to appear for work for he was an extremely good tracker in his own right. Added to this was his ability as a skinner. Not one of the company's skinners could match him in this endeavour.

Dengesai Makoni and I share a contented smile over a leopard, Dande, 1993.

Unfortunately for Makoni but fortunately for me, he did have a few flaws, and those resulted in me being promoted to his full-time apprentice. His first flaw was a poor command of the English language. Makoni's English was so poor that I had to verbally interact between him and his clients. To be able to communicate with clients in a relaxed, friendly, and knowledgeable manner is one of a professional hunter's most important requisites. Something as simple as this can either make or break a hunt. A professional hunter is, in many respects, little more than an entertainer. His job is to keep clients happy and to give them a good time. The ability to communicate competently is deemed essential to becoming a professional hunter. Makoni's communication skills were undoubtedly lacking, and I was tasked to assist him in this way.

Another flaw was his driving skills, or better stated, the lack thereof. He was, in fact, a terrible driver. His incompatibility with four-wheeled vehicles led Ian to take away Makoni's driving privileges and hand them over to me, but before that happened, Makoni managed to destroy two Land Cruisers. On one occasion it was an unbearably hot October day, and Makoni decided to drive a Land Cruiser up the Zambezi escarpment. Ignoring the red warning signs clearly indicated by the vehicle's temperature gauge, Makoni continued to drive up the slope until the engine finally seized.

On another occasion Makoni was traveling back to camp from a leopard blind. It was late in the evening and he was driving much too fast through a particularly thick patch of bush commonly referred to by the Zambezi Hunters' staff as "Pedza" *jesse*. This area of thick *jesse* bush is well known for being a safe haven for irate elephant cows.

There is a spring deep within the Pedza *jesse* thicket that ensures a regular elephant presence, so driving through the area is extremely dangerous especially at night because that's when most elephant cows prefer to drink. Driving through the area at this time is referred to as "running the gauntlet," and I've been chased on a number of occasions by irate cows. Well, as luck would have it, Makoni managed to hit an elephant cow one particular night. The cow suddenly emerged from the *jesse* right in front of the vehicle and the Land Cruiser hit her behind both knees. This caused her hind legs to buckle, bringing her backside down on the Land Cruiser's bonnet!

Under the immense weight, the Land Cruiser's front suspension collapsed and the engine was flattened. Fortunately, the elephant appeared uninjured. Having righted herself, she fled off into the dense thicket with a terrible scream. The result was a somewhat startled Makoni and an uneasy and nervous client who had to walk through the remainder of the gauntlet all the way back to camp!

It was after these two incidents that Ian banned him from driving, and I was promoted to the position of Makoni's full-time driver. In that position I began to accompany him on all of his hunts, from start to finish. To be honest, I have to admit being grateful for Makoni's downfalls.

For an apprentice this was unusual. Under normal circumstances an apprentice only joins the occasional hunt as he is far too occupied with the mundane and often unpleasant dogsbody work necessary for the successful day-to-day running of a safari camp. Apprentice professional

Makoni (left) with his favourite tracker, Hans, on the Zambezi River.

hunters are commonly known as "gophers," as in "go fetch this" and "go and do that." Thanks to Makoni's imperfections and the fact that he conducted most of the company's hunts, I got to do a great deal more hunting and a lot less "gophering"!

As mentioned earlier, Makoni had the most "return" clients, and Ian took advantage of this by underpaying Makoni yet giving him the lion's share of the hunting season. I certainly did not complain for my seasons were packed back to back with dangerous-game hunts that resulted in giving me invaluable professional experience, the type of in-depth knowledge and understanding that's kept me alive and in good shape to this day. I will say, however, that in true Scottish fashion, Ian honestly underpaid Makoni for his services.

Another of Makoni's flaws was his shooting. While a poor shot, Makoni was fearless when it came to hunting all types of dangerous animals, with the exception of the elephant. After surviving two close calls, he developed a healthy respect for the elephant. This was understandable for he was once knocked to the ground by a bull before it absconded. If the truth be told, Makoni's respect for elephants bordered on fear.

Throughout his hunting career he used an ancient FN .458, which he cleaned annually by plugging the barrel with a wine-bottle cork then filling the barrel to capacity with engine oil and leaving the rifle standing vertically overnight. The following morning he would remove the cork, drain the oil, and pull a rag though the barrel! It was with this rifle that Makoni faced numerous close calls. Surprisingly the rifle never let him down despite its lack of basic maintenance and care.

One day a message came through to Zambezi Hunters' headquarters with the news that a buffalo bull had killed a local woman who had been working in a field. In problem animal control situations such as this, we were obliged to assist where we could. Upon arriving at the field, we found Ian R., another of the company's professional hunters, covering the body of the unfortunate woman with a motley coloured patched blanket.

Ian, Makoni, and I followed the buffalo's tracks to an area of thick and impenetrable *jesse* bush. Ian stated outright that he had no intention of entering the thicket and insisted that I refrain as well. This left Makoni out on a limb. Fearless as always, he disappeared into the thicket by himself while Ian and I sat on a nearby anthill waiting with bated breath.

Less than five minutes later there was a blast from Makoni's .458 followed by the sound of the bull crashing through the thicket. It sounded as though the animal was heading in our direction, which indeed turned out to be the case, for a few seconds later out came the bull running straight toward us. Ian and I fired at the same time and, thankfully, the huge beast fell to the ground stone dead not more than a hundred yards from where it had killed the woman.

Concerned about Makoni and expecting the worst, Ian and I climbed down the anthill and headed for the thicket. Much to our relief and surprise Makoni came hobbling out the *jesse* with a bunch of grass protruding from the rifle's barrel. His face was swollen and his two front teeth were loose!

In re-creating the events, we learned he had followed the bull's tracks down a narrow trail with *jesse* so dense that visibility was down to a few yards. Sensing, as all good trackers do, that the bull was close, Makoni looked up. There it stood, right in front of him . . . giving him the beady eye. The bull's head was sticking out of the *jesse* bush, only yards away. So close was the animal that Makoni realized he would not have enough time to raise his rifle, so he fired from the hip, Audie Murphy style, his bullet hitting the animal in the chest.

In a frenzied rush, the bull erupted out of the bush, bowling Makoni over and knocking both him and the rifle into the dirt. The old *dagga* boy then ran straight over Makoni, planting one of its hoofs into his face before continuing its escape out of the *jesse* and into the open. The bull then ran straight toward the anthill upon which Ian and I were patiently waiting, and that's when we both fired. At last the bull was down. I would think most people would be a bit shaken by a near-death experience such as this, but not so Makoni. Amazingly, he appeared rather amused by the incident.

As a buffalo hunter, Makoni was undoubtably the best of the best. He had little or no respect for the animals that he hunted year-in and year-out. In an average season he would successfully guide around thirty buffalo hunts. When one considers he hunted continually for twenty-odd years, his tally would equate to something like six hundred buffaloes killed.

While never particularly concerned with the spread of a buffalo's horns, he was invariably successful in getting his client a good old bull. Makoni's buffalo-guiding career coincided with the time when Ian Piercy owned a share in Safari-Willscher, a German booking agency. This was, indeed, fortunate because Zambezi Hunters' predominately German-speaking clients, unlike Americans, shared Makoni's lack of interest in horn spread and the record book. As long as the bull was old and had a big boss, the German client was happy!

Makoni had the uncanny ability of knowing where the buffaloes were heading. While we were tracking, he would often leave the spoor and wander off in a different direction. When questioned about his behaviour, he would click his tongue and, with a disdainful look, ignore me completely and proceed as though I wasn't there. Invariably, not only did we catch up to the herds but more often than not we'd also come out ahead of them. Such occasions resulted in a number of perfect ambushes.

I never figured out how he knew where the buffaloes were heading. It was like a sixth sense. Call it what you may, but he had an inherent gift of anticipation and a deep understanding of the buffalo's mind. It was this combination that contributed to his achievement as a truly consummate professional.

One of the advantages of hunting with Makoni was his willingness on occasions to let me take charge, thereby helping me to learn a lot faster. Above all else, he hated sitting in a lion or leopard blind. Once he had confidence in my ability to take care of some cat, he would happily sit by himself in the vehicle waiting for the sound of the gunshot. This would be the signal for him to come with the Land Cruiser, which was one of the few times he was allowed to drive.

On one occasion he left me in charge of a client who was after a leopard. The client and I were sitting in a blind overlooking a bait that we'd hung. The setup was not very far from the camp, and we had already established the bait had been hit. That evening, just before the sandgrouse flew in to drink at a nearby spring, my client and I heard a bushbuck bark, a sure sign something was about to happen!

Materializing out of nowhere was not the leopard I was expecting, but an emaciated lioness. Fortunately there was still sufficient light for me to

It was a mercy killing to shoot the emaciated lioness that was starving toward a slow death.

get a good look at her. Pathetically thin and gaunt, she was obviously in a bad way. Through my binocular I noticed a couple of porcupine quills embedded in her mouth. Unable to eat, she was simply starving toward a slow and certain death. Here was obviously a situation that called for a mercy killing to end her misery.

In the early days of my career, common sense still prevailed among the Zimbabwe's Parks and Wildlife's staff, so I was sure the officials at the department would understand my actions when they saw her condition and back my decision to shoot the poor creature. As the lioness turned broadside on, a well-placed bullet behind the shoulder brought her suffering to an end. When seen up close, she was nothing more than skin and bones.

The gunshot also brought forth a happy Makoni, whose broad smile froze when he saw a dead lioness lying below the bait tree instead of a leopard! Thinking I had made a mistake and concerned his license was on the line, Makoni was, to say the least, shocked. I actually had never seen him in such a state. It was only after showing him the lioness's appalling condition and her suffering that he finally calmed down. Thankfully there were no repercussions; in fact, the Parks staff was most understanding.

Makoni was an amiable person who almost never held a grudge against anyone. The exception was a gun-ho Afrikaner whom he had once had bad experience with. Unfortunately, Makoni tended to generalize from this one incident the viewpoint that all South African professional hunters were poorly trained.

Here's what happened: Makoni and this Afrikaner had been following a wounded leopard, and the tracking was particularly difficult because the leopard had sustained a flesh wound from being shot in the leg. As a result there was only a weak blood spoor to follow. Makoni was bending down in front of a patch of tall grass trying to determine whether the wounded animal had passed that way when suddenly the snarling beast leaped onto his back. Makoni yelled out, galvanizing the South African into action. Unfortunately, to kill the beast, the South African had to shoot at the leopard with a shotgun from twenty yards away. He succeeded in killing the leopard, which was all to his credit, but at the same time he also sent multiple buckshot pellets into Makoni's back and rear end! This episode had a long-lasting effect on Makoni, and from that day forward he regarded professional hunters from the other side of the Limpopo with intense displeasure.

While I gained invaluable hunting experience from Makoni, he was poor in identifying the various birds that inhabit our hunting areas. A good knowledge of these birds is an important part of obtaining a professional hunter's license Upon seeing a raptor on my first day out with Makoni and inquiring as to its identity, he shook his head.

"Buzz," he replied. "I know a guinea fowl and a francolin because I can eat them."

Thus ended my tuition on the identity of birds. Regrettably, this lack of instruction resulted in ornithology being a weak point for me.

******

It was a rare privilege, indeed, to have spent the better part of three years working alongside Makoni. He came from a humble background where most black youngsters in their wildest dreams could expect at most to become a tracker for a professional hunter or a safari company. The best these individuals could hope for was a life of hard labour behind an ox-drawn plow, tilling an overcropped piece of land in a poor rainfall area in a futile attempt to make a living out of maize and cotton.

Makoni achieved unimaginable heights by becoming a fully licensed and well-respected Zimbabwean professional hunter—the cream of the crop when it comes to Africa's hunting professionals. For Makoni to have achieved this can be compared to a rural African becoming the President. As a result he was looked upon in awe, not only by his fellow tribesmen but also by the ladies. In this respect he was often entertained. . . . Sexual favours were readily forthcoming and gratefully accepted!

Unfortunately for Makoni, it was his misfortune that these favours took place during the time the AIDS epidemic was spreading like wildfire throughout Zimbabwe. Sadly Makoni did not escape its eager grasp. He contracted this disease when antiretroviral drugs were not as readily available as they are today. Despite living with the HIV virus for many years, Makoni's condition eventually developed into full-blown AIDS, and thereafter his condition rapidly deteriorated.

For me, this was a most upsetting time as I had to witness his slow and tragic demise, the end of a fantastic man and competent hunter. But Makoni's legacy lives on. Of his many sons, Lovemore is now a licensed professional and we employ Muno as a camp manager and yet another son, Crispen, as our head cook.

I shall never forget Makoni. He had a huge influence on my life, and looking back I realize that where I am today would not have been possible without him and the guidance he so willingly gave me.

PRACTICAL

CHAPTER THREE

Obtaining a professional hunting license in Zimbabwe for an aspiring applicant is a long and thorough process. Respected the world over, this license takes a minimum of three years to attain, but the norm averages closer to the four-year mark. The process not only includes an apprenticeship with a recognized safari operator but also several written exams. Having passed the written exams, the would-be professional hunter is then subjected to a shooting test and finally a practical exam.

The practical exam takes place over seven days in a chosen area determined by Parks and Wildlife Management Authority. There the applicants are put through vigorous tests in the field, overseen by two examiners, one from Parks and Wildlife and the other from the Zimbabwe Hunters Association. The exam questions cover a vast range of subjects including the identity of trees, birds, tracks, and star constellations at night, among other things. The examination also entails the setting up of a bush camp and the basic logistics of running one. On the hunting side, the applicant is required to track and shoot a buffalo, an elephant, or both, and then to successfully skin the carcass.

Having managed to pass my written exams, I set off for my first shooting test and practical exam full of youthful arrogance. I arrived at the test site in the Gonarezhou National Park confident that I was more than prepared because of my apprenticeship with Makoni. I was brought firmly down to size by promptly failing the test.

The reason given was that I was too young. I remember being furious. I felt it was unfair to fail someone because of his age, especially if he'd had sufficient experience. Looking back at it now I totally understand the examiner's decision, despite the fact that I probably had had more experience at the time than he did himself. I was twenty years old at the time.

Dave Petzal with his dagga *boy in the Save Valley, 2017.*

I qualified a year later, and my first clients often commented that they had grandsons older than me. In fact one of my first clients, Dave Petzal, a renowned gunwriter and the editor of *Field & Stream* magazine, picked up my .416 Rigby that still looked brand new and said with his dry sense of humour, "This certainly doesn't instill much confidence!"

When Dave hunted with me some twenty years later, he shot a fine old buffalo. I had only recently sold my .416 Rigby, which is too bad given his previous comment, for seeing its condition might have instilled in him a feeling of supreme confidence. By that point, the old weapon had seen twenty years of hard work in the Zambezi Valley and certainly looked like it.

On my second attempt at the practical exam, our group was told we would have to track a herd of elephants, and then for my part of the exam, I was instructed to approach the herd and shoot a cow using a frontal brain shot.

We hadn't been searching long when we found fresh tracks and steaming dung on the main security road. We were soon hot on the tracks. Half an hour later we caught up to the herd in fairly open mopane scrub. There was a large, single-tusk elephant at the back of the herd, a perfect situation that I took advantage of. A quick check of the wind showed it to be in my favour. I wasted no time and walked up behind the elephant. When I was about fifteen yards away, it heard me and swung round, ears spread, head held high. I raised the rifle and pulled the trigger and down it went, the back legs folding, the trunk and head thrown back, a perfect brain shot!

Arrogantly I walked around my brained cow thinking I had finally done it, my license was now fully guaranteed. But there was yet another twist to this story, for when I wandered around to the rear end of the elephant, I stood rooted, shocked and disbelieving: There protruding between the huge animal's legs was a penis!

I tried to cover the penis with my first-aid bag, something we all had to carry on the practical, but to no avail, for the examiner had already seen the offending appendage! Thankfully, I was not given an outright failure but a partial restriction, which meant I had to shoot another three elephants before my license would be upgraded. This meant I did not have to return and retake the practical examination, which was good news. The restriction was quickly removed the following season after I shot three Problem Animal Control elephants.

Thus began my career as a fully licensed professional hunter.

ZAMBEZI

CHAPTER FOUR

Most of my hunting has been done in the Zambezi Valley. Through this beautiful valley flows the Zambezi River, and it would be amiss not to give a brief description of this mighty river that has captivated me since my first hunt along its banks in 1992.

The Zambezi River rises out of a black marshy bog in a hilly forested area of northwestern Zambia. It is the start of a sixteen-hundred-mile journey through some of the most beautiful country in Africa. The Zambezi follows a course through Angola, along the borders of Namibia, Botswana, Zambia, and Zimbabwe, then on through Mozambique where it empties into the Indian Ocean.

Along its course through Angola, the Zambezi is joined by more than a dozen tributaries of varying sizes. Shortly before reentering Zambia the river suddenly widens before flowing over Chavuma Falls. It then flows through a shallow valley of marshy plains, one of which is the well-known Barotse. The main tributaries intersecting these plains are the Kabompo River from the east and the larger Lungwebungu River from the west. Farther on, the Zambezi enters a stretch of rapids that extend from Ngonye Falls south of Katima Mulilo where it forms the border between Zambia and the Caprivi Strip in Namibia.

From then on the river meanders widely to where it receives the floodwaters of the Chobe. After flowing past a small section of Botswana, the Zambezi forms the boundary between Zambia and Zimbabwe. At Kazungula, the Zambezi is joined by the Kwando River. Farther on it reaches its greatest width of 4,550 feet before, in a thunderous roar and a cloud of spray the upper Zambezi, it ends as its waters plunge over the world's largest waterfall, Victoria Falls. This is known as the upper Zambezi.

Having meandered for one hundred and twenty miles through a series of deep gorges and rapids below the falls, the river is then harnessed by the Kariba Dam. The wall of the dam is built at the head of the Kariba Gorge, which is part of the Zambezi escarpment and the uppermost region of the great East African Rift Valley.

The river then enters the Zambezi Valley and meanders between Zimbabwe and Zambia while receiving additional inflow from the Kafue River, its largest contributor. This part of the river's course ends at the Cahora Bassa Dam in Mozambique and is known as the middle Zambezi. From there it begins its descent to the coastal plain. It enters the Tete basin and flows for forty miles before rushing through the Lupata Gorge to emerge onto the Mozambique plains where the water spreads out to a width of three to five miles. Near Villa Fontes the river receives its last great tributary, the Shire River, which drains the waters of Lake Malawi. At its mouth the Zambezi splits into a wide, flat, marshy delta obstructed by many sandbars. After flowing through a series of channels, the Zambezi finally enters the sea. This section is known as the "Lower Zambezi."

During its long journey to the sea, the Zambezi encounters a wide range of differing topography, flora, and fauna. When it flows over Victoria Falls, the river continues to descend until it reaches Lake Kariba. Prior to its Kariba's submersion in water, this great basin was part of the Zambezi Valley. It is along the river on the Zimbabwean side of the lake and lower toward the "middle Zambezi" where the contents of this book mostly concentrates.

What's left of the Kariba basin is an area of flat land rising gradually to a range of mountains that, in turn, becomes part of the central Zimbabwe plateau. The Kariba basin is divided into tribal land and wildlife areas. At the top end of the lake is the Chizarira National Park and farther down are the Chete Safari Area and the Matusadona National Park. At the top end of the lake close to Kariba is the Charara Safari Area while farther inland along the main road between Makuti and Kariba is the Makuti Safari Area. Surrounding these wildlife areas are tribal lands, and along the lake itself

The magnificent Victoria Falls.

can be found remnants of the Batonka tribe who were displaced by the rising water of the new dam but now eke out a living from fishing.

The flora is typical Zambezi lowveld. A thick cover of grass grows along great ridges of land where baobab trees stand like lone monuments of the past guarding the mopane forest beneath them. Along the edge of these ridges, Combretum *jesse* bush and acacia thorn trees provide welcome cover and a refuge for the many animals that live there.

Kigelia trees, with their familiar sausagelike pods, and lush green natal mahoganies grow along the banks of the many gullies that transport summer flood waters from the highland into the lake. Farther inland towering mountain acacia trees cover the rocky hills that form the Zambezi Escarpment.

The area along the edge of the lake abounds in wildlife. Elephant, buffalo, lion, leopard, and many other species are common here, albeit under

A male leopard in the late evening sun.

A typical sunset over Lake Kariba.

constant pressure from poaching. The lake itself is a mecca for tourists who have the unique privilege of viewing big game along the shoreline from the luxury of a houseboat.

It is also a paradise for the angler. The waters abound in indigenous species, like the well-known tigerfish, nkupe, chessa, and vundu, a member of the catfish family. Certain species of tilapia are also indigenous, but other varieties of the same species were stocked once the lake was full.

A small sardine-size fish, indigenous to Lake Tanganyika, named kapenta was introduced to Lake Kariba and form the basis of a successful and prosperous fishing industry. These little fish are caught at night using powerful mercury lights, which attract the fish to them. A circular net suspended beneath the water under the lamp is used to scoop up the congregating fish. During daylight the fish are spread over suspended wire nets and dried in the sun; they are an important source of protein for the local Zimbabweans.

As the water rushes through the hydro turbines and possibly an open flood gate, it continues through the Kariba Gorge until it reaches the topmost portion of the Zambezi Valley. Here begins a series of national parks and safari areas, the first one being the Hurungwe Safari Area. Having passed under the bridge at Chirundu, the river opens up onto a vast plain that encompasses the Mana Pools National Park.

At the southern end of the valley is a vast mountain range, called the Zambezi Escarpment, that runs due east until it levels out in northeastern Zimbabwe near Mozambique, a distance of four hundred miles. The main road to Zambia enters the escarpment at Makuti and begins a gradual descent along a windy road bordered with thickly forested hills of mountain acacia trees until it reaches Marongora where the Zimbabwe Parks and Wildlife Management Authority has its main office. A few miles farther on, a sharp bend in the road circuits the last hilly obstruction to reveal the Zambezi Valley in all its splendour. A brief stop at a roadside lay-by discloses the vast valley spreading out as far as the eye can see.

In the distance can be seen the mountains of Zambia under which the Zambezi flows. And eastward the escarpment continues unabated until it disappears in the distant haze. But only from this height can the variety of flora in all its magnificence be truly appreciated.

Massive baobabs stand among the forest of mopane trees. Jagging through this forest are natural gullies that take the flood waters off the escarpment and channel them into the Zambezi. Kigelia sausage trees and dark green, leafy natal mahoganies grow along the banks and serve as stark sentinels that outline these gullies. Between the mopane forest and the river a thick almost impenetrable Combretum bush, commonly referred to as the *jesse* bush, can be seen. This dense thicket provides sanctuary to the herds of buffaloes and elephants that frequent the area.

From the lay-by, the road descends the escarpment steeply until it reaches the valley floor, where it continues in a straight line to Chirundu, the border between Zambia and Zimbabwe. Branching off the main road at the base of the escarpment is a dirt track that traverses the full length of the escarpment, finally linking up with the road to the town of Mukumbura, close to the border between Zimbabwe and Mozambique.

A dagga *boy with the ever-present tick birds.*

Elephants crossing the Sapi River in April, early in the season.

From its beginning this dirt road passes through a number of wildlife areas and tribal settlements. The first of these areas is the famous Mana Pools National Park, well known for the vast plain that before man's interference in the building of the Kariba Dam, flooded annually during the rainy season. Unique and beautiful, this huge floodplain resembles a parkland. Beneath a forest of towering *Acacia albida* trees and the occasional patch of Combretum bush, antelopes, elephants, and buffaloes can be seen.

Lone bull elephants and numerous family groups browse upon the seed pods of the albida thorn trees, while herds of buffaloes make their way from the sanctuary of the *jesse* bush to cross the floodplain in a cloud of lingering dust on their way to the Zambezi to drink. Numerous herds of impalas move slowly across the plain, this year's youngsters frolicking among the females while rutting males, outside the perimeter of the herd, clash horns in a constant battle for supremacy. Small groups of two or three zebras add colour to the tranquil scene.

Two camouflaged-to-perfection kudu bulls give away their positions as they reach for succulent Combretum leaves, their long, twisting horns glinting in the sunlight. Out of the same thicket a family group of warthogs suddenly appear, trotting with upright tails toward a shallow mud pan, the water turned to a quagmire by old buffalo bulls that cover their hairless hides in the mud to prevent being bitten by tsetse flies.

Close to the pan two male baboons squat on their haunches deliberately ignoring man's presence by looking arrogantly in another direction. In the branches above them the troop feeds upon succulent fruits while being frequently interrupted by the squeals of reprimanded youngsters and the chatter of their elders.

Under the shade of an acacia, a pride of lions is resting from the burning midday sun. Since early morning they have been following a herd of buffaloes that are now watering at the river. An alert lioness is facing the river waiting for the herd to reappear. She is aware of a sickly buffalo cow that is struggling to keep up with the herd. The rest of the pride is stretched out under the tree, waiting patiently for their evening meal to appear.

Down at the river, the buffalo mill about nervously, aware of the crocodiles lying on the many sandbanks that dot this stretch of the river. Numerous pods of hippos can be seen half submerged in the water, their snouts and the tips of their noses the only sign of their presence apart from the occasional series of reverberating grunts or the opening of massive yawning jaws.

As evening approaches, the herd of buffaloes, trailing a lingering cloud of dust, makes its way back to the safety of the *jesse* bush. The lions await. The male lions try to split the herd with short and ferocious rushes, but the buffalo guard bulls repel them. Meanwhile the lionesses wait patiently for their moment.

In the confusion the sickly cow, aware of her vulnerability, has moved away from the rest of the herd and is close to a deep donga. The lionesses are on her in a flash, and they drag the defeated cow down; only a piteous bellow is offered in response. As the last of her struggles cease and her legs slowly stiffen, the lions join the females and the feast begins.

After the lions have had their fill and move away, the animals of the night appear. In the inky darkness around the buffalo carcass, jackals bark, hyenas chatter and howl, and a leopard coughs. All night the rumpus continues unabated as these scavengers vie for each morsel. Come dawn little remains for the many vultures that appear out of the sky, swooping down like hunchbacked old men to perch upon the carcass and do battle for what little remains. So begins another unforgettable day in Mana.

******

From the Mana Pools National Park the Zambezi continues its course through narrow channels of fast-flowing water, past many sandbanks and vegetated islands. The river is now over a mile wide, flowing parallel to the northern section of the escarpment in Zambia.

The dividing line between Mana Pools and the Sapi Safari Area is the Sapi River itself. Sapi is similar in every respect to Mana with a floodplain separating the river from the *jesse* bush thicket, after which comes the forest of mopane woodland that continues inland up to the base of the escarpment.

The area was designated a Safari Area many years ago and is used by local hunters under the patronage of the Zimbabwe Hunters Association.

On the eastern boundary, the Chewore River separates the Chewore Safari Area from Sapi. Chewore is used by professional safari operators offering hunts to overseas clients. Like Mana, Sapi and Chewore have many species to offer. Great herds of buffaloes are common. Sable antelopes and zebras exist in satisfactory numbers but are not as common and plentiful as kudus, elands, waterbucks, and impalas, bushbucks, duikers, and grysboks.

Elephants abound throughout the Zambezi Valley. As with Mana, Sapi and Chewore are well known for the small family groups of tuskless elephants that are smaller in stature than their counterparts with tusks. What they lack in hardware, however, is more than made up for in ferocity. Over the years, poaching and over-hunting has reduced the size and weight of the tusks of resident bulls. Gone are the big tuskers of yesteryear when seventy or eighty pounds a side were common. Nowadays thirty-pound tusks are considered rewarding.

Forty years ago, the rhinoceros was a common resident. In those days to be treed or chased by a startled rhino was considered a normal daily occurrence. However, to man's eternal shame, the rhino has been completely wiped out by poaching, and today, only forty years later, the rhinoceros no longer exists in the Zambezi Valley.

Elephant bulls at Mana Pools.

Not far from the confluence of Chewore and the Zambezi there is a hill feature called Pfumbe. Around this feature are a number of nyalas, an uncommon species in the Zambezi Valley.

The Zambezi River continues to flow past Chewore before reaching the Dande Safari Area, another hunting concession used by professional hunters. The Dande has a common boundary on its western side with Chewore but is otherwise surrounded by Tribal Trust Land. Pockets of thick bush in the TTL still house small herds of marauding buffaloes and elephants that plunder the commercial crops of the tribal land. The Dande is where a lot of my stories in this book take place.

Slightly eastward of Chewore and north of Dande, the Zambezi leaves Zimbabwe and enters the Cahora Bassa Dam in Mozambique, after which it continues its fascinating journey through all types of terrain before finally entering the Indian Ocean. In Zimbabwe the Zambezi flows entirely through low-lying country. Intense heat, high humidity, and heavy rain induce thick and lush vegetative growth during summer, but the areas are uncomfortable

The red cliffs—the border between Dande and Chewore North.

and often unbearably hot for humans. However, in winter, temperatures are above those of the high veld, where frost and cold conditions are the norm. By contrast, the Zambezi Valley and surrounding areas are cool in the evening but pleasantly warm and sunny during the day.

The Zambezi River and the areas through which it flows can only be described as a paradise of contrasting features. From its source in the Zambian highland to the great estuary in Mozambique, it flows through great marches, under well-known bridges, and over great waterfalls, the largest and most famous of all, the Victoria Falls.

Through manmade interruptions, the Zambezi River has flooded vast areas of natural valleys to form two of the biggest man-made lakes in the world, Kariba Dam and Cahora Bassa.

The rapids below the Victoria Falls and farther down in Mozambique are spectacular as are the great floodplains of the Zambezi Valley. The magnitude and beauty of these features climax in an estuary that is several miles wide as this most famous river ends its long journey to disappear into the Indian Ocean.

This is the Zambezi Valley, a place I have been fortunate enough to hunt most of my life. Through judicious and far-sighted management, the Zambezi River and its environment have been left a paradise. It is up to future generations to ensure the legacy continues.

Buffalo Hunting

Chapter Five

The buffalo is considered by many to be the most dangerous of the African Big Five, for it has the reputation of charging without provocation. Many of my first-time clients approach a hunt for buffalo with great trepidation. The feeling they'll be mown down at any moment and, God forbid, the possibility of having to follow a wounded one has the prospective client re-writing his will and having sleepless nights. I have no idea how the poor buffalo has gained such a fearsome reputation.

Having hunted buffalo for more than twenty years in the Dande Safari Area, which probably has the highest concentration of the animals in the Zambezi Valley, I have gained considerable experience. As a learner

One of many PAC buffaloes I took in Dande, 1993.

hunter I was put in charge of Problem Animal Control (PAC) throughout the communal lands in the valley where, at that time, there was a high concentration of *dagga* boys.

Dagga boys, as they are fondly known, are the older bulls that have been evicted from the breeding herds. At this stage of their lives, many such bulls "retire" into the thickets close to, and often in between, the scattered villages within that communal area. At night they would leave their safe havens to find an easy meal in the villager's fields. As dawn approached, they would return to the *jesse* thickets and dense riverine bush that grew between the villages, there to rest up in the heat of the day. This became their daily routine, much to the annoyance of the local villagers.

Unable to effectively protect their crops, the villagers would retaliate, and serious conflicts would ensue between man and beast. The use of dreaded wire snares, muzzleloaders, and old .303 rifles that the villagers were legally allowed to own for "crop protection" ensured the increase of ugly incidents.

A herd of buffaloes in the Zambezi Valley.

Jeffery Hicks and I in Dande, 2016.

Several people a year were killed or gored by these old rogue bulls, and it became my job to kill them as "problem animals" whenever the Parks and Wildlife Management Authority deemed they were repeat offenders.

In one season alone I killed twenty of these old bulls in the Angwa section of the valley, an area that is not more than ten square kilometres. They were among the most exciting hunts I ever had for a number of reasons. First of all, I was at that time still young and inexperienced, and I most certainly did not realize the risks involved. Secondly, it was "my hunt" rather than my guiding a client. On these occasions it was just the trackers and me.

For an eighteen-year-old such occasions had "adventure" written all over them. The hunts were exciting, for they were predicated on danger. More often than not these old bulls were wounded, sometimes from snares round their legs or necks and sometimes from bullets, with the latter ranging from old .303 slugs to muzzleloader projectiles. The reasons for the wounds were many: Perhaps the villagers had wounded a buffalo in desperation while trying to chase the buffalo out of the fields, or perhaps poachers after meat

A worn-down old dagga *boy.*

would leave the animal injured. Harassed in this manner, it's not surprising the old *dagga* boys were unpredictable.

The PAC hunts I conducted would begin after an incident was reported. These incidents usually involved a buffalo goring a villager or perhaps a particular buffalo was deemed a potential threat to the villagers. It was then that I was called. Unfortunately, this system was often abused. A number of "innocent" buffaloes were labeled "problem animals" by the protein-hungry Parks and Wildlife Management Authority wardens and staff. I am embarrassed to admit that I never questioned this arrangement. Getting the green light from the warden to hunt a buffalo was for an eighteen-year-old similar to some youngster being told he didn't have to go to school that day if he didn't want to.

I would pick up the tracks where the incident occurred or where the buffalo was last seen, after which my trackers, Morgan and Crispen, would begin weaving their magic. Within a short space of time, we would be following the tracks in single file through thick *jesse*, bush, which was frequently riddled with the dreaded buffalo bean. The bush was often so thick that we were constantly weaving and ducking along the trail and where visibility could be measured in feet.

This type of bush was the buffalo's safe haven. We would creep along at a snail's pace straining our eyes and ears to get a glimpse of the animal, for we knew that old bulls did not usually go far into the thickets. We would listen intently for sounds of movement or breathing. It was important to locate the bull before he knew he was being followed. If we were lucky enough to locate him, we would then try to distinguish what part of the bull was visible. Once that was established, I would take a shot over the top of the trackers who would be crouching low in order for me to do so. On many occasions though, the buffalo would snort and crash off through the *jesse*, often barely metres away, without presenting the chance of a shot. In such instances, the hunt would continue until we eventually got a lucky break and killed the animal.

Unfortunately, there were occasions when I wounded a bull. Considering the fact that they had every advantage over us in such thick bush where the opportunity to charge was heavily stacked in their favour, this hardly ever happened. In all my time as a professional hunter, I have only had five serious charges.

One reads many buffalo stories published in hunting magazines where the vast majority of charges are considered "life and death" situations where either hunter or buffalo will definitely meet his maker. Granted, this makes for exciting reading, but I regret to say that most of these stories are exaggerated. These magazines imply that if by chance a buffalo happens to take a few steps toward its aggressor, then lo and behold, it's considered a charge!

A full-blooded buffalo charge is unmistakable, and when it does happen, the buffalo is a formidable opponent. Only a perfectly placed brain shot or a shot that breaks the spine will stop him. Unlike elephants and the cats, if a buffalo is not dropped, he is unlikely to turn and make off, so a heavy-calibre rifle like a .458 or .470 shooting a 500-grain bullet would be my preference.

A particular charge that I once experienced taught me a valuable lesson in how to stop a charging buffalo. We had been tracking a herd for most of the morning without seeing a shootable bull, so we

A 45-inch buffalo bull from Dande.

I'm shown here with Dan Tindal's 44-inch buffalo, taken in Chewore North, 2008.

decided to call it off and head back to a road that runs parallel to the Manzamtanda River. In a shady spot we unloaded our rifles, made them "safe," and called in the Land Cruiser. Hungry after our morning's exertion, we enjoyed lunch at the spot. During the interval we decided to head downriver to a spring that I knew from past experience was about a kilometre away.

We refilled the water bags, grabbed our rifles, and set off. While walking in the dry riverbed toward the spring that was situated on a ridge above the river, we came across a lone *dagga* boy's tracks heading toward the spring. To hasten the follow-up, we abandoned the spoor and made haste for the spring, for I knew he would have stopped there to drink and we could resume tracking from there. When I casually climbed over the ledge, I really did not expect him to still be at the spring during the heat of midday, so I was surprised to find the old *dagga* boy lying in the water facing me from about twenty yards away.

This is John Senekal's 46-inch buffalo from Dande North. It scored 136 SCI points and ranked No. 5 in the SCI record book.

As soon as he saw me, he stood up and charged. In such a situation, a rush of adrenaline takes over. Everything seems to move in slow motion. I can clearly remember thinking I had more than enough time to shoot before he was on me. I started raising my .416 Rigby to my shoulder while at the same time pushing the safety catch forward to the firing position. To my horror I found that the safety was already off, and in that instant realized I had not reloaded my rifle after lunch.

Hastily cycling the bolt, I rammed a cartridge into the chamber and re-shouldered the rifle . . . but I had lost valuable time. When I lined up the sights, I can distinctly remember thinking: *This is an easy shot.* At that very moment my foresight was sitting between the buffalo's eyes and the muzzle was barely feet away from his head. When I pulled the trigger, the bull came crashing down. In fact he landed on my slops, the very pair that I had lost

This was the buffalo that nearly got us in Chirisa.

moments before as I hastily jumped back to avoid being knocked over by the already dead animal.

The lesson that I learned by default that day is that if you have the presence of mind, firmness of nerve, and intestinal fortitude to wait to the bitter end, a killing shot on a charging buffalo is not only easy but also one with far less chance of a badly placed bullet. Since that time I have always withheld my shot until the last moment possible.

However, this was when I was using a bolt-action rifle. Now that I use a double-barrel weapon, I have the advantage of being able to fire my first barrel as and when I please, holding my second shot till I am sure I cannot miss. This is, of course, the great advantage of using a double-barrel rifle and why they are the weapons of choice for most professional hunters when dangerous game is involved.

Yet another buffalo charge where we were lucky enough to emerge unharmed occurred in Chirisa. This was before I had learnt to wait to the bitter end before shooting. On this occasion we followed a large herd of over two hundred buffaloes that had drunk at Sipani Pan. We managed to get in front of them and into a shooting position as they filed past.

My client took a shot at a mature bull but unfortunately hit the animal too far back. We followed the wounded bull as he left the herd, which is always a good sign, and pursued him for several hours. It was about lunchtime when his tracks cut across a road. I decided to call a halt. I asked Royal, my driver, to get the food basket from the back of the vehicle, and we settled down on the side of the road to eat lunch. Unfortunately, we had finished all our water, so I got Crispen, my tracker, to fill the rucksack he was carrying with cans of Coke. This was the only liquid refreshment that was left, and I felt a Coke would be better than nothing.

Crispen took the lead. By that stage of his life Crispen was in his seventies and his eyesight was failing. On several occasions while tracking wounded buffaloes, he had "cried wolf," imagining he had seen the wounded animal when, in fact, nothing was there at all. We were barely fifty metres from our lunch spot when Crispen suddenly stopped, pointed at a patch of thick bush, and exclaimed with excitement, *"Nyati!"* (buffalo)

Not expecting the buffalo to have been that close to where we had lunch, I only took a casual look. All I saw was a dark patch that looked like a rock. Regrettably, I once again cursed the old fellow. Crispen, however, was convinced the buffalo was there, and as he leaned forward to point at the so-called dark patch, the Coke cans fell tumbling out the rucksack, landing on the ground with an almighty crash.

The noise was immediately followed by a high-pitched scream, a sound I have never before, or since, heard from a buffalo, and out of the bush at full tilt came the enraged animal. Both my client and I fired at exactly the same time, and thankfully the buffalo went down. Close inspection revealed that one of our bullets had passed harmlessly through his ear while the second bullet had luckily struck the animal through the spine. This, of

The Lippmanns' end-of-the-hunt picture, Dande, 1994.

This beautiful old dagga *boy is a magnificent trophy.*

course, is what dropped him. Had he not been shot through the spine, it is unlikely either of us would have had time to reload.

******

I have been on many successful buffalo hunts, beginning with the time I was an apprentice under my mentor, Dengesai Makoni, and I've come to certain conclusions on hunting the African buffalo based on these many and varied experiences.

In those early days the Dande had up to one hundred buffaloes on license annually. When I was Makoni's apprentice, we would take multiple buffaloes on a single safari; at least that's what happened for a majority of these hunts. In fact, one of our clients, Fritz, used to come out to hunt with us every year. He did this for eight consecutive years, and on each occasion he hunted eight buffalo bulls. Then one year he returned and announced that he was divorced and that from then on he would only be hunting four buffaloes. When asked why, he explained that his wife had taken half of all he owned, so now he could only afford to shoot four.

Note the soft top on this bull; he still needs a few years to become a trophy.

While buffalo hunting is not my favourite type of hunting, it is undoubtedly, a good, honest hunt, and I can understand why clients return year after year to hunt these great bovines. I enjoy the actual hunting part because it is similar to hunting elephants, which means it is strictly a tracking game. Once the herd of buffaloes that's being tracked is finally caught up with and a good bull been selected, one needs to get into a decent position.

This is not as easy as it sounds, for unlike elephants, the buffalo does not have poor sight and average hearing. On the contrary not only do they have outstanding eyesight, but their sense of hearing is also equally as good. They are, in fact, graced with excellent senses in every department, be it sight, hearing, or smell. This often means doing the "buffalo butt shuffle," a self-explanatory maneuver, in order to achieve a good shooting position. It's an exercise that, I regret to say, I'm not particularly fond of.

As far as I am concerned, the term "shootable bull" or "trophy buffalo" implies a bull with a hard boss. Buffalo bulls obtain hard bosses when they are fully mature, and in the Zambezi Valley this occurs from their eighth year onward. Breeding age or tenure lasts for three years, and by the time these bulls have had a chance to spread their genes, they are heavy in the shoulder and neck with a noticeable dewlap beneath the chin. By this age their horn tips are blunt and they bear numerous scars of a hard life. Such bulls are formidable animals, indeed.

Better still are the old *dagga* boys! *Dagga* is a Shona term for mud. These old bulls have often lost all the hair on their backs and down both sides of their bodies. In order to rid themselves of troublesome flies and other insects, they have an obsession for rolling in mud, which when dry, keeps them free of the pests. The old warriors are generally around eleven years or older and, in most cases, have been forced out the herd. Some of them choose to live solitary lives, but for the most part they seek company with other like-minded bulls. In reaching that venerable age, they have been "around the block," so they are wise, cautious, and very cunning. They have survived drought and harsh seasons, experienced relentless pursuit by hunters on many occasions, and in all probability they have fought off lions and hyenas. Without a doubt, they are proven survivors, and they all have the "attitude" to prove it. To me these old warriors represent the ultimate buffalo trophy.

In my opinion, horn spread makes no difference with regards to trophy quality. I would MUCH prefer to shoot an old, worn-down "*dagga* boy" or, better still, a "scrum cap" rather than a forty-six-inch soft top!

Much has been written by the acclaimed hunter and writer Craig Boddington, some of which has been first-class, while other writings are debatable. But without doubt, Craig's greatest accomplishment has been to change the attitude of his fellow American hunters on the subject of trophy bulls. In the early years clients focused solely on shooting a buffalo with a forty-inch-plus horn spread, regardless of the bull's age. Today, with the help of Craig's writings, most clients come out to bag a good "*dagga* boy" with a massive hard boss. For this I salute you, Craig!

A great dagga *boy trophy.*

A big boss bull from Dande North, 2008.

Your goal on a buffalo hunt should be to track and observe as many bulls as possible before deciding on your trophy. When a shooting opportunity arrives, it is preferable to shoot an old *dagga* boy. Regardless of horn spread, an old buffalo is a great trophy that also presents an equally great experience. Many of my clients return to Africa time and again just to repeat their memorable quest for a venerable old bull.

Buffalo hunting is, as I like to call it, an honest hunt. This implies the hunt will take place on foot and will invariably be a challenge. Speaking as a professional hunter, it is also our "bread-and-butter hunt" because most aspiring trophy hunters who visit Africa come here to shoot a buffalo.

The Tale of Bernard's Ankle

Chapter Six

I once hunted with a Frenchman who like many of his kind had a liking for red wine, and a lot of it. Bernard was accompanied by his friend Luc. They were on a fourteen-day hunt, and both wanted to shoot a buffalo and a leopard. I was hunting with Bernard who was one of life's characters despite being overweight, extremely unfit, and undoubtedly an alcoholic! Because I had a day overlap with clients who were finishing their hunt, I asked Makoni, my former tutor and our second professional hunter, who would be guiding Luc and his wife, to take all three clients out for their first day of hunting while I finished up with my former clients.

As luck would have it, they came across an exceptional buffalo bull on the first morning out. The bull was too good to turn down, and Luc was successful in bagging it without any difficulty. The buffalo was among the best I have ever seen, a particularly fine specimen. Along with a forty-two-inch spread, the horns were elegantly twisted above an impressively large boss.

By the time I joined them round the campfire that evening, the two Frenchmen were showing signs of excessive wine consumption, and by ten o'clock Bernard had consumed on his own the entire contents of a five-litre box of red wine, the equivalent of seven regular bottles. At first I thought the Frenchmen were simply celebrating the bagging of Luc's buffalo, but it subsequently turned out I was mistaken, for over the next thirteen days, Bernard consumed a five-litre box of red wine every evening.

On the way back to his tent that first night, the somewhat unsteady Bernard tripped over a guy rope and fell flat on his back. Upon hearing his outburst, which I presumed was a selection of choice French swear words, I rushed over and found him sitting on the ground holding a rapidly swelling ankle. All I could do to assist was to give him a few anti-inflammatory

Bernard and the leopard that was eaten.

tablets and some of our precious ice to pack around his ankle. I then helped him into bed.

At dawn the following morning I sat beside the glowing embers of our campfire enjoying a cup of coffee, captivated by the beauty of the sun rising over the Zambezi River. Suddenly my thoughts were interrupted by the sound of moaning which, in many ways, resembled a wounded buffalo about to charge. Heading toward the campfire waddled Bernard using a folded camp chair as a crutch. Having seated him by the campfire, I examined his swollen ankle. It appeared obvious we would not be doing as much walking that morning. In fact, I doubted we would be doing any walking at all for the next few days as poor Bernard's ankle was black and blue and swollen twice its normal size.

Being only day two of a fourteen-day hunt, I was not unduly concerned, for there was still sufficient time for Bernard's ankle to recover. So, instead of chasing buffaloes, we decided to concentrate on bagging his leopard since this would not involve excessive exercise. All we had to do was shoot a couple of impalas from the hunting vehicle to use as bait, and the rest of the time we could spend checking the baits until we had a "hit." This would

Peter Smidt and his leopard that had its stomach eaten by another leopard.

give Bernard's ankle sufficient time to recover, after which we could resume the next stage of the safari and concentrate on his buffalo.

On the third day we were thrilled to find that our closest bait had been hit by what appeared to be a large tom leopard. We built a blind about twenty-five yards from the lure, a good deal closer than normal. I did this because Bernard was averaging three shots for every impala killed, so I was not entirely convinced that Bernard's shooting skills were sufficient to hit a leopard from a greater distance. We hung the carcass in such a position that when the leopard came in to feed, it would offer a perfect broadside shot from inside the blind.

As luck would have it, the hit bait was hanging in a communal area where the rules and regulations are somewhat different to those stipulated in the Parks and Wildlife Management Authority–controlled safari areas. In communal areas it is legal to hunt leopards at night with the aid of a spotlight. In safari areas only natural light may be used, meaning that hunting can only commence a half-hour before sunrise and end a half-hour after sunset, this being deemed the period of natural light. As we were hunting in a communal area, we could use a spotlight.

It was around 7 P.M. and totally dark when we suddenly heard the leopard's telltale "sawing" close to the bait. Soon after came the unmistakable scratching sounds as the leopard climbed up the tree, followed by the leopard chomping on the remains of the carcass.

It was clear from his rapid breathing that Bernard was overly excited, so much so there was no point in my turning on the spotlight until he calmed down. For a full five minutes we sat in absolute silence, listening to the leopard tearing at the bait. It seemed like an eternity, but eventually, when I felt Bernard had calmed down sufficiently to take a shot, I turned on the spotlight. Illuminated in the glare was the leopard, but instead of being broadside-on as I had anticipated, its backside was facing us. Precariously balanced, the big tom was trying to pull the impala carcass onto an upper branch.

As the only target presenting itself was the leopard's rear end, I whispered to Bernard to wait. The big cat was totally relaxed now, and it appeared only a matter of time before it would tire of its balancing act and stand broadside-on, thus giving Bernard the opportunity of a lethal shoulder shot. Despite my whispered instructions to "wait," a shot rang out, and the leopard was thrown off the branch and hit the ground with a meaty thud. The telltale growls of a wounded and very angry cat wafted over to us on the evening air. Moments later we heard the injured leopard crashing off through the undergrowth.

Despite the fact that there had only been a view of the leopard's backside, Bernard proclaimed in his broken English that he'd placed a perfect shot into the leopard's shoulder. I knew otherwise. I also knew we were in for an interesting evening.

Leaving Bernard in the blind, my trackers Crispen and Morgan and I followed the leopard for several hundred metres. Drops of thin, watery blood indicated that Bernard had shot it in the stomach. After enduring several blood-curdling growls from as close as five metres in thick bush, I decided the wisest move would be to abandon the follow-up until next morning.

We set off after the wounded leopard at first light. A somewhat relieved Bernard stayed in the vehicle after I assured him I would not be offended if he remained there. To be fair, the bush where we had abandoned the tracks was extremely thick and his ankle was still very swollen. In such situations, Bernard would only have been a liability. I was relieved at his decision to stay behind.

We found Bernard's leopard already dead. It had traveled about a kilometre from the tree and must have died during the early hours of the morning. What was surprising, however, was that another leopard had eaten part of the dead one's stomach. I have subsequently witnessed such cannibalistic behaviour on two additional occasions. Bernard was ecstatic with his trophy, for it was a very big male. I, however, was concerned about the up-and-coming buffalo hunt.

By the seventh day of the hunt, Bernard's ankle had returned to normal and only a feint blue tinge remained visible. Despite the improvement, he still hobbled around using choice language and declaring that in his predicament there was no way he could possibly track a buffalo.

I went to great lengths to accommodate Bernard's condition. My first thought was to rent a donkey upon which he could ride while we pursued the buffalo. I rejected this idea almost immediately because we were in the heart of lion country, and the donkey and Bernard would present too attractive a target for a hungry lion. My next idea was to push him in a wheelbarrow. This plan was shot down by my trackers, one of whom was in his seventies. They unanimously refused to track a buffalo while pushing the overweight Frenchman in the wheelbarrow.

I realized that if we were to bag Bernard's buffalo, we would have to get him as close to the animal as possible. In the end I decided to leave my two trackers in one of the villages every evening with a radio; their job was to track the old *dagga* boys that raided the village crops during the night. At first light they were to follow these bulls and report back to me. These particular animals seldom went far from the villages before lying up during the day, which would give us the opportunity to get Bernard close enough for a shot.

The following morning we left camp and called up the trackers on the radio. They said they were on tracks and not far away from an old bull. On hearing this I parked the Land Cruiser beneath a shady tree and waited for their return call to tell us they'd caught up with the animal. But there was no response. Thinking they were busy on the follow-up, I waited for an

Old dagga *boy resting during the heat of the day.*

hour, and when I still had heard nothing, I called them again. This time they replied by telling me they were still on the tracks. Strangely enough I thought Crispen's voice sounded a little slurred, but this I put down to poor radio communications, a not uncommon occurrence in the valley.

On my third call I was told the buffalo was still "very far away." This time I distinctly heard drums beating in the background. Suddenly the penny dropped, and I knew what they were up to. They were at a beer drink! Luckily, it was not too difficult to find where the closest beer drink was taking place. So, along with a hand-held radio, I made my way to the village in question. There I discovered Crispen and Morgan in the company of communal members of the opposite sex, both of them elegantly seated upon a fallen tree trunk while holding calabashes of the local brew in each hand.

I stood out of sight and not more than fifty metres away from the rowdy party, and I radioed again to ask how the follow-up was going. I watched as Crispen, putting on a big act for the crowd, set down one of the calabashes to answer the radio. He told me the buffalo bull they were following had scented them and run away, but he added they were still on its tracks. His statement was followed by hysterical laughter from their inebriated lady friends.

Shouting loudly, I called out their names. In their drunken state it took a few moments for them to realize that the voice calling them had not come from the radio but, in fact, from directly behind where they stood. Suddenly the ladies saw me and in a bewildered flurry scattered in all directions while Morgan and Crispen, in utter confusion, dropped their calabashes and stood rooted to the spot. That occasion was the closest my trackers ever came to getting fired, but in spite of their insubordination I had to admire their gall.

The safari was rapidly drawing to a close, and our several attempts to get Bernard his buffalo had all failed. Bernard's ankle was the problem. After his customary five-litre box of red wine each evening, he seemed to cope very well on the ankle, yet each morning he would hobble and complain and curse vehemently. To me, his ankle looked fine, so I was becoming unsympathetic toward his dramatics and felt he had pushed his performance too far.

On the second to the last day the trackers spotted a buffalo only a hundred metres off the road. The great animal was resting in a thick patch of bush. This was possibly Bernard's last opportunity, so I dragged him, hobbling, complaining, and cursing toward the resting buffalo. After a

Bernard's (left) end of the hunt picture was taken on the Zambezi River.

Bernard and his dagga *boy.*

great deal of verbal support and encouragement, we finally got close enough for him to take a shot.

It was a fine mature buffalo, and on that occasion Bernard surprised us all by giving it a perfectly placed heart shot. The buffalo ran fifty-odd yards before keeling over and, much to the relief of our team, letting out a mighty death bellow. It was success at last for Bernard, who collected a fine forty-two-inch buffalo for himself. Granted it was not as pretty as Luc's, but a great trophy nonetheless.

A month or so later I received a letter and some pictures from Bernard. The first picture showed him with his leg and foot in plaster. The poor guy had, in fact, broken his ankle in three places! I felt embarrassed by my lack of sympathy but consoled myself with the thought that his painful cries and hobbling had, in the end, been amply rewarded. Below is a copy of his letter.

Buss,
Thank you good safari. I now look a good lion with big mane.
You find lion I bring wine!
Your friend,
Bernard

OVID

CHAPTER SEVEN

Our clients were three brothers from the United States who were after buffalo. Ovid was the eldest; he was also very overweight and really did not appreciate walking too far!

One evening a skinner came running to the dining room to inform us that a leopard was in the skinning shed. Armed with torches and cameras, we went to investigate. Sure enough, there it was, eating a piece of leftover meat from a buffalo that one of the brothers had shot earlier that day. When we shone the light on the leopard, it scampered off with the chunk of meat in its mouth and climbed up a nearby tree. There it continued to feed undisturbed, despite the torch beams and all of us watching.

Ovid decided to take a picture of the feeding leopard, but he first needed to get into camera range. Slowly he edged forward while we continued to keep the leopard fixed in the beams of our torches.

"Get a little closer, Ovid," encouraged his younger brother with a gentle nudge.

In the darkness, with our attentions focused on the leopard, none of us noticed that there was a huge hole right in front of us. This hole was a massive dump site where the skinner disposed of all the rotten guts and bits and pieces of sinew and bone left over at the end of each day.

With what can only be described as a combination of a loud yell and a terrified yodel, Ovid disappeared into the open hole where he began to wallow in its slimy, stinking contents. Every time he managed to get his massive body halfway out of the pit, he would fall back again into the filthy mire. His slapstick attempts to extricate himself were masterpieces of pratfall humour and so hilariously funny that soon everyone was rolling around, crying with laughter. Think Buster Keaton meets the Three Stooges.

Ovid took his buffalo in Makuti, 2011.

Eventually the camp staff arrived, and Ovid's dignity suffered a further insult. Like us, the staff took one look at the situation, and they, too, doubled over with laughter. Poor Ovid covered in smelly guts and nasty waste was a hilarious sight, indeed.

In the end it took a massive combined effort of hunters and staff to haul the unfortunate fellow out. It soon became obvious that Ovid did not appreciate being centre stage of the humour, but after a long hot shower, a fresh change of clothes, and a couple of large whiskies, his mood changed for the better and eventually he did see the funny side of it.

ELEPHANT HUNTING

CHAPTER EIGHT

In the early years during my apprenticeship I gained a lot of experience doing PAC (Problem Animal Control). This was done in the off-season, which coincided with the main growing season for crops. This involved tracking and shooting young bulls that made a nuisance of themselves by raiding the locals' crops night after night. In a single night these bulls could literally finish off an entire crop that was intended to sustain an entire family for a year, so you can appreciate how devastating this could be.

Having just qualified, I would, like all other young professional hunters, accept whatever hunt I was lucky enough to be offered by an operator. This is beneficial in that it offers the young professional the opportunity to gain hunting experience over a wide spectrum, especially with those animals considered to be dangerous.

After I had had a number of successful years hunting elephants, the safari operators with whom I dealt began to offer me the exclusive rights to their elephant hunts, which was just what I wanted. This afforded me the opportunity to choose the hunts I particularly wanted to guide. Over the next twenty-odd years I have almost exclusively hunted elephants, and in some seasons I guided in excess of thirty hunts a year. I have also produced four DVDs on the same subject, the most recent being completed twenty-four years after I shot my first elephant.

My infatuation and, indeed, my love for elephants started when I was very young. Growing up in Rhodesia, now Zimbabwe, we were privileged to have access to the country's wonderful and diverse national parks. Observing an elephant from the comfort of a vehicle in a national park or from the luxury of a houseboat on Lake Kariba is one thing, but approaching an elephant on foot in a hunting area is a totally different ball game.

Here I am with an elephant bull that has a huge body, Kazuma, 2014.

As a budding apprentice, approaching my first elephant on foot had a profound effect on me. It was the sheer size of the animal that captivated me, and it was not long before my schoolboy impression of tame elephants—the loving creatures that would never intentionally harm anyone—was soon shattered. I learnt very quickly that the "harmless jumbos" of the national parks are not how elephants are naturally meant to be. That is an artificial situation created by man and propagated by the existence of the national parks.

Man has hunted elephants for as long as literature has been written. An elephant in its natural environment fears humans, and as a result becomes an aggressive animal, one to be respected and hunted at one's peril. Their sheer size makes them formidable opponents, and when combined with a

I shot this PAC elephant bull right among the crops.

great sense of smell, decent hearing, and the ability to travel many miles in a day, the elephant makes for the ultimate hunting experience, especially when the pursuit is carried out on foot, following the spoor.

I have often been asked how I can kill such a magnificent animal when I claim to love and have an affiliation to them. This is always difficult to explain, but it helps if people can understand the hunting process. It is more than just the kill—it is the hunt itself that's important: the tracking, the pursuit, the excitement, the unknown, all leading up to the final moment, the kill itself. Critics of hunting only see the kill, yet if they could be part of the whole experience, they would have a better understanding of the process that draws me and other professionals to hunting elephants.

On average I guide about twenty hunts a season, which equates to about one hundred and seventy days in the field. This means following and interacting with many hundreds of animals on a daily basis. Apart from the thrill of the tracking process, which is the essence of a true elephant hunt, I have had the privilege of spending more quality time than most with these great animals, unobserved, in their own environment and under every imaginable situation.

When you follow a particular elephant bull, you become part of his daily routine. You see where and what he feeds on, the trees he breaks, the grasses he pulls out, and the leaves upon which he browses. You watch where he rests in the heat of the day or where he stops for an evening nap. You take notice where he rolls in a mud wallow or quenches his thirst at some remote spring. You watch where he meets up with the cows and how they chase him away, resisting his stubborn advances . . . and, if you're lucky, you might observe his acceptance by a cow. You see him in musth and smell it clinging to the thick bush through which he has just walked. You observe him joining other bulls and watch where he jousts with the younger ones; you also take notice as he leaves the group and plods on his own way again. As you draw closer, his dung becomes fresh, revealing what he's been eating. To hunt a bull elephant the right and proper way is to become part of his life. It is the involvement with this process that first attracted and then later trained me in the pursuit of the elephant.

Here is the sequence of an unprovoked elephant charge. First, the shot.

The hit.

The result.

Another picture of the last few seconds of a successful end to an unprovoked charge.

After many hours of amazing tracking, you finally catch up to the bull while he is resting in thick *jesse* bush. There the visibility can sometimes be measured in feet. You edge your way to an opening, conscious that the wind might change at any time, and if it does, in a flash he might be gone or, worse still, he could turn and charge. Suddenly you are there, within twenty feet of the most amazing animal. What a magnificent sight a bull elephant is at such times, a sight that will remain with you for the rest of your life.

There you have it in a nutshell, my own opinion of what constitutes a successful elephant hunt. Now come the variables. What is the size of his tusks? Are they big or small? Are the shapes different or are they symmetrical? Does he have both tusks or has one been damaged or removed completely? Is he an old bull? Is he too young to remove from the gene pool? Is he the bull you really want? Many times the answer to these questions is "NO." In such situations you carefully back away, leaving the bull undisturbed and resting in his little haven, totally unaware of your presence. And THAT is what elephant hunting is all about.

Beware of tuskless cows!

On most occasions, after many days of endless tracking and lots of painful blisters, you become emotionally drained from numerous thick *jesse* bush approaches. That's when you finally find the "right" bull. It is only at this point that you change from being a naturalist to a hunter. Time goes into slow motion as you lift your rifle to evaluate which clean killing shot the bull is offering you. At such moments, nothing else in life seems to matter. In fact nothing else exists on the planet except you and the huge elephant facing you, twenty yards away!

At the shot, his hind legs give way first, and then his front end buckles forward and sinks onto the ground with a thud. He is dead . . . killed in an instant, often without even knowing you were there. When the dust settles, the reality of what you've just done sets in. You have killed Africa's most iconic animal. It is a time not only for rejoicing but also a time for reflecting on the enormity of your actions. Such times can also be sad ones when a feeling of melancholy overshadows the happiness of a successful hunt. This is the way it should be. Sadness pays tribute to Africa's ultimate animal and Africa's ultimate hunt.

There are two types of elephant hunts in Zimbabwe: those for trophy bulls and those for tuskless elephants. While the law states that any elephant that does not have visual ivory is deemed tuskless, the reality of finding a tuskless bull is very remote, indeed. In all my years of hunting, I have only come across three tuskless bulls. So when a client books a hunt for a tuskless elephant, he is essentially booking a hunt for a cow.

A lot of people view tuskless elephant hunts with contempt, saying they do not constitute a real elephant hunt. Granted, such hunts are not for a big bull with impressive ivory, but I can assure you they can be every bit as exciting and demanding as going after a bull elephant. Apart from the sheer danger and emotional toll of approaching a tuskless elephant up close in thick *jesse* bush, the tuskless hunt is also physically demanding. Without a doubt, tuskless cows or cows in general are far more dangerous to hunt than a lone bull or a bull with a companion or two.

This 50-pound elephant bull is from the Dande in the Zambezi Valley.

This bull has beautiful long ivory and is a much sought-after trophy.

Tuskless cows will invariably be part of a herd, and as we all know, there are close family ties within the elephant family. Low and behold, if you are seen as a threat to them, things can get really nasty in a hurry. You need to be on your toes when hunting tuskless elephants, for a charge at any time is all part of the deal. In my opinion, elephant cows are without a doubt the most dangerous of any unwounded big-game species to hunt. They are highly intelligent, unpredictable, and often outrageously malicious.

On occasions having made a successful getaway, the cow elephant will reverse the hunter/hunted dynamic. I've had some cows deliberately hunt me down by following my scent. There can be no doubt about this, for on one particular occasion I was able to view the goings on from the safety of an elevated position. Her intention was clear, and I managed to escape only by climbing a rocky outcrop that she was unable to negotiate. Unfortunately, over time, I've been forced to shoot a number of elephants in self-defense, and all but two of them were cows.

Only 3 percent of the Zambezi Valley's elephants are tuskless. This statistic alone means that you have to look over a lot of cows to find a tuskless one, and when you eventually do, the animal should be mature without a dependent calf at her side. The combination of these factors means that, on average, you will probably look at and approach roughly three hundred elephants before you find a suitable tuskless cow.

Hunts for tuskless cows are a lot more affordable. Currently a trophy bull elephant hunt averages around $40,000, and there are not many people out there who can afford that. A tuskless elephant cow hunt, on the other hand, is actually the cheapest big-game hunt to be had. It's even cheaper than a buffalo hunt. This is where the appeal really lies: lots of adrenaline bang for not too many bucks.

In the early years operators and even the Zimbabwe government did not realize the true value of a tuskless elephant. In fact, they often thought them undesirable and almost impossible to sell. Fortunately, I had several clients who, like myself, thought otherwise. On a number of occasions we

Luis and I celebrate his 55-pound elephant bull from Dande North.

Walter Edar with his 60-pound elephant from Dande North.

were fortunate enough to have operators sell us a ten-day hunt for as many tuskless elephants as were on quota. On a number of such hunts, thanks to awesome trackers and good elephant numbers, we successfully hunted and shot seven or even eight tuskless cows on a single hunt. But those days are long gone, and as it currently stands, only a single tuskless cow can now be hunted on a ten-day hunt.

My elephant bull hunts can be divided into two brackets. The first are the bulls that are hunted in the Zambezi Valley. These hunts involve tracking a single bull or, if we're lucky, a small group of approximately four bulls. During this time the bull's spoor will take us through some of the most beautiful country God has created. The second category is for those bull elephants we hunt in northwestern Zimbabwe, around Hwange National Park; these areas in northwestern Zimbabwe are known as the forestry blocks of Ntundhla and Kazuma. These hunts involve tracking groups rather than single elephants.

There are some real differences in the elephants and the way we hunt them in these two areas. In the Zambezi Valley there are many more cows than bulls. Genetically, the elephants in the valley are smaller in body and have smaller tusks than the elephants in the northwestern areas. Interestingly enough, the ratio of cows to bulls in the northwestern areas is completely the opposite to that of the valley: In the forestry blocks there are more bulls and a fewer number of cows.

Tracking in the Zambezi Valley is more demanding because the elephants travel greater distances over much harsher terrain; this is in comparison to tracking in the northwest where the terrain is sandy soil, which makes tracking easier. On a typical fourteen-day, Zambezi Valley elephant bull hunt, we will track and approach an average of around thirty bulls before a suitable one is found. Then it takes a minimum of five hours of tracking before there is even a likelihood of getting close to the elephant we are after. In the northwest, by comparison, we can expect on a similar hunt to track and look at about three hundred bulls.

David Jones with his 68-pound elephant from Kazuma.

Mac Jenkins with his 68-pound elephant from Dande East.

Zambezi Valley ivory is very attractive—long and slender and with an average tusk circumference of sixteen inches at the lip. I think it is obvious that these measurements are not conducive to weight. Bulls in the northwestern region are among the biggest-bodied elephants in Africa. They also have shorter, thicker, denser ivory, and the average circumference for these elephants is eighteen inches at the lip.

Another noticeable difference is the smaller head on the Zambezi Valley bull when compared to its northwestern cousin. The Zambezi bulls have on average two-and-a-half feet of ivory embedded in their skulls while their cousins from the northwest have on average three feet of embedded ivory. In the Zambezi Valley, a forty-pounder is considered a fine trophy while in the northwest we hope for at least sixty pounds a side, and sometimes even better.

Both types of hunts are highly rewarding, but for different reasons. I love the Zambezi Valley hunts primarily for the challenge they present in tracking. The "Valley," as we call it, has very little sand, and that makes tracking extremely difficult. Apart from the floodplains close to the Zambezi River, the other hunting areas consist of rocky ridges interspersed by sandy gullies, thickets of *jesse* bush, and valleys with tall, flattened grass. Only the very best trackers can operate successfully in this sort of terrain.

On many occasions, my clients have walked great distances without seeing a sign of the elephant we were tracking. This reminds me of what an elderly client once said to Rich Tabor when they were hunting a bull elephant in the Zambezi Valley. After an hour of following a bull's trail, the old fellow turned to Rich's tracker, Norest, and said, "Young man, have you any bloody idea what you're doing?"

"Yes, sir," replied Norest, pointing to a steaming pile of elephant dung. "We are following this elephant bull and we hope you will shoot it, sir!"

The Zambezi Valley and the Dande Communal Land in particular are in wild, rugged country that contains many stunning valleys dotted with numerous springs. Bull elephants love these areas, and the best way to see them is to let a set of elephant tracks take you there. The adage, "You hunt an elephant with your legs" is very true, but few realize what beautiful country can be seen along the way.

Bull elephants in hunting areas are too smart to get caught out in the open during daylight. As soon as it starts to get light or warm up, they enter

This was Gus's second elephant; the longer tusk weighed 58 pounds and the broken one weighed 48 pounds.

Dave Adams and good-looking 55-pound elephant from Kazuma.

the dreaded *jesse* bush, which is comprised mainly of Combretum bush. This bush becomes extremely thick in places, so much so that at times it is barely penetrable, and the only way to pass through is to stick to the narrow elephant paths that wind their way through the thickets. Deep inside these shady thickets of *jesse* bush are many rainwater pans, a favourite haunt of the elephant. The difficulty of hunting bull elephants in these areas is further compounded by the valley's notorious fluctuating winds that occur during the heat of the day. All these factors contribute to providing the ideal resting place for an elephant. This is a place where they feel safe and secure, and more often than not, it will be in the depths of this deep and tranquil environment that a hunt for a Zambezi Valley bull elephant will finally end.

In the northwest of the country, the hunt will involve following larger groups of bulls, with their numbers reaching as many as forty and more in a single group. As the hunt progresses, they will split up into smaller groups of about ten animals. On occasions the hunt will start on a single bull's track, but very rarely will you catch up to your target before he's joined up with a group.

The northwest areas are essentially an extension of the Kalahari Desert. There the gusu sand makes for easy tracking and the open terrain makes visibility much easier. There are no blocks of *jesse* bush, no rocky ridges, and no gullies to contend with; instead, the landscape is comprised of sparse, open grasslands dotted with teak trees. It is under these trees that the elephants rest up during the heat of the day. Good visibility makes the final approach a lot easier than in the valley, and even if the wind is unfavourable, it is usually possible to maneuver into a downwind position before the bulls pick up your scent.

It is the sheer size of these elephants that makes them so attractive. They are huge, Africa's largest without doubt, and they make you feel small and insignificant when they raise their heads and look down their trunks at you from no farther away than fifteen yards. To the uninitiated, the sheer size

Gus Alvera's 70-pound elephant from Kazuma had an unusual spread.

Here we are approaching a herd of elephant bulls in Kazuma, 2016.

of these bulls is intimidating, so much so that clients need to be mentally prepared for the encounter. If not, things can go pear-shaped in a hurry.

If I were asked which of the areas I prefer, I would have to say that they are so different they can't be compared. In the Zambezi Valley you have the stunningly beautiful terrain, which is of great consequence to me and an aspect in which the northwestern regions cannot compare. Also in the valley, as I've said, it's all about tracking in some of the toughest terrain imaginable. For me, that is the key issue to the overall challenge and appreciation of the entire hunt.

Elephant bull hunts in the northwestern regions are different, the tracking is easy, the bulls and their tusks are much bigger, and the sight of so many elephants gathered together is a spoiling factor for me. On the positive side is the slight possibility of bagging a bull with one hundred pounds of ivory a side.

Another notable difference between the bulls of the two regions is that the valley bulls are MUCH harder to approach. These bulls have been on high

Here I am with a beautiful 60-pound elephant from Kazuma ,2017.

Success.

alert for countless years due to heavy poaching, mainly from neighbouring Mozambique where they often travel. It has been many years since I have shot a bull that has not carried at least one projectile from a poacher's gun, be it an AK-47 rifle bullet or a lead ball fired from a homemade muzzleloader. As a result, the Zambezi bulls are much more unpredictable, making them a lot more dangerous than their cousins from the northwest. There the bulls have had the havens of national parks that adjoin the hunting blocks to lull them into a sense of security, making the hunter's approach easier and, perhaps, more predictable.

Regardless of which area one chooses, if the hunt is conducted on foot with first-class trackers, it will be challenging and memorable. Hunting elephants is never easy, but rest assured when you finally secure a fine bull elephant, you will have earned it.

CHAPTER NINE

CLIFF HANGING

I had finally attained my license, and I was booked the following season to commence my first elephant hunt as an actual professional and no longer as a "tag-along" apprentice. With youth and enthusiasm on my side, I set off to scout the area and look for elephant movement the week before my client was due to arrive.

My client had booked a bull elephant and a buffalo hunt. It was the first hunt of the season, so I decided to look for a worthy bull around the villages east of the Dande Safari Area. This is a remote area that borders Mozambique. I had received word by the famous bush telegraph system that there were a number of bull elephants raiding the villagers' maize and pumpkin crops, so that's where I headed.

The Dande is not well known for the size of its elephants, but occasionally some better-than-average bulls cross the border from Mozambique to raid the villagers' crops. Long before first light, the culprits would normally re-cross the Angwa River and return to their safe haven in Mozambique, but that was not always the case. Occasionally driven by greed for the tasty pickings available, some bulls would linger until dawn. Should this happen, rather than taking the risk of crossing the wide Angwa River in daylight, the bulls would head west into a very thick area of *jesse* bush known to the locals as the *maitumbu.*

On the day in question my tracker and I found the spoor of a large elephant bull that had caused havoc the previous night in a maize field belonging to an old villager. The bull had literally destroyed the crop upon which the old man relied to feed himself and his family over the coming year. From the devastated field, the tracks headed due west and into the *maitumbu*. Initially the elephant had moved rapidly to put as much distance as possible between himself and the maize field he had so effectively destroyed.

The *jesse* bush is a mecca for elephants. In this inhospitable environment the bull has all the advantages of thick cover, unstable winds, shade, and numerous pans in which to wallow and drink. Having penetrated the dense block of *jesse* bush for a couple of kilometres, the bull began to slow down. Feeling secure in the thick and dense environment, he started to meander and feed at the same time. Because he was no longer traveling in a set direction, following his tracks became considerably more difficult.

He began to wander to whichever bush or tree took his fancy, and as he did so his tracks began to overlap, a sure sign he was no longer in a hurry. We were now rapidly closing the distance, but, unfortunately, and just when I expected to hear the noise of his feeding, his tracks suddenly joined those of a large group of cows.

This further complicated the tracking. Under such circumstances, trying to pick out a single bull's tracks from those of many cows and calves requires immense concentration. To make matters worse, the *jesse* bush in the early part of the season is thickly covered in foliage that reduces visibility to a couple of feet. Believe me, tracking elephants in these conditions can be extremely trying on the nerves and highly dangerous to boot.

Tracking the herd that now contained the crop-raiding bull by following the trail of destruction left behind by the feeding herd, however, was easy. Despite these easily visible signs, my tracker had to remain vigilant and on the lookout for signs of the bull breaking away from the herd. Occasionally the slowly feeding elephants would cross an open patch and we could see their spoor more clearly, including the spoor of the bull as it dwarfed the tracks of the cows.

The deep cracks and worn-down heels clearly indicated that our bull was advanced in years. Ivory continues to grow throughout an elephant bull's life, so the chances of an old bull having long and heavy tusks are good. As my mind wandered on the possibility of a fine tusker, his tracks took us through a dry, rocky riverbed and up a steep bank. Just as we started to climb the opposite bank, we heard the elephants. We were now so close that we could hear their communicating rumblings and the occasional breaking of a branch.

An elephant bull disappearing into the maitumbu jesse *block.*

This was the sign for my tracker to fall back. Alone I climbed the bank, on top of which I encountered an impenetrable wall of *jesse*, so thick that all I could see of the elephants was an odd leg and a swishing tail about twenty yards away. To my left and slightly higher up the bank there was an open gully. I decided that I could get a much better view of the herd and with a bit of luck identify the old bull we were after if I made my way there.

Typically the wind at midday throughout the Zambezi Valley tends to swirl, so I needed to proceed with care. Making regular checks with my ash bag, I edged slowly forward along the bank toward the better vantage point. I was halfway there when I heard an angry scream. Bearing down the ridge and heading straight toward me rushed an irate elephant cow with a tiny calf at her side.

In such situations adrenaline takes over and time seems to slow down. Even so, there was no doubt as to her intention as she came barreling along the ridge toward me. That she wanted to turn me into a strawberry jam look-alike was obvious, but I can still recall my sense of reluctance to shoot her because of the small calf at her side. Every professional hunter develops his own methods of dealing with an elephant charge. Makoni, my excellent tutor to whom I had been apprenticed, helped me develop mine.

Instinct took over as I tried in vain to shout the cow down. In similar situations shouting had been enough to turn stampeding cows, but this one was different. Raising my .416 Ruger, I shot over her head, which normally is enough to halt a mock attack, but to my dismay the warning shot only appeared to quicken her pace. I realized then that there was nothing mock about the charge; she was coming for me with deadly intent. There I was, standing on the edge of a vertical five-metre drop with an empty rifle in my hands.

Frantically I tried to reload my Ruger, but in my inexperience I badly misjudged how long it would take. I was still recycling the rifle's action when the cow flattened a *jesse* bush right in front of me. So great was her momentum that she ploughed straight through the thick bush. Now thoroughly alarmed, I noted her massive trunk rolled up and all ready to swat me like a fly.

I watched as her trunk uncoiled like a massive spring, and in that split second she hit me across the chest with incredible force. Thankfully I was still holding my rifle diagonally across my body in my frantic effort to work the bolt and chamber a new cartridge. The cow's trunk hit my rifle in the pistol grip area with enough thrust to crack the stock, and as it snapped the rifle, I was knocked backward off the edge of the vertical drop—very much like a cork being popped from a champagne bottle. As I flew backward, I had enough presence of mind to complete the reloading process, and by the time I landed with a bone-jarring, tooth-snapping thud on the ground, my rifle was reloaded and the safety catch on.

As I hit the deck in a sitting position, I heard an ominous cracking sound. I thought it was the stock of my rifle breaking, but instead it turned out to be my coccyx fracturing. Initially, there was no pain, probably due to the massive surge of adrenaline pumping through my body. I immediately stood up, fully expecting the vertical bank to collapse on top of me from the weight of the irate cow. As luck would have it, she had somehow managed to stop herself at the edge. Had she not halted in time and had she followed me over the vertical drop, my professional hunting career would have been a very short one, indeed.

For what seemed an eternity, the cow just stood on the bank looking down at me. Immobilized, I stood with the foresight of my .416 rifle resting on her forehead well below the level of her eyes. This was to compensate for the angle of the bullet to reach her brain. Just as I was deciding to shoot, she let out a defiant scream and then turned to follow the rest of the herd as they crashed off through the *jesse* bush.

It was at this point I collapsed, so great was the pain from my fractured coccyx. I was lying on the sand in agony when my ashen-faced tracker reappeared. He later admitted to thinking I was dead. What followed was an excruciatingly painful five-kilometre piggyback ride on the back of my bony tracker to the Land Cruiser. This was followed by an even more painful, seven-hour drive to Harare over the bumpiest of roads as I lay in absolute torment on a mattress in the back of the vehicle.

After what seemed like forever, I finally reached the hospital where I was diagnosed with a broken coccyx and torn groin muscles. My first-ever solo elephant hunt could not have been a more disastrous beginning to my professional hunting career. To make matters worse, I was forced to spend the subsequent two months in rehabilitation where the boredom nearly killed me. Not being able to hunt for this length of time was harder to endure than the pain from my injuries.

In retrospect, being knocked off a vertical, five-metre-high bank by an overprotective elephant cow and landing in a sitting position in the sand and rocks below is probably the reason I've never attained my height potential. In fact I've come to accept that thanks to that irate cow, I will for the rest of my natural life remain a short-arse.

The occasion did, however, teach me a valuable lesson. To this day I still employ the same technique for charging elephants. Shouting an elephant down is my first line of defense, but as for a warning shot, I no longer do this. Too much can go wrong in those tense final moments. To be in such a situation with an empty rifle makes no sense at all. No professional hunter wants to shoot an elephant in self-defense, but if you have to, your rifle needs to be loaded. If a warning shot does not work as anticipated, then you need to shoot to kill. Having to reload before doing so takes far too long, as I painfully came to realize.

RUN FASTER, MADAM!

CHAPTER TEN

The busy 2008 hunting season had finally come to an end, and it was time for some well-deserved R&R (rest and recuperation). At the time I was going out with a girl named Laura who I'd known from my high school days. I had always fancied Laura, who was a really good-looking girl. After leaving school, Laura went to Dubai where she found employment training horses for one of the many sheiks. It was in Dubai that she met and fell in love with a Zimbabwean pilot who was flying for Emirates Airlines. However, the relationship only lasted a couple of years, and after a difficult and traumatic breakup, Laura cut her losses and returned to Zimbabwe. Around the same time I, too, was ending a relationship, so in a fortunate stroke of serendipity, Laura and I got together and soon we were dating.

With nothing specifically planned for the Christmas holiday, I decided to take Laura to the Mururu Camp in the Zambezi Valley. Mururu is one of my favourite places. It's a spectacular chalet-styled camp, nestling under a cluster of massive old mahogany trees along the bank of the Manyemu River. Nice and secluded, Mururu was, in my opinion, the perfect place for a romantic holiday.

Having enjoyed a privileged colonial upbringing where African staff was always on hand for cooking, washing, cleaning, and making up beds etc., I decided that Royal, who at the time was my driver and right-hand man, should accompany us on our romantic excursion. It was the off-season and the regular Mururu camp staff would be away over the festive period. With Mururu being so remote, there were no villages nearby to recruit temporary camp staff, so Royal was appointed camp cook, bottle washer, and general handyman.

The drive down to Mururu proved challenging as the annual rains had already set in, making many parts of the Zambezi Valley nearly impassable.

Mururu Camp in Dande.

The access road into Mururu camp runs through a section of mopane forest where the soil consists of dark brown clay, commonly referred to as "cotton soil." When saturated, the soil takes on the consistency of slimy chocolate pudding. Driving in these areas during the rainy season is well-nigh impossible because the vehicle continually sinks up to its axles in the muddy clay. Thankfully in our case, with the aid of a winch and shovels and by packing the ruts with branches, we managed to pull and push and dig ourselves out of trouble.

Laura's stint in Dubai had starved her of the African bush and its wildlife, something that those of us who were lucky enough to grow up in Zimbabwe learn to love. Of all the Zambezi Valley wild animals, the one she missed the most were elephants. In fact she was desperate so see a few elephants during our time in the valley. Lady Luck smiled upon us that day. As we were getting close to Mururu camp, a herd of elephant cows and calves ran across the road in front of us, then carried on down into a small valley below the road. The bush was very thick, and in no time the herd had been swallowed up in the lush green foliage that's so abundant during the rainy season.

It was an opportunity not to be missed, so I decided to follow the herd into the bush. I already knew from past experience that the herd would not go far in these lush conditions, and, besides, it was an ideal opportunity to show Laura what a tough and rugged professional hunter I'd become! So I grabbed my rifle and off we went, in single file, down a narrow game trail. Laura wore a white tee shirt, skimpy shorts, and flip-flops, not exactly the best form of dress for such excursions. Anyway, just as I'd expected, we hadn't gone far when we came upon the herd at the bottom of the valley. The bush was very thick there and our view of the elephants restricted, but as luck would have it, we found a well-used elephant path that gave us a much better view of the herd as they trooped away from us in single file.

Bringing up the rear was the herd's matriarch, a massive old cow. If I hadn't been showing off so much in front of my new girlfriend, I would have recognized the tell-tale signs that trouble was just around the corner: As the cow ambled slowly away, her head was held high and slightly cocked at an angle. This afforded her a good view of us from over her shoulder, a sure sign she was fully aware of us and that she felt something was amiss. I'm embarrassed to admit I was distracted by Laura's presence, especially her skimpy shorts, but I have absolutely no excuse for failing to detect those warning signs.

As if she was reading my thoughts, the cow suddenly whirled around and down the path straight toward us she thundered, her head held high, her massive ears extended. To the inexperienced, an elephant blasting down a narrow path can be a frightening creature, indeed.

Shouting at Royal and Laura to run for their lives, I stood my ground to confront the angry old cow. I tried to shout her down, but my best efforts were unsuccessful, and on she came. Eventually, when she was dangerously close and still coming, I realized something drastic had to be done to stop her. In such situations there are only two options: The first is to kill the cow with a frontal brain shot or, second, to shoot over her head in the hope that this will change her mind and stop the charge.

After an unpleasant experience at the beginning of my career when a warning shot had failed to stop an irate elephant cow, I had long given up on warning shots as charge-stopping deterrents. It had been a painful lesson and one I had taken to heart. The cow had knocked me off a high bank, fracturing my coccyx in the process. On this occasion, however, I was carrying my double-barrel rifle, so I sent a bullet just over the top of her head. Had she still not stopped, there would have been enough time for me to drop her with a shot from the second barrel. This is the advantage of a double-barrel rifle.

Thankfully my warning shot had the desired effect. As she felt the shock waves of the bullet passing closely over her head, accompanied by the deafening roar of the rifle, the old cow locked her legs, applied the brakes, and slid to a halt right in front of me. With a defiant shake of her huge head and a piercing scream, she whirled around and set off back up the path to catch up with her rapidly departing family.

Realizing the situation was under control and the danger gone, I turned around to see how Royal and Laura were faring. Before my eyes was a truly amazing scene and one that could only happen in the wilds of Africa. There was Laura in full flight and leading the way up the track. As I watched, she jettisoned her flip-flops in midstride with both flying off in different directions. At the same time, Royal was nipping at Laura's heels, whacking her with the flat of his hand on her trim little backside and shouting at the top of his voice, "Run faster, madam, please run faster!"

I couldn't help but to burst out laughing.

Laura, a typically feisty Zimbabwean female, was not amused at all, not in the slightest. In fact, she completely failed to see the humorous side of the situation. What's more she claimed I'd orchestrated the whole affair and by doing so had acted like a complete idiot. As a result, the romantic Zambezi Valley holiday, which I had so carefully planned, fizzled completely. I guess that proves even serendipity has its limits!

The Luc Elephant Saga

Chapter Eleven

My brother, an airline pilot, once told me there are many "young and bold pilots but very few old, bold pilots." I suppose the same can be said about professional elephant hunters. I should know. I almost fell into the trap of becoming a statistic that proves the adage: "very few old, bold professional elephant hunters." When a professional hunter becomes overly confident, when he challenges the status quo, when he seeks more and more excitement from each subsequent hunt, that is the time to reassess his priorities, as this saga will show.

What does it mean to be a professional elephant hunter? In all honesty I'm troubled by the title "professional elephant hunter" and in many ways I'm reluctant to call myself one. In my eyes, the title "professional elephant hunter" refers to two categories of hunters: The first is the acclaimed hunters of yesteryear, of whom I would not be so presumptuous as to compare myself. The likes of Karamojo Bell or James Sutherland come to mind. These were professionals who hunted at a time when there were few game laws and boundaries between nations were porous.

Later on yet still part of this first category were the so-called hunters that some might rightfully call poachers. They, too, made their living by killing elephants for their ivory, but these men hunted in the days when there were game laws and when borders between nations were fixed. To give them their due, they were flamboyant characters, comparable to the "Robin Hoods" of the criminal world today. The likes of Ian Nyschens and Pondoro Taylor come to mind when I think of hunters in this category.

The second category is composed of professional hunters who specialize in conducting elephant-hunting safaris. In the glorious days of yesteryear, an exceptional trophy elephant was an animal that carried a hundred pounds of ivory or better. I remember watching an interview with an old

The infamous Ian Nyschens with a tracker.

and well-known East African professional hunter who was asked how many elephants he had shot during his career.

"Only twenty," was his reply.

The interviewer was confused by the low number and commented that surely he must have shot more than twenty elephants during his illustrious career.

"My dear boy," replied the old hunter. "I'm only referring to the ones that carried over a hundred pounds of ivory a side."

Despite the absence of elephants carrying this sort of weight of ivory in Africa today, I have dedicated the past twenty-odd years of my career almost exclusively to hunting elephants with clients. Yet, even though I realize that the expectations surrounding elephant hunting have drastically changed over the years, I still feel a bit of a scam artist when referring to myself as a professional elephant hunter. What we all must realize, however, is that it's unrealistic to expect to do today what the elephant hunters of yesteryear felt to be the norm.

That said, over this twenty-year period I have consistently averaged in excess of twenty elephants per season. While a good number of this tally have been trophy bulls, the majority have been tuskless cows, which provide, without doubt, the most dangerous form of elephant hunting available. So, while there's a dearth of hundred-pounders today, there's certainly an abundance of danger when it comes to hunting tuskless cow elephants.

Professional hunters who focus primarily on hunting elephants, tuskless cows in particular, all seem to follow a similar progression throughout their careers. This evolution is consistent whether you care to label him a professional in this field or not. Initially, the hunter starts off by being overly cautious, and then, as he gains experience and reaches a level of competency, he emerges into a knowledgeable professional who hunts elephants both safely and successfully.

What follows next is the "dangerous stage." This is when the professional hunter becomes overly confident, when he challenges the status quo, and when he seeks more and more excitement from each subsequent hunt. Elephant charges and close calls become frequent, and disaster is averted only by luck or through good shooting. Such "gung-ho" attitudes, fueled by an adrenaline addiction, continue unabated. For example, where once the perfect distance to administer a frontal brain shot was twenty yards, the adrenaline addict progressively reduces the distance from fifteen to ten paces and then even closer. Dangerous situations and charges become more frequent and accepted as normal.

I'm not proud to admit that I, too, became a victim of such arrogance and self-belief. All too soon I found myself dropping charging cows from a distance of only five yards. Never did I give such hair-raising situations a second thought other than to consider it another thrilling occurrence. Tomorrow was another day and, perhaps, an even more exciting experience just waiting to happen. I never once lay in bed at night thinking what the consequences might have been had I not perfectly brained that charging cow at five yards. In short, I had become the perfect example of a self-centred and "gung-ho" professional elephant hunter. I'm embarrassed that some of this cavalier, unprofessional attitude can, to the trained eye, be observed in my earlier elephant hunting DVDs.

Guided by Richard Harland (in back), Victor Vester shot the magnificent Dhulamithi II, which had 120 pounds of ivory per side, in the Zambezi Valley in 1967. Dhulamithi means "Taller Than the Trees."

For me, the turning point came on a safari with good friends and clients, J.B. and Luc De Runz. J.B. is an avid bow hunter. The previous season we had arrowed a trophy elephant bull from twenty yards. J.B. was using a one-hundred-pound draw-weight bow and a thousand-grain arrow. This was a lethal and legal combination, but, unfortunately, his arrow hit his bull a little too far back on a broadside shot. Amazingly, the arrow exited just in front of the bull's rear leg and shattered on a tree directly behind. This conclusively proved to me that this combination, provided the arrow hits the heart/lung area, most certainly has the penetration capability to get the job done.

On that occasion, however, J.B.'s arrow had been poorly placed, and the result was a nonfatal but, nevertheless, wounded elephant bull that was unlikely to die soon. We followed the bull for three hours that day until sunset forced us to abandon the tracks. It was only after an additional nine hours of tracking the next day that we finally caught up to the bull. He had joined up with a herd of about fifty elephants. To his credit, J.B. wanted to put an end to the bull's suffering as soon as possible, so he abandoned his bow to shoot the bull with a .375 rifle. By killing the elephant this way, he could not claim it as a bow kill. Being such an avid bow hunter, it remained on J.B.'s bucket list to cleanly kill an elephant with his bow one day.

So J.B. rebooked for the following season. This time he wanted to bow hunt two tuskless elephant cows, and after accomplishing that, we would move on to Mozambique where we would hunt crocodiles and hippos on Lake Cahora Bassa. Ironically, even though cows are cheaper to hunt than bulls, this turned out to be our first mistake. First of all, in order to hunt an elephant successfully with a bow, the shooting distance should be no farther away than twenty yards, and that's with the elephant in question standing broadside on or preferably slightly quartering away when the shot is taken. These positions allow the shooter to place his arrow into the front leg crease in order to penetrate the heart. Then there's a distinct probability that there will be other members of the herd close-by since this is a hunt for an elephant cow. That's another risk. Looking out for other cows requires careful watching. Finally, there's the necessity to confirm that the cow is definitely tuskless and that she doesn't have a dependent calf at foot.

All these limitations suggest that numerous approaches in thick *jesse* bush are required before the ideal shooting situation presents itself. Given all the various factors, it's a situation where things can turn nasty in a heart-beat. To sum it up, hunting a tuskless elephant cow with a bow is certainly the most difficult and dangerous form of hunting. Period!

When hunting a trophy bull, you are contending with a single animal or at most a bachelor group that will normally, on becoming aware of your presence, prefer flight rather than fight! Cows, on the other hand, and especially those with dependent calves at foot, very much prefer fight over flight! This is why hunting a tuskless elephant cow is not for the faint of heart.

******

Luc, an accomplished hunter in his own right, was accompanying his cousin J.B. as an observer. On that fateful day in the Omay Safari Area, we started tracking a group of about twenty cows that had raided a village's crops the previous night. While tracking the herd, we heard several gun-shots, which I suspected were poachers. It is my opinion that elephants in the Omay and surrounding areas are more aggressive than those in other parts of the country due to the pressures from the high levels of poaching.

After at least two hours of tracking, we caught up to the herd that, luckily, included a shootable tuskless cow. My tracker Criton was up front; I followed closely behind; then came J.B.; and finally Luc was in the rear

J.B. and Luc with Luc's elephant bull.

as the observer/cameraman. While carefully observing the herd, I noticed they were slowly moving up a gully that gradually narrowed into a small funnel. With a bit of luck and quick maneuvering on our part, I planned to get us ahead and above the herd, and that would place us at the required bow-hunting shooting distance as they filed past us. When the chosen cow finally came abreast of him, J.B. would then get the opportunity of a shot.

We got ourselves into a downwind position on the side of the gully, but unfortunately things immediately went wrong. The first cow appeared in the gully and was perfectly broadside-on from about twenty paces, but she saw us and immediately mock charged. Luckily, I managed to shout her down, and she stopped about seven yards away, raised her tail, then turned and made off at haste along with the front members of the herd.

The cow following behind the leader was looking at us over her shoulder. I had experienced this type of behaviour on previous occasions, and it was bad news. Whenever elephant cows run away from a threat, they usually push their head forward, shift into top gear, and rapidly put distance between the potential threat and themselves. However, when a cow looks back at you from over her shoulder as she walks away, it means she has still not made up her mind as to whether she truly wants to run or whether she wants to fight. That is exactly what this cow decided to do. It never ceases to amaze me how

Too close for comfort!

quickly a three-ton animal can swing around and come bearing down at you at full tilt when she's made up her mind to pulverize you into dust.

In such situations panic must be avoided, and this despite the fact that the cow will be covering the twenty-odd yards in a matter of seconds. Under such stress, the whole world devolves into slow motion and you become totally tunnel-visioned. All that matters at that moment is that you have no doubt whatsoever you are going to kill the elephant rampaging toward you, and why not? Heck, this is a situation you have been in many times before—and you've successfully handled them all.

Automatically, like second nature, my trusty .416 comes into my shoulder and I push the safety catch forward at the same time. The foresight bead appears as if by magic, correctly nestling at the bottom of the V-shaped rear-sight, right between the cow's eyes. *Bang*, and down the cow goes in a cloud of dust, right at my firmly planted feet! Another amazing, heart-stopping experience to add to the others in my memory bank. . . .

However, not so on this occasion. As the rifle exploded, I saw the cow's eyes roll back as she took the shock of the 400-grain solid bullet, but she did not fall. Because I was so close, I had only a fraction of a second to sidestep her. I was so close that the cow's vision of me was impaired, so she charged on, narrowly missing J.B. who scrambled off to the left and the safety of a thick *jesse* bush. This left poor Luc, who was still busy filming, right in the path of three tons of fury!

With a high-pitched scream and a flick of her trunk, the elephant knocked Luc to the ground. Such was the force of the cow's trunk that it knocked Luc about ten yards backward. By the time he came to a stop, the cow was on him. She then proceeded to kneel over him, trapping his body between her thick legs while at the same time doing her utmost to drive one of her long, slender tusks through the center his chest!

Luckily for Luc, his video camera case was still slung across his chest, and this was supported by a thick, wide, and extremely strong nylon strap. By great good fortune the point of the cow's tusk hit the strap, thus preventing it from entering Luc's chest. As he struggled to free himself from under the cow, the strap, together with the tusk boring into it, started to move across his chest. Eventually the tusk slipped off completely, tearing his shirt in the process and pegging itself into the ground beneath his armpit. There it completely snapped off from the sheer force of the thrust.

Screaming for dear life, Luc desperately tried to push himself away from the cow, which by that stage was attempting to shove him into the ground

Luc recovering after being attacked by an enraged cow elephant.

with her forehead. So desperate was his effort to push himself away from the cow that he shoved one of his hands into her mouth. Unfortunately the thumb became trapped between her molars and was subsequently squashed flat like a ripe tomato when she snapped her jaws shut.

These proceedings all happened in seconds, by which time I had reloaded my .416 Rigby. I could see Luc trapped and struggling frantically beneath the elephant, and I realized that I would have to kill her instantly to save him. A heart shot would not kill her quickly enough, only a brain shot would do, but in saying that, I still had to put her down without shooting Luc in the process. The opportunity finally presented itself, and I killed the cow with a side-on brain shot through her earhole. Thank goodness, she fell away from Luc rather than on top of him.

Much to my relief I saw Luc scramble to his feet and make a dash for safety while emitting the most blood-curdling and spine-chilling screams imaginable. Not only will those terrible screams remain with me for the rest of my life, but they also changed my outlook. I'm a more cautious and wary professional hunter these days, my "gung-ho" attitude over forever.

To add insult to his injury, Luc's "death run" to escape the maddened cow landed him entangled in a wait-a-bit thorn tree! The thorns on these trees are vicious—curved and incredibly sharp. To be stuck in one is a most painful experience, and the only way out is by retreating very slowly backward, something the panic-stricken Luc didn't do. The result was a torn lip together with a severely scratched and bloody scalp. He looked so bad, in fact, that Morgan, one of the trackers, who incidentally had discreetly made himself scarce during the rumpus, took one look at poor Luc's torn and bloodied face and assumed that during the commotion I had accidently shot him!

My immediate reaction was one of relief on seeing Luc still alive, but my jubilation was short lived. I suddenly remembered the death of a local man who had died from internal injuries after being gored by a buffalo. At that moment Luc was struggling with his breathing, but when the shock finally subsided, the painful side of his injuries set in. I suspected several broken ribs, but I was alarmed that he might also have sustained internal injuries.

My GPS told us we were four kilometres in a straight line from the nearest road, and I estimated a further two hours' drive to the closest air-

Luc and his hippo bull from Mozambique.

strip. My immediate concern was that Luc might not survive a trip of that distance and time.

The only way to make Luc comfortable was to sit him on the ground, back to back with J.B. I then radioed my driver, Eddy, and instructed him to call Kirsty on the satellite phone and ask her to contact MARS, our Medical Air Rescue Service, and ask them to get airborne as soon as possible.

Having completed his task, the ever-resourceful Eddy raised a collection of villagers with axes to cut a recovery road to the injured Luc who was in no state to walk. By the time we had run back to the main road, we found Eddy waiting for us with the extra hands. The hectic, at top speed overland trip that then ensued would have impressed any 4x4 specialist!

Only the biggest trees obstructing our path were cut down while the odd bad drainage line and erosion gully were quickly made passable by the numerous villagers, who, it appeared, were only interested in getting their hands on a good supply of free elephant meat. Poor Luc's condition was the very last thing on their meat-hungry minds!

Due to a severe wash-away that would have taken too long to fix, the closest we could get the Land Cruiser to Luc and J.B. was about a hundred metres away from where they were seated. Moving Luc to the vehicle over this distance was pure torture for him. Initially we laid him on a mattress, which one of the villagers had kindly thought to bring along, and tried to carry him out. This proved too painful, so he eventually walked to the Land Cruiser supported by Criton and J.B.

The only way we could travel in the vehicle was to have Luc seated between me and J.B., with J.B. keeping Luc as straight as possible by pulling upward on his shirt collar. This seemed to relieve the pressure on his broken ribs, but the slightest bump in the road hurt so much that he nearly passed out with the pain.

To cover the four-kilometre distance from the main road to the incident took twenty minutes. This included cutting down the few trees that were in the way as well as filling-in a couple of gullies. The trip out, however, took over an hour. Our progress became painfully slow when it became necessary to stop on numerous occasions just to allow Luc to recover. The effort required to keep him in an upright position was also causing J.B.'s supporting arm to cramp severely.

At long last we finally reached the main road, only to face a two-hour drive to the nearest airstrip over Omay's exceedingly bumpy roads. Luc was incredibly brave during this part of the journey, wincing at every little bump in the road. Throughout the entire ordeal, Luc received no painkillers. All I had in my medical aid box were aspirin-based, and I was concerned that should he have internal injuries, and I was convinced he did, aspirin would have thinned out his blood and compounded the possibility of internal bleeding.

After what seemed like an eternity, we eventually arrived at the remote bush airstrip where I was thankful to see a Navajo twin-engine aircraft and a doctor and two nurses patiently waiting. I cannot express the relief I felt at handing over Luc into the capable hands of qualified personnel, people who are trained to deal with such situations. While all professional hunters are required to obtain a certain level of medical expertise, we are not trained to deal with situations that involve internal injuries or critical emergency care.

The doctor and nurses were professional, calm, and competent. After checking Luc's blood pressure, they quickly dispelled my darkest fears by proclaiming his condition to be stable. This meant he was not suffering any major internal injury. After the medical team settled him in the aircraft in

Luc and his massive croc from Mozambique.

a sitting position, Luc and J.B. took off for Harare, then on to the Avenues Clinic where Kirsty had already organized a bed with a specialist waiting to see him.

As the dust settled and the plane disappeared into the setting sun, the reality of the situation began to set in. That Luc had survived an elephant attack was a miracle. Despite this, I remained concerned as to what a full medical report would reveal. Fortunately, the airstrip was only two kilometres from our camp, and the first thing I did on arrival was to pour myself a generous tot of whisky!

Sleep did not come easily that night, and well before dawn I was on the road to Harare. I arrived at the Avenues Clinic after morning visiting hours were over, but I did learn that the nursing staff had kindly put a bed in Luc's ward for J.B. so that he could act as a translator as none of the nurses spoke French!

Luc ended up spending several days in the Avenues Clinic's intensive care unit, and both he and J.B. were complimentary on how thorough the doctors had been. As luck would have it, Luc's thoracic specialist was an imposing Cuban-trained specialist who spoke fluent French.

The Cuban doctor explained to Luc that in addition to his crushed thumb, his encounter with the elephant cow had resulted in several broken ribs and a collapsed lung. The Cuban doctor told Luc that about two-and-a-half litres of blood needed to be drained before his lung could reinflate on its own accord. I could see that Luc was understandably concerned. When I asked the Cuban what were Luc's main concerns, the doctor flabbergasted me by replying that despite his condition, Luc was more concerned about being able to continue with the second half of the safari, which included the crocodile and hippo hunt on Lake Cahora Bassa in Mozambique! He had told the specialist, and I suspect with a twinkle in his eye, he was concerned that should he have the misfortune to fall out of the boat during the hunt, his deflated lung would not keep him afloat!

Amazingly, Luc checked himself out of the Avenues Clinic as soon as his lung was functioning normally. He further insisted on commencing the second half of the safari, totally disregarding my advice that he should return to France to recuperate with his wife and beautiful daughters!

Despite being in considerable pain from his broken ribs—all on the right side of his body, which happened to be his shooting side—we managed through trial and error to devise an ingenious plan whereby Luc would be able to shoot his .375, thus achieving his ambition of shooting a crocodile and a hippo. We accomplished this by seating Luc on a sturdy dining-room chair and bracing it with a four-foot-long plank that we attached to the arm of the chair. The plank was then jammed into the ground upon which I would put my weight. This enabled Luc to put his shooting arm around the plank and to mount the butt of his rifle on the plank itself. In this manner, he could then shoot relatively naturally with the plank taking the recoil.

With Luc, the plank, and the chair all loaded into a far-from-steady mokoro (a dugout canoe), the hunt was on. Over the next few days he managed to shoot a monster crocodile and hippo, confirming the fellow's willpower and sheer determination. A lesser person would have headed home and possibly instigated legal action against me. There's little doubt that if Luc had not been fortunate enough to have the camera bag's strap across his chest, the cow's tusk would most certainly have gone completely through his body, killing him instantly. Luc recounted later how he knew he was in deep trouble when the viewfinder of his video camera became totally gray.

I recently received an email from both J.B. and Luc. It was entitled "The Revenge of the Elephant." In it both Luc and J.B. expressed their intention to return and put their fear of elephants to the test by each shooting an elephant cow in the *jesse* bush.

This tragic tale has a silver lining. While being examined in Harare, the specialist picked up that Luc had a seriously dangerous heart condition. As a consequence, he has recently undergone triple bypass heart surgery, and by all accounts he is recovering well. It would appear at the end of the day, being tusked by an elephant cow might well have saved his life. In addition to this, there are not many people in the world who can claim to have been tusked and had their thumb chewed upon by an African elephant and still be alive to tell it.

Smelly Affair

Chapter Twelve

I was hunting with Mike, one of Charlton McCallum's most loyal clients. We were hunting in Chewore North, specifically to bag a lioness, which incidentally, prior to the "Cecil" debacle, we were permitted to hunt. We were based in the "Big Five" main camp at the junction of the Zambezi and Mawanja Rivers. I decided to get an early start one morning and be on our way by daybreak as I intended to focus our efforts well south of the camp in an area on the Chewore River called the Mariastore Gorge.

This particular gorge is spectacular, with numerous springs that surface along the otherwise dry Chewore riverbed. The beauty of the area makes for a memorable hunt. The access to a plentiful supply of water during the dry season results in a high population of game animals that, in turn, attracts a number of lions and lionesses to the area. In this case, rather than use the baiting method to bag our lioness, I decided to track one.

We arrived at the gorge around 8 A.M. and set off down the riverbed looking for tracks. We had only been going for a short time when, low and behold, as we rounded a sharp bend in the riverbed, there in front of us was a pride of lions feeding on a kudu kill. Unfortunately, the lions saw us and immediately bolted, so we set off in hot pursuit and spent the better part of that day on tracks. On numerous occasions we caught up with the lions, but every time we got near, a few of them broke away.

With late afternoon upon us, we decided to head back to the dead kudu to see if the lions had returned. I was convinced that this is what they'd do, but when we arrived near the kill, not a lion was in sight. So we positioned ourselves about sixty metres downwind of the bait on a slight bluff that gave us a good view of the dead kudu and then settled down to wait. We had barely made ourselves comfortable when the first lioness arrived, a young-looking animal with spots still visible on her

Mike and his exciting lioness from Chewore North.

legs. Not long afterward two more arrived, one of them an old cat, which we decided to take.

Mike shot her a shade too far back, and with a grunt she rushed across the riverbed and into the Sapi Safari Area, out of our jurisdiction. A decision needed to be made as to whether we should follow her tracks, for in theory we needed permission to enter the area. This meant going back to the Parks and Wildlife Management Authority headquarters at Marongora to get permission. The long delay would have seen us returning to camp in the dark, and that would have ruled out a follow-up that day. Leaving any wounded animal in the bush overnight is a huge risk as the valley is full of scavengers, hyenas being the worst. In all probability, a follow-up the next morning would result in us finding a mutilated carcass or, indeed, no trophy at all. Then there's the problem that we'd be leaving the poor animal in pain for so long.

Thankfully, my Parks and Wildlife scout gave us the go ahead, and we caught up and duly shot her before she had a chance to charge. With much excitement, we carried her back to the river, took some photos, and loaded her onto the back of the Land Cruiser just after darkness had set in. There was much singing from the trackers in the back of Land Cruiser, which prompted Mike to ask if he could travel with them and enjoy the moment. I was more than happy to oblige.

It was dark now, and as we still had a long way to go, I was driving very fast. We were speeding through a thick block of *jesse* bush along the Chewore River when suddenly a hyena appeared in the headlights. One look at the oncoming vehicle and the ugly scavenger turned and bolted down the road. The trackers and Mike, shouting at the top of their voices, were urging me on as we sped after the fleeing animal. Due to thick bush on both sides of the road, as well as the glare of the Land Cruiser headlights, the poor creature was forced to keep running along the same track.

Mike and the crew were roaring "Go! Go! Go!" as I got closer and closer. Every now and then the terrified animal glanced back at its pursuing tormentor, and seeing us so close, increased its pace, only to be caught up again farther down the track.

In sheer terror of its unrelenting pursuer and the relentless clamour from the mob, the poor animal released the full contents of its bowels onto its fleeing back legs, straight onto the windscreen and into the faces of Mike and the trackers. Suddenly there was a great pounding on the Land Cruiser roof together with cries of "Stop! STOP!"

Before I could get out of the vehicle, Mike stuck his head through the window. His face was contorted in disgust and covered in hyena excrement. He asked if he could get in front with me for the rest of the journey. Trying to keep as straight a face as possible, I wrinkled up my nose and politely declined.

******

Another smelly affair occurred several years earlier. I had an elderly client who had booked a bull elephant hunt. He was accompanied by a girlfriend who was considerably younger than he, a fairly common occurrence in the safari business. Sadly, she was rather hopeless around the camp and walking was definitely not one of her stronger points. She also carried a knife on her belt that would have made Crocodile Dundee proud. When I asked her what she intended to do with it, she said, quite

Elephant bull with very similar tusks to the one we were after.

adamantly, that should there be any trouble in Zimbabwe while she was here, then if needs be she would cut her way to Namibia. I did not have the heart to tell her that Namibia was about a thousand kilometres away, which would have taken a lot of cutting.

Just prior to my client's safari I had seen a large bull elephant not far from camp, and the day they arrived I found the tracks of a bull that we were confident was the same animal. This bull was a monster, and we estimated he could be carrying ivory in the seventy-pound range. The spoor was not fresh, but we felt with effort and determination we could catch up with him. There were several bulls in this group and after a few hours of tracking, it became obvious they were slowing down and looking for a place to rest during the midday heat.

It was at this point that the girlfriend decided she needed a toilet break, so we dutifully waited while she went behind a bush. A few minutes later we were on spoor again, and after an hour of rapid tracking, we heard the bulls ripping branches off the trees just ahead of us. The wind was in our favour, and we were about to enter the final approach when there was a disturbance from the girlfriend.

Annoyed at the interruption during such a critical time, I asked her what was wrong. Evidently she had left her knife behind the bush where she had taken her toilet break. I told her we would go back and find her knife after we had finished with the elephant, but she would have none of it. In the end I had no option but to backtrack, and we found her knife behind the bush, exactly where she had left it. I was thoroughly annoyed and frustrated, and, of course, when we returned to the spot where we had caught up to the elephants, they were gone.

At this point my client was showing signs of dehydration and was struggling to walk. I was not prepared to give up the hunt, so I had him drink two bottles of water before we carried on. We got to the point when I knew the old chap could not carry on much farther. I was about to call off the chase when we arrived at the top of a ridge, and there in the depression below us was a beautiful spring. With an abundance of water around the spring, the bush was very thick.

As we looked down upon the oasis, there standing barely seventy yards away was our bull, slightly hidden in the undergrowth, but clear enough to make out the size of his tusks, which were so long they were nearly touching the ground. What an amazing sight he was! He did not have a particularly big body, but his tusks were close to eighty pounds, or so we estimated.

Inexperience on my part resulted in us not taking a shot at that amazing elephant. In those days I was convinced the only way to kill an elephant effectively was a bullet in the brain at close quarters. As a result, we turned down a golden opportunity of a perfect shoulder shot that would have penetrated his heart and killed him within a hundred metres of where he was standing.

Instead, with the wind strongly in our favour, we crept down the slope hoping to get into a good position closer to the bull. What we had not seen was a young bull drinking from the spring directly below us. Just as we went over the top of the ridge, the young bull saw us and immediately mock charged. There was nothing I could do other than to shout him down. With that he broke off the charge and made off along with the rest of the group, and that was the last we saw of our dream bull.

By that point, a combination of jet lag, dehydration, and exhaustion had overcome my client, and he could not carry on. It was a very disappointed party that hobbled to the nearest road where we sat and waited for Royal, my driver, to pick us up. While waiting for the vehicle, my client said he had a bad stomach and needed to go to the toilet. I dug out the roll of toilet paper from my pack and gave it to him.

Much to our disbelief and embarrassment, he hobbled across the narrow track and dropped his pants not more than five metres away. I hissed to my trackers to turn away so as to afford him a bit of privacy. A little later one of the tracker's urged me to take a look, which I refused to do, but he insisted. Reluctantly, I turned to see what it was all about, and to my horror I was confronted with a bizarre sight.

Evidently the old chap had squatted down and done what was necessary, but on getting up he had had a dizzy spell and had fainted, landing right on top of his business. Still a little groggy, he rolled about in the mess before regaining his footing. It was about this time that Royal arrived. I told him that the situation was beyond a professional hunter's duties, so, being the great chap that he was, Royal cleaned up the old man and dressed him in his overalls, after which we set off back to camp with a very embarrassed client.

Actually, he turned out to be an amazing old man. After adjusting to the heat and getting over his jet lag, he walked incredibly well considering his age. Sadly, we did not get an elephant on that hunt, but I did learn a few important lessons: never take jet lag lightly and always adjust to the capabilities of each client. These are essential to being a responsible professional hunter. Lastly, and most importantly, to remember that a good effective heart/lung shot on elephants is a vital option if the opportunity presents itself.

Had I learnt these lessons earlier, my client would have had his dream elephant. As a result, he never did get an elephant and is now physically incapable of hunting them. For this I feel responsible, and I wish I could wind back the clock. In retrospect, all I had to do was have him take a rest against a tree and take an easy heart shot at one of the most amazing bull elephants I have ever seen.

As for that marvelous bull, it is my earnest hope that he managed to dodge the elephant poachers and was able to spread his genes far and wide.

Criton's Close Call

Chapter Thirteen

Earlier on in this book I mentioned the incident of my client Luc getting squashed by an elephant. The unfortunate event changed my entire outlook on the hunting of dangerous game. From a cavalier, happy-go-lucky professional hunter, I suddenly realized that such arrogant behaviour can actually have life-and-death consequences. It was a lesson that taught me never to tempt fate. Criton's experience re-enforced my feelings on the issue. Furthermore, what happened to him made me aware that, in spite of taking the necessary precautions, accidents can still happen. After all, we are only human, and there will be occasions when we will be unable to pull off that "miraculous last shot." At such times fate is no longer in our hands.

My client was Mark, a super-nice gentleman from the deep American South and a man of few words, which in some instances was probably due to his habit of chewing tobacco. A nicer, more down-to-earth Southerner you could not wish to know. This time Mark was after a bull elephant, a buffalo, and a variety of plains-game species found on the Hammond Ranch in the Save Conservancy. I should add that this was Charlton McCallum's first season hunting in the Save.

The first few days of the hunt were spent checking out the availability of buffalo bulls while working along the ARDA (African Research Development Authority) boundary where there was also a lot of elephant movement. Earlier in the season while scouting in the area, I had seen a fine-looking bull with tusks in the sixty-pound range, and I hoped that Mark and I would get the opportunity to meet up with the bull again.

What surprised me about the Save was that the elephants congregated in large herds, some numbering up to two hundred animals. In the Zambezi Valley I was accustomed to following single bulls or small bachelor herds.

Even the tuskless cows in the valley only gathered in small herds, so the sight of these large concentrations of both bull and cow elephants were an eye opener, to say the least. Since elephant herds of this size do not occur in the Zambezi Valley, I knew that hunting these larger herds would require a different and bolder approach.

Large areas of the Save consist of flat, featureless mopane country, and this made me nervous. When you are trying to sneak your way through two-hundred-odd elephants on flat ground with little cover, it is only a matter of time before a confrontation will occur. Moreover, in mopane-scrub country there is limited visibility, so only a handful of elephants can be seen at any one time. In large herds there will invariably be elephants behind and on both sides of you that have been obscured by the head-high scrub. In such situations, it is nigh impossible to check the whole herd without being seen.

To make matters worse and a lot more dangerous in this case, it was the breeding season, so there was a lot of mating going on. Young and older elephant bulls full of testosterone were chasing the cows, all the while emitting high-pitched screams. These screeches made the tense situation hair-raising. When the elephants moved off in one direction, we would flank them or walk behind while trying to single out a good bull. Suddenly there would be a scream, and we would see a cow running in our direction followed closely by an amorous young bull. In such situations our only option was to beat a hasty retreat!

However, there were occasions when there was simply not enough time to escape. Fortunately, the elephants were so preoccupied with their sexual proclivities that we were sometimes able to find a bit of cover in which to hide. In that case, we would watch them racing past, sometimes only a few feet away. Such situations were a real test of our courage. Believe me, it took real presence of mind, steady nerves, and a whole load of guts to stand one's ground and not sprint away. Mark was such a person; he handled these tense moments like a veteran.

One morning Mark was late in arriving for breakfast. It transpired he was not feeling well and he requested we take the morning off. He said he wanted to rest until lunchtime, so off he went back to bed. Not one

Save is known for its big herds of elephants.

for being idle, I decided to see if there were any elephants around. It was not long before we found the tracks of a big herd, which we immediately began to follow. With such a large number, the tracking was easy and we soon caught up with them. Close inspection revealed a fine-looking bull. He was not the sixty-pounder we were looking for, but he had short, thick tusks that would easily go more than forty pounds a side. This was Mark's minimum weight.

I radioed Eddy, our camp driver, who was waiting at the Land Cruiser and told him to return to camp and find out how Mark was feeling. He was to tell Mark that I had found him a "shooter," and the elephant was not too far off the road. It was Mark's call. If he felt OK and would like to give it a try, Eddy was to bring him to a designated place on the side of the road where the trackers and I would be waiting. Eddy soon radioed back to confirm that Mark had decided to take advantage of the situation.

Twenty minutes later we were loading up with water, and with a rather pale-looking Mark in tow, we set off to the place where we'd left the elephants resting in a shady spot along one of the dry riverbeds. By the time we arrived there, however, the herd had already moved on, so we started tracking again. We caught up with them about a kilometre or so farther on down the river. The elephant we wanted was clearly visible, but we were unable to close the gap because a herd of buffaloes had inconveniently positioned themselves between us and the bull. Unfortunately, the wind was not in our favour, so we settled down to wait for the buffalo herd to move on after their afternoon siesta. After a while they did just that.

By moving on, the buffaloes had cleared our approach to the elephant, but we were now presented with another problem, actually a hair-raising one. We now saw that the bull we wanted was with a group of ten other bulls to one side of the main herd. To get into a suitable shooting position meant that we would come within ten yards of the other bulls. This was just a little too close for comfort, especially considering that there would also be bulls on either side of our group.

Despite the wind being irregular, we decided to go straight in for the kill. This meant disregarding the other bulls. We managed to get to within twenty-five yards of our targeted animal before he saw us and raised his head. I gave Mark the go-ahead to shoot, indicating that he go for a frontal brain shot. Mark's .500 Jeffery roared and the bull went down. Luckily, the other too-close-for-comfort bulls ran away in panic.

Unfortunately, Mark's bull had not been properly brain shot. I realized this when I saw his front end going down first, making it look as if he'd nose-dived into the ground. With a successful brain shot, the hind legs of an elephant will always collapse first as the head and trunk are thrown upward. As Mark's bull had not fallen in this manner, I knew he was only stunned. To add to the dilemma, the bull went down behind a thick bush that made him vanish from view.

It is customary whenever an elephant drops to the shot, to shoot it again for assurance purposes. Because the bull was lying behind a thick bush, we couldn't see to do this. Within seconds we saw him struggling to regain his footing, but the cover in front of him still prohibited effective back-up shots. Even so, we took whatever chance was available. Shooting through the bush, both of us hit him, and each of us managed a second shot into his rear end as he turned to run off.

We waited for a while and had a drink of water. After the water break, I asked Mark how he was feeling because he did not look at all well. He said that he was game to carry on and finish off his elephant, so we set off on the bull's tracks. Luckily, the bull had left the herd and veered off by himself, a sure sign he was hurting. Twenty minutes later we got a brief glimpse of him walking ahead of us. I was convinced he would not go much farther as he was staggering from side to side. This is normally a sign that he had been shot in the lungs and was about to fall over.

We closed the distance and got in two more shots. I honestly expected him to drop, and I was more than surprised to see him run off at pace again. The follow-up continued. It was getting late now, so we increased our tracking pace. I was getting concerned about Mark, who at this stage was as pale as a sheet and lagging farther and farther behind. Eventually we came across a road where Mark said he could go no further. So we called Eddy on the radio and told him to come collect Mark and take him back to camp. Meanwhile the trackers and I would continue following the bull as I was determined to put the poor animal out of its misery before dark. Despite being shot numerous times with two large-calibre rifles, the elephant was not leaving a clear blood trail. If by chance he began to mingle with other elephants in the area, we stood a real risk of losing him.

After Mark and Eddy had departed, my trackers, Criton and Nyati, and I increased our pace to a slow jog as we followed the bull's tracks. They were easy to follow despite the fact that there were only a few drops of blood to be seen here and there. The light was beginning to fade, and I was getting close to calling an end to the hunt when suddenly we caught sight of the bull. He was walking slowly away from us through the mopane forest.

I moved ahead of Criton and Nyati and closed the gap. In hindsight I should have shot him in the hip as he walked away from me. This would have anchored the bull. It's a struggle for elephants to walk on three legs, and I could then have administered a coup de grâce in the ear hole when he was thus immobilized. I felt really sorry for the old bull for having shot him so many times, and I desperately wanted him to turn so I could kill him quickly with a lethal brain shot and put an end to his suffering.

It was not long before the bull sensed we were close behind him, for I could see him raising his head and looking over his shoulder as he walked away. In hindsight I should have waited for him to turn broadside on or turn around completely and face me before shooting.

Instead and impatiently, I tried to take the difficult quartering-away brain shot as he looked back over his shoulder at me. This particular shot is the most difficult brain shot of all as it's necessary to calculate, in seconds, the correct angle for the bullet to penetrate the brain. Unfortunately, my shot hit him too far forward, and the bullet passed ineffectively in front of his brain.

I had no idea that a bull could turn so fast. The next thing I knew he was bearing down on me in a full-blown charge. I was not overly concerned as I was still about twenty yards from him and I had been in such situations before. I was confident there was enough time to reload my .416 Ruger and drop him with a frontal brain shot. It was only when my second round jammed and failed to feed into the chamber that I realized I was in serious trouble. In the heat of the moment, I must have short-stroked the loading action, and that caused the stoppage.

The bull that squashed Criton.

I desperately tried to free the jammed cartridge as the elephant bore down on me. During this time I realized that even if I did manage to clear the stoppage and reload, there was simply not enough time to shoulder the rifle and fire. With that I flung myself off to the side as the huge bull came flying past. I can clearly recall seeing his beady eye following me as he rushed by, his speed and sheer mass making it impossible for him to stop. My saving grace was that he did not turn and come back to finish me off. Instead he now turned his attention on the trackers as they tried to escape. Poor Nyati, much the older of the two, became the focus of the bull's attention as he lagged behind Criton who was running like the wind in front.

I can still remember looking between the bull's massive tree-stump-like legs and seeing Nyati running for all his worth directly in front of the charging elephant. Despite his impressive athletic effort, Nyati was rapidly being overtaken, and I realized in that fateful moment he hadn't a hope of escaping.

The massive bull was only moments away from knocking him down when lady luck intervened. Just as the elephant was nearly on him, Nyati ran past a lone mopane tree, and at full speed he stuck out his left hand and grabbed the mopane trunk. With his arm acting as an effective fulcrum, he was able to change direction by 90 degrees. The enraged elephant, itself unable to repeat Nyati's maneuver, rushed past him, and at this moment fate changed its course.

Criton, for all intent and purposes should have been safe, for he was by far the faster runner of the two as well as being the farthest away from the bull when it charged. He should have been the one to get away. But lady luck was not smiling upon Criton that evening. Suddenly Criton slipped on a patch of loose gravel, and before he could get back on his feet and continue his escape, the bull was on him.

In the blink of an eye, the massive animal was shoving Criton around on the ground while at the same time trying to trample and impale him. For his part Criton was desperately pushing himself off the bull's front legs in an effort to keep away from the two massive foot pads that were intent on squashing him into the ground. In horror I realized it was only a matter of time before the elephant stamped, knelt upon, or even thrust its tusk through Criton. That, unfortunately, is exactly what happened.

The enraged bull finally stamped on Criton's pelvic area, crushing his pelvis in the process. While the elephant continued its attempt to tusk him, it was, for me, as though the world and time itself had slowed down. In what felt like slow motion, I managed to locate my fallen rifle, clear the stuck casing, manually feed the next cartridge into the chamber, close the bolt, and shoot the elephant up the backside. This action diverted its attention from Criton and the bull swung around to face me. With my last cartridge I shot the bull in the brain. Lady luck finally favoured poor Criton, and the dead elephant fell away from him and thankfully not on top of him.

In such situations there is a terrible moment when reality sets in and you expect the very worst. As I ran up to Criton, I was horrified of what I might find. He was still alive, and for that I was very grateful. I remained fearful, however, at the prospect of finding a mangled lower body when I removed his overalls. Gingerly and very carefully I looked him over. I was thankful to see there was no sign of bleeding, but my next fear was that he might be paralyzed from the waist down. I was hugely relieved when I asked him if he could move his legs and he managed to do so.

With Nyati's assistance we made Criton as comfortable as possible. I quickly searched for my radio, which had fallen off my belt during my escape and evasion maneuvers, and having found it, I radioed Eddy. After a quick briefing I told him to bring the medical aid kit and a mattress on which to place Criton. I also instructed him to inform Graham, the camp manager, that we had a serious issue on hand and to see if he could get an ambulance to the camp while we were moving Criton out of the bush.

Eddy duly arrived, and by that time it was already dark. Fortunately, the incident had taken place not too far from a road, and with some difficulty, Eddy, Nyati, and I managed to lift Criton onto the mattress and load him into the Land Cruiser. Braced between Nyati and Eddy, lay a very stoic Criton, who despite being in obvious pain never complained once during the bumpy ride to the hospital in Triangle, about two hours away.

When we arrived, I was pleased to find a well-organized little hospital, staffed with very efficient doctors and nurses. In no time at all they had Criton sedated on morphine. A drip was set up, and he was treated for shock, and he was X-rayed and thoroughly examined. Thankfully, his condition stabilized within a few hours.

Criton's X-rays revealed a badly shattered pelvis. Such was the damage to my untrained eye that the pelvis resembled a smashed windscreen! I was fearful of internal injuries as there was blood in his urine. I was again thankful when the examination revealed no serious internal injuries and when I found out that the blood in his urine was the result of severe bruising.

The following day, Criton was transferred by ambulance from Chiredzi to the Avenues Clinic in Harare. I was relieved when the Harare doctors agreed that the only serious issue with him was his fractured pelvis. With the diagnosis confirmed, Criton was moved to a private ward in Parirenyatwa, the local government hospital, where he would stay until his pelvis had knitted sufficiently for him to be discharged. After that he could recuperate at home.

Criton was assigned two orthopedic surgeons to oversee his recovery. One of them was an elderly gentleman who had received his training in Zimbabwe and who had subsequently practiced for a long time there. The second surgeon was younger and had been trained in the United

Kingdom. I inquired about Criton's recovery and was informed that he would be put into traction and that every few days his pelvis would be X-rayed. Based upon this information, they would then determine whether to remove or add to the weights that were already attached to his leg. This procedure made sense to me, so we settled down for the long recovery process.

To help him with the boredom of being bedridden for such a long time, I purchased Criton a portable DVD player and several DVDS including my latest elephant hunting DVD in which he featured prominently. Criton's vanity has always been of great amusement to me. He played the DVD continually, and he deliberately paused the disc wherever he featured on the screen so that all the African nurses could see him in action. The process was repeated with every shift change and continued until every nurse in the hospital had seen the budding film star.

In the meantime I was becoming extremely irritated with the hospital and doctors. Criton's first set of scheduled X-rays were put on hold. This was because he needed to get down to the ground floor where the X-ray machines were situated. It so happened, however, that the lift designed to cater for beds and larger apparatus was broken. Manhandling Criton up and down the stairs to get him to the X-ray department was not an option lest the bumping and jarring should damage his pelvis and thus delay the healing process.

Eventually the hospital authorities repaired the lift, but then to add to our woes, Harare endured a four-day power outage. That meant no X-ray procedure for Criton or any other patient! To add further to our dilemma, when the power finally returned, the radiologist told me they had run out of film for the X-ray machine!

I'm embarrassed to admit at this point I lost my temper! In a rage, with my blood pressure gauge well into the red, I went and saw both orthopedic surgeons. The elder surgeon did not appreciate my attitude. Dragging me by the collar he literally frog-marched me to Criton's room. As he did so, he explained in the harshest terms that he had overseen the recovery of numerous fractured pelvises, the majority of which had healed successfully without the benefit of X-rays! In his learned opinion X-rays were a luxury in impoverished Zimbabwe and he was good enough a doctor to cure his patients without them!

The old saw-bones then proceeded to grab Criton's legs and move them about in all directions. As he did so, he kept asking Criton if this activity was causing him any discomfort. Criton answered in the negative, at which point the surgeon curtly explained that the reason it was not sore was that the pieces of Criton's shattered pelvis had settled in the correct position. He did not need an X-ray to confirm it! That the old surgeon had swiftly put me in my place is something of an understatement!

In the end Criton only spent three weeks in hospital. Upon discharge he endured a bumpy six-hour ride in the back of the Land Cruiser all the way down to the Zambezi Valley where he then went home to recover. The two surgeons had agreed that Criton would require a year or two to recover sufficiently to the point where he could hunt again.

How wrong they were! Within three months Criton and I were hunting elephants again and what was even more amazing was the fact that he immediately resumed the "point" position when we were tracking. This position required getting very close to the elephants. Sad to say, in my case, it took many more elephant hunts for me to regain my confidence.

Criton's trampling made me realize that to prevent such incidents from occurring again I needed to invest in a quality, suitably large-calibre double-barrel rifle. Had I been afforded the luxury of an immediate follow-up shot instead of having to cycle the bolt of my, up-to-then, faithful old .416 Ruger while the enraged bull elephant bore down on me, the ending of this story might have been a lot less dramatic!

Postscript

For many years my "back-up" rifle was a Ruger M77 Mk II, in .416 Rigby calibre. This was an effective and reliable combination. Based on the renowned Mauser '98 action, the M77 Mk II also has controlled feeding via a large, nonrotating claw extractor. The M77's ejector is somewhat different from that of the '98, which uses a fixed blade to eject the spent cartridge case as the bolt is pulled rearward. On the M77 action, the ejector, also a blade, is not fixed; instead, it is positioned at the bottom of the action where a small spring raises the blade while the bolt is in the process of being pulled backward.

This ejection system works well and efficiently when the M77's bolt is pulled slowly backward. This action creates time for the ejector blade to be lifted, thus ejecting the spent cartridge case. In panic situations, however, when there's a need to reload the rifle in a hurry, the bolt is sometimes pulled back too quickly for the ejector blade to be raised in time. When this happens, the spent cartridge case is not ejected as it would have been had the bolt been cycled a bit slower. Also, with time, the small spring that lifts the ejector weakens, and as it does so, the lifting process takes longer.

In retrospect, working my Ruger's bolt too quickly is most likely the cause of the stoppage in the incident just described. There is much wisdom in the cowboy-gunslinger adage: *"Slow is smooth; smooth is fast!"* When being charged by a dangerous-game animal, professional hunters are advised to keep this advice in mind!

ELEPHANT RECOVERIES

CHAPTER FOURTEEN

I have done most of my elephant hunting in communal areas where traditionally the villagers were hunter-gatherers. Often an entire family would set off into the bush for a week or more at a time, collecting honey, catching fish, and snaring animals. It was their way of life. It was not commercial, but it was sustainable in the fragile ecosystem of the Zambezi Valley.

However, in order to take advantage of the growth in commercial hunting, the villagers were required to make certain decisions. This they did through a project named CAMPFIRE (Communal Management for Indigenous Resources) whereby the people ceded the hunting rights to commercial hunting companies who paid for a sustainable offtake of animals through foreign-paying clients. Not only do these clients provide meat for the villagers, but they also pay trophy fees and daily rates, the proceeds of which fund numerous community-based projects like the sinking of wells and the establishment of schools and clinics.

In essence, the villagers have the best of both worlds. For example, if a client killed an elephant that was far from the villagers, we, the commercial hunters, would recover the carcass with the aid of a tractor and trailer and deliver the meat to selected villages on a strictly adhered-to rotation system. This ensured that each village received equal amounts of meat each year.

In many cases, however, elephants are shot close to villages as they are not only attracted to the crops that grow there but also to the relative safety afforded them from poachers. Reluctant to carry out their activities in proximity to human populations, poachers prefer to engage in their clandestine activity as far from prying eyes as possible.

As soon as an elephant is shot, the bush telegraph comes alive. Very soon the first villager appears out of nowhere, followed shortly by dozens

Crazy scenes cutting meat from a dead elephant.

of excited and protein-starved inhabitants who wait impatiently for us to complete the task of removing the ivory and skin. As soon as the last portion of skin is removed and dragged away, a free-for-all begins: The multitude descends upon the carcass using knives and axes in a frenzy of slashing and cutting until, in a remarkably short time, all that remains are a few bones and a patch of bloodstained earth.

It can be disturbing to those clients who have not experienced this performance, for it is the fittest and strongest who get the most, while the old and young get little. To the Western eye, the scene is chaotic. One can be forgiven for thinking the villagers are a bunch of meat-hungry savages and that a more civilized approach would be to delegate the butchery to a selected few. Under a supervised system, the resultant meat could then be distributed fairly to all. However, if you take a step backward and realize that, unlike us who can eat steak twice a day if we so wished, these village folk have probably not eaten meat in a month. With that in mind, I would probably act in the same manner in order to provide my family with as much meat as possible when it becomes freely available.

It was at one of these meat recoveries in Mozambique that I saw a hilarious incident, followed, in turn, by a very sad one. The funny incident involved a young boy of about ten who was desperately trying to get into a position whereby he could cut a few chunks off the carcass. But try as he might, he was unable to push through the tide of meat hackers. Eventually, he worked his way to the rear end of the dead elephant, where most of the meat is. There he found himself backhanded by a burly young man. This young man had positioned himself in a prime position on a back leg and was busily cutting large chunks of meat from the carcass and putting them into a sack that was situated between his legs.

Looking forlorn, the young boy was about to head home empty-handed when he appeared to have a brain wave. Casually positioning himself behind the burly young man, he knelt down and cut a hole in the young fellow's sack. Each time the burly fellow put a large chunk of meat into the sack, the lad would remove one and put it in his own sack. The youngster even had the presence of mind to appreciate that his con act

Elephant or chicken for dinner?

could not last forever, so realizing that under the circumstances how well he'd done, the lad quietly withdrew and disappeared from the scene.

A few minutes later the burly young man decided he had gathered about as much as he could carry. Thus, thinking his sack was full, the young man braced himself for the full weight of the bag and heaved it up. Such was his momentum that the empty bag flew past him and into the sky. Seeing his loss and unable to control his temper, the burly fellow took out his misfortune on the other meat cutters by lashing out with fist and boot, convinced that it was they who had stolen the meat. By this time the young lad was halfway home with his bounty!

At the same recovery was an old woman, possibly in her seventies. Like most tribal women of that age, her body and face reflected a lifetime of child bearing, of toiling in the fields, and plain hard work. The poor woman was desperately trying unsuccessfully to find a gap between the multitude in order to garner a few scraps of meat. Thinking there was an opportunity, she found herself behind a young man who was hacking wildly with his ax. For those of you familiar with the African ax, the blade is wide and sharp on the operating side then tapers down to a point. The point of this triangle is then burnt through a round wooden handle, exiting an inch or so on the other side.

It was the backswing of this ax-wielding young man that struck the old lady in the forehead, hitting her with the protruding point of the ax. The point penetrated her skull and knocked her down into the bloody mess of the elephant's stomach. She lay there for a moment then slowly struggled to her knees still immersed in the filthy mess. Then, as though it was second nature, she casually raised her hand, touched the bleeding wound, shook her head, and then bending down gathered a handful of the mixture of mud and guts and plugged the hole in her skull. As though nothing had happened, she rejoined the others and continued to struggle to find an opening among the crowd where she hoped to find a few measly scraps to feed her family. Such is the desperation of protein-starved Africans.

On a lighter note . . . I was hunting a nontrophy elephant bull on my last hunt before completing this book. We had picked up the tracks of five elephants, and several hours later we caught up to them very close to some nearby villages. I could not believe it when one turned out to be a big

Elephant meat is an important source of protein for the villagers.

George de Bell with his tuskless bull, surrounded by villagers.

tuskless bull—it was the perfect, non-trophy animal. In twenty years of hunting I have only come across three tuskless bulls, and on all occasions I was hunting trophy animals, so they were of no interest to me. Here, however, was just what we were looking for. A short stalk brought us up to a twenty-yard frontal brain shot, and down he went.

It wasn't ten minutes before the horde of villagers arrived. One young man asked me where the tusks were, and off the bat I told him the tusks had fallen out on the impact of the bullet and that I would be most obliged if he and the rest of the villagers could help us search for them. When I told them the tusks had fallen in the grass nearby, the entire collection of villagers set about scratching and searching through the grass like a flock of hungry guinea fowls. Such is the ignorance of many rural Africans.

For better or worse, being present on an elephant recovery near a village is a sobering experience. It is on these occasions that one realizes how pathetic and misguided organizations like PETA are. They have no idea how the local populations view elephants and wildlife in general. As far as the local population is concerned, a wild animal that has no financial or food value to them should be exterminated as they are simply competition in an already hard way of life.

My Worst Safari

Chapter Fifteen

Having gained something of a reputation for producing the goods on elephant hunts, I was contacted by an infamous South African operator who hunted in an area on the south bank of Lake Cahora Bassa in Mozambique. He wanted me and my cameraman to accompany a high-profile Russian client on a bull elephant hunt. The area had previously produced several large bulls, so I was more than happy to accept.

There were to be two clients, mine for a trophy bull elephant and a second one who wanted to shoot a fifteen-foot crocodile. The latter client would be accompanied by a South African professional hunter. It should be mentioned here that there are monster crocodiles in Cahora Bassa, so the fifteen-foot crocodile the client wanted to shoot was well within target range.

The "operator" who offered me the hunt was one of the first of many South African professionals to offer "canned" lion hunting, a sordid practice. In essence, this involves taking an unsuspecting client on a lion hunt where he unwittingly shoots a tame and newly released-from-a-cage lion. To add to the disgrace of this disreputable practice, the lion is often drugged.

In view of his dubious reputation, I decided to travel down to his game ranch in South Africa, which is about an hour south of the Zimbabwe/South Africa border. The purported reason behind this trip was to have some much needed work done on my Land Cruiser, which the operator would pay for as an advance against my fees. I did this because I had a strange feeling that it might prove difficult to get my fees from him at the end of the hunt. So, just in case my suspicions were confirmed, I had the work done on the Land Cruiser, and, fortunately for me, it proved to be a wise decision in the end.

While the vehicle was being worked on, I stayed in the operator's guest lodge, which was situated in one of his hunting areas. On a walk around the property one afternoon while I waited for a new winch to be installed on my vehicle, I came across a *boma* in which there were four oryx gazelles, also known as gemsboks. All four animals had hose pipes stuck onto the tips of their horns, quite obviously to protect them from being broken in the *boma*. As a so-called ignorant Zimbabwean, I presumed the South African's intention was to breed these rare and beautiful animals as they are not naturally found in that part of South Africa.

When the work on my Land Cruiser was completed, I went to the operator's office to get a run-down on the up-and-coming hunt. It was confirmed my client, who was, indeed, a high-profile Russian, would be in company with his crocodile-hunting buddy, along with two lady "observers." I was looking forward to the hunt: The area was not only well known for the size of its elephants, but it also included about fifty kilometres of lake frontage. Then there is Cahora Bassa, home to some very large, man-eating crocodiles. All things being equal, it looked as though the Russians were in for a brilliant safari. We decided that I should collect them in three days' time in the little northern town of Tete, which happened to be closest to the hunting area.

Prior to setting off on the long return journey to Tete, I asked the operator about his oryxes. With an element of pride, he declaimed that the gazelles would be released the following day to be shot by four Czech clients who had booked them. He also mentioned that he would be collecting an additional three the following week for the next safari. With much difficulty I managed to hold my tongue. Somewhat later I learned that this practice is common in South Africa; it's called "put-and-take hunting." It has resulted in a huge trade in wildlife with vast numbers of animals being sold at auction to facilitate this so-called method of hunting!

As I was heavily loaded with supplies, the drive down to the hunting area through Zimbabwe took the better part of two days. Deon, the South African professional who was to guide the crocodile hunter was already in camp, so I decided to call in and drop off the supplies before proceeding to Tete to pick up the clients. Once there, I was told there had been a change in plan. Instead of the south bank, the hunt would now be conducted on the northern side of the lake in an area run by a Portuguese man from whom the South African "operator" had purchased the required quota. Who was I

A huge tuskless bull.

to argue about the change of plan? I incorrectly assumed that the Russians had already been informed.

We arrived, some fifteen hours later, at what I assumed was the staff compound, but to my horror, I was told it was the main camp. The seedy-looking place consisted of several rotting grass structures that served as the clients' sleeping quarters. There was a rusted bucket that served as a pull-up shower and a single long-drop toilet that you could smell from any part of the camp. To make matters worse, the smelly "convenience" served the entire site, including the staff. To add to the camp's so-called character, the blown-up remains of an old Land Rover, evidently a relic from the civil war, was prominently displayed on the site. It was the shelter for several scrawny chickens, which were to be our daily wake-up call. There was also a pet pig, affectionately called "Chop" who became our companion whenever we were in situ. These initial signs clearly told me that I was in for a challenging safari.

The clients arrived on schedule, and it was Sean's, my cameraman, intention to film them as they emerged from the dilapidated Tete airport. His actions were greeted by the wild flaying of the clients' arms accompanied by frantic shouts of, "Stop camera! Stop camera!" We were later to learn that the two high-heeled lady "observers" in designer safari clothes were neither wife nor girlfriend but expensive call girls. Neither Mikhail nor Nikolai wanted any photographic evidence that could compromise them at a later stage. Their request would make Sean's job a lot more challenging.

From Tete to the hunting "camp" was a five-hour drive, so we had ample time to get acquainted. When I mentioned that we were headed for the north bank of Cahora Bassa rather than the south bank, they were rather surprised but gave the operator the benefit of the doubt, assuming the hunting would be as good there as it was in the south. Then they asked me about the camp because they had told their "observers" that they were going to a luxury outfit where they would be comfortable and safe. Considering the two lovely ladies, one of whom bore a remarkable resemblance to Julia Roberts, had never previously left Moscow, the camp was important to them. My conscience would not allow me to lie or even attempt to play down just how awful it was, so even though I told them what I thought, when we arrived at the camp and they saw what it was like, there were two very unhappy hunters and two extremely shocked women.

We had a quick guided tour of the camp with Mario, the sleazy Portuguese operator, but the tour was cut short by Mikhail. He sat down with Deon and me in the dining room and told us in no uncertain terms that this was not the safari he had booked or, indeed, had been promised. It was at this point that I made it perfectly clear to both Mikhail and Nikolai that I was a freelance professional hunter and was in no way involved in the change of plans. Deon then explained that the south bank quota had been filled, despite Mikhail having booked his elephant hunt some three years previously. He went on to inform the unhappy Russians that the hunt would have to be done on the north bank or not at all. After complaining bitterly about their treatment, the two Russians eventually decided they had little option but to continue the hunt. We unpacked and settled in for the next twenty-one days in what was truly the worst camp I had ever seen.

The next three weeks proved to be an interesting safari for me. Our hunting area was huge, and no one, not even the game scout, knew where the boundaries were. Mikhail was an accomplished hunter, but from his perspective, the hunt was a complete failure. The main problem was a lack of roads throughout the vast track of bush. The only road in the half-million-acre concession was a major tarred highway that meandered its way up to Malawi. This formed the southern boundary of the concession.

Most recognized safari areas have decent networks of roads that make it possible to cover an area thoroughly by vehicle, but in this case it was a question of stopping at any given point on the only road and walking blindly into the bush in the slim hope of coming upon fresh elephant tracks. In twenty-one days we only tracked and came up to three elephant bulls, two of which were youngsters in the twenty-five-pound-a-side bracket while the third bull was tuskless. Fortunately Mikhail was extremely fit so walking long distances was not a problem for him.

Early one morning we came upon a huge set of tracks, and to add to our jubilation, the dung was still warm. I confidently told Mikhail we would catch up to the bull within an hour. How wrong I was! It was also obvious how little I knew of Mozambican elephants' behaviour. In their never-ending effort to beat poachers, they simply keep on moving and seldom, if ever, rest in the heat of the day as elephants normally do.

We tracked that particular bull until sundown and never once did we even get a sniff of him. His tracks took us through some amazing country that included the largest bamboo forest I have ever seen. While tracking him, we bumped into three lions at very close range, which created an adrenaline rush of note. On that particular day Crispen and Morgan tracked the bull at an incredible rate, so much so, we eventually lost radio contact with the vehicle, which, unfortunately, only worked on line of sight. We then became disorientated in the featureless bush, and to make matters worse, not only was it getting dark, but the party was also divided as to which direction we should head in order to get to the road.

In the end, Crispen, the clients, and I headed in one direction while Morgan and the game scout headed the opposite way. We agreed that the party to get to the road first would then radio the other group. It turned out that Crispen had guessed correctly; in fact, we were not that far from the road, but in any case, we struck it at around 7 P.M. that evening. In total I estimated we had walked about forty kilometres that day.

We tried to contact Morgan, but unfortunately the battery in his radio had run flat. I then ran back toward the vehicle until I made radio contact with Royal, my driver, who then came and picked us up, but poor Morgan and the game scout were only found the following afternoon. After tramping for hours through the endless bush, they eventually came upon a village near the Malawi border where they were given directions to the main road and then back to the camp.

Deon and Nikolai were not faring much better in their hunt for a crocodile. Not that this was a surprise, for there was only a single stream running through the entire area, and at its widest point it was only ten yards, so the likelihood of finding a fifteen-foot crocodile in such a small body of water was virtually zero. Understandably Nikolai was totally browned off, and in the end after much threatening from the Russian, I decided to phone the South African "operator" to tell him that Nikolai, who incidentally was a person of note in Safari Club International, was threatening to make life most unpleasant for him. Accordingly, I suggested that he get his act together and arrange to have Deon take him and his female "observer" to the south bank of the lake where they would at least have a chance of shooting a decent crocodile. Thankfully, he agreed to my suggestion.

Before dawn the following morning, Deon, Nikolai, and the big-breasted blonde set off on the ten-hour drive to the south camp, arriving there about 4 P.M. that afternoon. Nikolai was so excited to see the mighty stretch of water that he insisted on boarding the boat immediately for a reconnaissance of the area. His blonde observer decided she would stay in camp until they returned, so out onto the lake ventured Deon and Nikolai.

An hour later, and a good distance up the lake, the boat's engine conked out, and despite Deon's best efforts it failed to start again. Eventually after paddling with their plastic lunch plates—of course there were no oars aboard!—they reached the shore just as the sun was setting and swarms of hungry mosquitoes were preparing for a feast. The intrepid croc hunters finally got to the shore and pulled the boat out the water.

By good fortune, not far away a seminaked fisherman was preparing his nets for the night. Deon discussed the option of their getting into the fisherman's dugout canoe and heading for camp, but after seeing all the crocodiles and hippos, Nikolai declined. They decided the next best option would be for the fisherman to paddle to the camp and collect some sleeping bags plus Nikolai's cigars and whisky that he'd left in the tent.

So the fisherman set off and arrived at the camp an hour later. When the fisherman unzipped the tent to get the whisky and cigars, he was promptly jumped upon and stabbed with a pair of nail clippers by a terrified Russian lady. In all fairness to the large-breasted blonde, the final straw was having a seminaked African try to get into her tent. It was, understandably, just too much.

To cut a long story short, Nikolai eventually shot a monster crocodile and the three of them returned to join us on the north bank for the last two days of the hunt.

Our hunt concluded without shooting an elephant, disappointing to say the least. We were physically exhausted, for not only had we walked great distances each day, but also both Deon and I were awake at four o'clock every morning to make sure the camp staff was up cooking breakfast and preparing packed lunches.

One morning I went to wake up the cook, an African woman. When I reached her quarters, I found Mario, the sleazy and useless owner of the concession in bed with her. Mario was also giving me a hard time about getting reimbursed for the fees he had paid. In Mozambique it is customary to pay the license fee in advance for each animal on the tag. Regarding the bull elephant that we had failed to shoot, the government license was five thousand dollars, which Mario had already paid on the understanding that the South African "operator" would reimburse him at the beginning of the hunt.

Despite repeated promises from the South African that his manager from the south bank camp was on his way with the money, the last hunting day passed without him putting in an appearance. Mario pulled me aside and warned me that there would be trouble if the money was not paid by the time we got to Tete. I phoned the operator who promised me that his camp manager would be at the airport with Mario's money, so off we set for Tete.

I was very relieved, as was Mario, to see the camp manager waiting for us when we arrived at the airport. Our good spirits were short lived when he told us there was no money. Mario was furious and off he went, cursing in Portuguese into his cell phone. Before the clients had a chance to clear Customs and board the plane, we were all arrested by the Mozambican police. We were told that until Mario was paid his five thousand dollars we were all going to jail.

Eventually, I managed to persuade Mario to take possession of the South African's Land Cruiser, which Deon had been using, as collateral until Mario had been paid his dues. As a result the clients and I were free to go, and I did not stop until I had crossed the border into friendly Zimbabwe.

Despite the disappointing experience, my client Mikhail, his agent Alexei, and Vera, the Julia Roberts look-alike, were extremely nice people. Hunting aside, we had a wonderful time, and since then I have hunted with Alexei and a number of his clients.

CAT HUNTING

CHAPTER SIXTEEN

Most of my cat hunting has been in the Dande Safari Area, and on the whole I have been fortunate to have had a relatively easy time of it. This has particularly been the case with leopards. I think I've had such good fortune because they are very common in Dande and not nearly as alert as those in the other areas of Zimbabwe.

THE LEOPARD
PANTHERA PARDUS

The Zambezi Valley provides the ideal habitat for what I consider to be Africa's most beautiful trophy, *Panthera pardus*, the leopard. For the last twenty years, the Dande Safari Area has had on license an annual bag of twelve leopards, and if I'm not mistaken, there have only been two or three occasions during the time I've hunted there that this number of leopards has not been taken each year. This equates to almost two hundred and forty leopards over a twenty-year period. This significant number is testimony to the ideal habitat of the Dande for the leopard. That we have remained almost 100 percent successful in achieving our annual quota over the past two decades also suggests that the annual removal of this number of leopards is sustainable.

Max and Maria Mayer-Malnof with a nice cat we took in Dande.

Generally speaking, leopards are not big cats. A good Zambezi Valley tom will weigh in around 135 to 140 pounds; a 150-pound "valley" tom would be considered exceptional. However, body weight is an unreliable indicator of size. As a leopard is capable of eating as much as 25 percent of its body weight in a single meal, it stands to reason that a full stomach can easily create confusion when discussing the topic of weight with respect to size. Because of this issue, body length is a fairer indicator of size. A good-size Zambezi Valley tom leopard will average 6 feet, 8 inches in length. These animals are shorter than their cousins in the south of Zimbabwe, where a big tom can get close to 8 feet in length and weigh in at a staggering 200 pounds.

The success rate with leopard hunting in the Dande, or, indeed, the Zambezi Valley as a whole, is much higher than in the south of the country. Furthermore, to secure a good tom on a mixed-bag, Zambezi Valley safari usually requires less time being spent on the animal than elsewhere in the country. The difficult part of leopard hunting in the Zambezi Valley is trying to lure a good quality tom to the bait, but when success is finally achieved, it is almost a certainty that the leopard will be in the "salt," so to speak, not too long after dark, with still enough time to enjoy a whiskey around the campfire before bedtime. In my opinion, the reason for the difference is that valley leopards are uneducated compared to their cousins in the south of the country, areas which were or still are devoted to cattle ranching.

Considered a threat to livestock on these ranches, leopards in the south of Zimbabwe have been persecuted for generations. Over many years, persistent trapping, bait poisoning, and hunting have created a unique awareness among the survivors, and those that remain have become very wary. In the southern part of Zimbabwe, professional hunters are forced to become equally as cunning in order to bag a good leopard. This often requires double blinds, assisted hearing devices, and many nights spent in the blind, which to me is absolute torture.

In reality, there are only two ways to hunt a leopard successfully. The first method is to bait while the second uses dogs. The Dande Safari Area is infested with the dreaded tsetse fly, which transmits trypanosomiasis, better known as sleeping sickness. The disease is invariably fatal to all

Will Park with his monster leopard he shot in Save Valley with Thierry La Butt.

Hendrik Schuckman and I with a big Zambezi Valley cat.

domestic animals, so that rules out using dogs in the area to hunt leopards. Baiting, therefore, is the only option.

The baiting procedure requires the shooting of an impala or using suitable portions of other game meat, usually obtained from a buffalo kill. The baits are then hung in places where leopards are known to live. Territories vary in size from area to area depending on the availability of the food source. In the Zambezi Valley where there is a relatively low concentration of plains game, I estimate the average territory size of a dominant male leopard to be about twenty-five square kilometres.

It's my usual habit to set up at least ten baits at any given time, and once that chore is done, the monotony of leopard hunting begins! All baits need to be checked on a daily basis. This entails mile upon mile of hard driving, in my case over the Dande's rough and rocky dirt tracks, in order to see if any of the baits have been "hit."

If any individual bait remains intact, the area around that carcass needs to be dragged with *matumbus*, the smelly abdominal contents from the animals that were originally shot for bait. These stomach contents are stored in a bucket and carried from lure to lure in the back of our Land Cruiser.

One can imagine what this bucket smells like when its contents are a week old and the October temperature is in the region of 50 degrees Celsius (122 degrees Fahrenheit) in the sun. My driver Eddy has the distinction of being called Mr. Matumbu as it is his job to re-drag the baits that have not been touched. To his everlasting credit, Eddy never complains as he goes about his business, dragging and smearing the rotten, maggot-infested *matumbus* throughout the baiting area!

The first item that needs attention after the bait has been hit is to determine if the leopard responsible is male or female. Females are not hunted; they are ignored. If the leopard happens to be a male, you need to decide if it is worth shooting. In the early days of my career, we would make this decision purely on the size of the leopard's tracks, which is not all that easy to do. Things are much easier these days thanks to the use of trail cameras, which not only help to identify the sex and size of the leopard but also the time he came in to feed and what time he left. This information is essential in safari areas that prohibit night shooting.

The Dande Safari Area is divided into two parts, communal and safari. The use of artificial light is allowed in the communal areas but not in the safari area. For the latter, the law states that leopards can only be hunted during the hours of natural daylight: a half hour before sunrise to half an hour after sunset. Thus, the area in which you are baiting affects the choice of your baiting sites.

Baiting sites in the safari area need to be carefully chosen, a lot more so than those in the communal areas. Due to the daylight-hour restriction in the safari area, a concealed approach to the blind is essential. This ensures that if a leopard is already feeding on the bait, your direct approach will not be seen. The path to the blind also needs to be carefully cleared then raked and marked with white toilet paper. These actions will make it much easier to follow the path since you will be arriving at the blind in the darkness in order to be ready for first shooting light. A cleared and well-marked path will also be useful after last light, especially if the leopard has not made an appearance, and a quiet exit is necessary should he be close-by. Disturbing a leopard at this time could well result in failure in future predawn raids, the wily leopard having sensed your intention.

A nice Zambezi Valley leopard on bait in early morning.

In the communal area, however, where the use of artificial light is legal, you can sit for as long as you like in the blind. In such situations it is almost guaranteed that the leopard will eventually arrive at the bait, and you will have your opportunity to shoot it. In such situations there is no need to consider concealed approaches or carefully cleared paths.

From past experience I have found the "prime time" for leopards to arrive at the bait is just before darkness and until 7:30 P.M. After this time your chances recede dramatically, and I now no longer sit later than 9 P.M. If the leopard is not in the bait tree by then, in all probability he will not be coming at all.

Blind building is a time-consuming affair. Positioning is important as it is essential that the blind is situated downwind from the bait and not infringing upon the leopard's incoming or outgoing routes. It also needs to be well camouflaged and made comfortable for the shooter, for he has to sit for long periods at a time next to a reliable "rifle rest," which is used to steady his aim.

When the "moment of truth" finally arrives, the actual shot at the leopard is not that difficult. The shooting distance is usually no farther than sixty yards away, and, of course, the shot is taken from a steady "dead rest." To make things even easier, the bait and the hide are so situated that the leopard will be feeding in such a position as to provide the hunter with a broadside-on shot.

In spite of this perfect set-up, there are still a high number of wounded leopards. This can be attributed to the following reasons: First is the adrenaline problem. When a leopard finally appears in the tree and begins to feed on the bait, it is only natural for the shooter to become overly excited. Even I, who have witnessed dozens of leopard kills, get animated when I first see the animal. During these initial moments, it is important to restrain the client from shooting on impulse. A prehunt advisory talk helps to ensure he or she remains suitably restrained during those key moments. The hunter is encouraged to sit patiently and take in the splendour of the moment and wait until his excitement is under control. These nerve-settling moments ensure the placement of a steady and well-aimed shot.

The second reason is the light factor. Leopards are generally nocturnal animals, and they often arrive at the bait at last light. When hunting in a safari area where no artificial light is permitted, a client can be tempted to take a marginal shot as darkness approaches. Such situations can and do occur whereby the client, through human nature, imagines he can see the leopard clearly enough to take a shot, but, in reality, he can hardly see it at all. This premature action often results in a wounded leopard. At such times the difference between a good-quality scope and a poor one can

Trail camp pictures take the guesswork out of it.

make the difference between success and failure. It should also be noted that an illuminated reticle can also be a huge advantage in rapidly failing light.

Many clients consider sitting in a blind for hours on end tedious. During these extended periods one has to sit as motionless as possible. As I said, the longest period I will sit in a hide in the Dande communal area is from 4 P.M. to 9 P.M. and from 4 P.M. to last light in the safari area, which, during the winter hunting season is around 6:30 P.M.

Personally, I get much pleasure from sitting in a blind at this time of day. Our baits are frequently positioned near water, and that invariably attracts a multitude of species of birds at twilight. The most impressive of these birds is the sandgrouse. These little guys jet in from all sides, sometimes in large numbers, minutes before sunset, announcing their arrival with electriclike "Star Wars"–type calls. And they leave just as quickly as they came, taking enough time to relieve their thirst and immerse their frontal feathers in the water to take back to their chicks waiting patiently on some lonely rocky ridge farther inland. Listening carefully as day slowly changes to night is a peaceful experience yet spiced with the excitement and expectancy of suddenly seeing an elusive leopard appear under the tree or in the branches above.

We are usually forewarned of the pending arrival of Mr. Spots by the sound of baboons or the sudden bark of a bushbuck or kudu. Even squirrels,

Here I am with two male leopards that we took one night in Dande.

I consider the leopard to be Africa's most beautiful trophy.

monkeys, or ground birds, like the francolin, express with equal ferocity their hatred and fear by screeching a warning at the arrival of the enemy. Any one of these sounds is enough to put you on high alert, with your senses honed to a fine edge!

On the other hand, it is true that more often than not the leopard will arrive without a sound. One moment the bait tree is empty and the next time you look . . . there the leopard is sitting in the tree, as if by magic. Such is their stealth. What an amazing sight leopards are at such times. Little wonder then that this moment sets the heart racing.

This is the crucial moment for restraint. One's natural instinct is to reach for the rifle and shoot, for the assumption is that the leopard might disappear as quickly as he appeared! This is the very worst thing to do. The leopard will still be on high alert as he scans the territory from his vantage point, looking for any possible threat. The slightest movement in the blind could well draw his attention, and in a flash he'll be down the tree and gone.

Difficult as it may seem, this is the time to remain still. Keep watching this beautiful cat and wait until he starts feeding on the bait. It's only then that he's decided the coast is clear. Now is the time to slowly shoulder your rifle, which is already mounted and aimed at the bait. Carefully position the cross hairs just behind the shoulder, and squeeze off the shot. *Boom!* As he falls to the ground, you realize you have just secured one of Africa's most beautiful trophies.

A wounded leopard follow-up is every professional hunter's nightmare. The chance of getting mauled by a wounded leopard is very high, indeed! In fact, I would estimate that you have a 50 percent chance that a wounded leopard will get you before you can stop him. Rest assured, he will eventually charge at some stage during the follow-up. My preferred weapon for such situations is a 12-gauge, double-barrel shotgun loaded with nickel-plated double-zero buckshot. Nickel-plated pellets are essential as I have found that lead pellets often flatten on impact and do not penetrate. On a wounded leopard follow-up, I insist that the trackers remove the blades from their axes. In the heat of the moment, when an irate and wounded

We tracked Evolt Wilms's lion in Dande; note his huge body.

Jorge Borg with the lion he shot in Matetsi, 1992.

leopard is paying close attention to an unfortunate member of the team, a badly aimed ax blow can easily detach a limb or two.

The Lion
Panthera leo

Of all the dangerous wildlife species I have hunted, the animal of which I have the least experience is the lion. Although the Zambezi Valley has a sizable lion population, they seldom have the huge manes. The exception to this is a lion we took when I was an apprentice in Matetsi in 1992, as seen in the picture above. There are a few reasons for this. Personally, I consider it a genetic issue combined with an environmental one. The vegetation found in the valley is thick *jesse* bush, and as the lion moves through this thick *jesse* bush, the mane catches on the bush and hairs are stripped away.

Another possibility could be the temperatures in the valley. This is a low-lying area where winters seldom get excessively cold. (Summers in the valley are another story. Then it can get unbearably hot, with temperatures soaring into the 40-degree Celsius (104 degrees F.) range. Unlike the

The lion, the king of the beasts.

Kalahari where overnight temperatures can drop well below zero, that doesn't happen in the valley, so lions do not need long manes to help keep them warm. I feel certain these are the reasons why the lions of Dande are a little short-changed in the mane department.

As with leopards, the most successful way to hunt lions is to bait them. Baiting is the accepted method and the most successful by far. However, in my opinion the most satisfying lion hunts have been those where tracking has been used. Unlike the sandy soils of the Kalahari, which make tracking comparatively easy, the Zambezi Valley is vastly different. With its thick bush and variable soils, the valley presents some of the most difficult country for tracking in Africa. I have often said that I would love to witness the famed Kalahari Bushmen tracking an elephant or a lion in the Zambezi Valley, for in this environment I have my reservations that they would be better or even comparable to our local trackers.

Over the past twenty-five years I have successfully tracked and shot several male lions, and all of them rate highly as my most satisfying and enjoyable hunting experiences. Put simply, the odds are heavily stacked against you when you attempt to hunt a lion by tracking. First of all,

We tracked Pavel's lion and shot him on the last day of the hunt.

Guy de Peep and his lion that we tracked in Maonde Valley of the Dande.

without a team of expert trackers, it is doubtful you will get farther than a hundred metres without losing the tracks! Secondly, lions have such incredible senses that they will normally hear, see, or smell you long before you sight them . . . giving you no time to evaluate whether the lion is a good specimen or even old enough to shoot. If by chance the answers are in the positive, you rarely have time enough to shoot.

In other areas where visibility is better and the terrain more friendly to the hunter as far as the noise perspective is concerned, it is a lot easier to sneak up to lions. In the Zambezi Valley this is never easy, and I have found from past experience that the only decent chance of a shot is through the element of surprise. You need to get as close as possible while the lions remain unaware of your presence. You need to be lucky to catch the lions resting in a dry riverbed or to surprise them while they are in a gully. Finding them in these situations will force them to expose themselves as they climb up the opposite bank to make their escape. As slim as they are, it is in these situations that you get your chance at a shot. If by chance you catch up to them on level ground, rest assured, in the valley, you will not get in a shot, for they would have made their escape long before you see them. In normal circumstances the first sign of their presence is the release of a deep growl, a sure indication that they have seen you and are departing the scene with speed.

Once a lion knows that he's being followed, he is very difficult to track, his intention being to put as much distance as possible between himself and you. Under normal circumstances, lions follow the path of least resistance, for they are basically lazy animals. As they go about their normal day-to-day routine, they tend to take the easy route by following roads, game trails, or sandy riverbeds. This routine makes tracking easy.

The situation changes dramatically when a lion knows he's being followed. At such times he will depart the scene in haste, invariably in a straight line, and that often takes him over rocky terrain and through dense bush. This makes tracking very difficult and dramatically reduces your chance of success.

As I have limited experience in lion hunting, one of my greatest fears is following a wounded one. These magnificent cats are incredibly fast. A lion has the ability to camouflage himself behind a small tuft of grass, and when he charges he does so with unbelievable speed. I'm reliably told a lion can cover a hundred metres in four seconds. If you should fail to stop his charge and if you are on the receiving end of his fury, it is highly probable you will be departing to greener pastures in a very short but painful time.

Never Pull a Leopard by Its Tail

Chapter Seventeen

Not long ago the Chirisa Safari Area was considered one of Zimbabwe's premier big-game hunting areas. It has a common boundary with the Chizarira National Park and is bisected by the Sengwa River. The area once held a great quantity of game, but, unfortunately, the Parks and Wildlife Management Authority abused the pristine wilderness by over-shooting the elephant and buffalo populations for their own purpose. This atrocity combined with safari operators who never put a cent back into the area quickly led to Chirisa's downfall, to such a degree that professionals no longer hunt there, leaving the door wide open for poachers who have all but decimated the remaining stocks of wildlife.

I was fortunate to hunt in Chirisa in its heyday, before the tragic annihilation of its wildlife. My first Chirisa safari found me hunting with a strange individual named John. We were hunting buffalo, leopard, and a few plains-game species. At that time buffaloes were plentiful in the area, and we looked over hundreds of the animals before following a large group of about three hundred from the well-known Sipani Pan. After two hours of easy tracking, we caught up to the herd, and John shot and wounded an old bull.

We followed the animal for several hours, and when we finally caught up to him, he immediately charged. I was thankful that we managed to drop the bull a few feet from where we were standing, but as I related in an earlier chapter, that was only after an amusing incident involving Crispen and a backpack full of Coke cans. When Crispen bent over to show me that he had spotted the bull, his backpack fell onto the ground and out came the cans with an almighty crash right in front of the bull's nose, thus initiating the charge.

With the buffalo "in the salt," so to speak, and with plenty of meat on hand for baiting purposes, we set about laying a number of leopard baits.

The final bite.

Being my first-ever hunt in Chirisa as a fully qualified professional, I had gathered as much inside information as possible about the area from a local hunter named Dean who had been a resident there for a number of years. Like most Zimbabwean professional hunters, Dean was more than willing to assist a rookie like me with advice, such as to the best spots to lay our baits.

One of Dean's recommended sites was in a large *vlei* called Chiweshu. An absolute monster of a tom leopard was known to frequent the area, but the animal had become wise and very cunning, so much so that he had avoided several attempts to kill him. The leopard had been affectionately named the "Chiweshu Monster" by all the hunters who knew of him, and like many before me I was determined to see if John and I could put him "in the salt." Two days later, on checking the bait we had so carefully hung in the *vlei*, we were excited to discover that a big leopard had fed on it. With great enthusiasm we quickly constructed a blind and settled in to see what lay ahead.

A lot earlier than expected the silence was broken when a flock of cackling guinea fowl burst out of the bush close to the bait tree, and moments later a beautiful male leopard leapt up onto the branch. Despite his appearance so early, the leopard appeared nervous, and for a moment it looked as though he was about to ignore the bait and leap back into the bush. With the leopard's incredible eyesight, I suspected he might have seen movement from within our blind.

The leopard was, indeed, a large tom, but was he big enough to be the Chiweshu Monster? I had my doubts, and if I was correct, it meant the leopard was an intruder into the so called Monster's domain. This could well be the reason he had arrived early and why he appeared so nervous. As we watched him, the leopard turned and started running down the branch. It was at this moment that John fired, hitting the cat in the stomach. Grunting as it ran away, the big tom almost instantly disappeared into the thicket.

I've said before that following a wounded leopard is a professional hunter's nightmare, and so it is. As it was still light enough, we picked up the spoor and began tracking. I was especially cautious on this occasion due to a near disaster that had happened on a recent leopard hunt. I had been with a Mexican who had also wounded a leopard. The result was that Morgan, my tracker, and Richard, a learner professional, had both received a mauling! In this case and quite understandably, trackers Morgan and Crispen were both on high alert.

When finally we caught up with the tom, all I saw of him was a blur of spotted yellow as he disappeared into the bush. In desperation I shouldered my shotgun and took a "Hail Mary" shot, but all I succeeded in doing was peppering the leopard's backside with pellets. Regrettably, they did little harm other than to annoy him even more.

By that stage the light was fading fast, and it was becoming difficult to track, but there was still enough light to make out that his spoor had entered a very thick patch of bush, which looked about four times the area of my Land Cruiser. The bush was so thick that gut instinct warned me the situation meant trouble—big trouble. Since we were all convinced the tom was still in there, we very carefully circled the area, only to find there were no exiting tracks from the thicket. The leopard was still in there, of that I had no doubt.

The law clearly states there is to be no hunting during the hours of darkness. In this case, as it was too dark to continue, we headed back to camp

While a very large leopard, I had my doubts that John's leopard was the Chiweshu Monster.

with the intention of resuming the follow-up at first light next morning. Over a rather subdued dinner, Dean asked me if I thought the leopard was, indeed, the "Chiweshu Monster." I still remained doubtful because the so-called "Monster" was aptly named, having an estimated weight of two hundred pounds. To make John feel better, I told him the wounded leopard awaiting our attention was, indeed, a very big male.

The following morning I asked Squirrel, a fellow professional, to assist us with the leopard because John had decided to stay in the Land Cruiser. I was more than relieved by John's decision as it is well known that on a wounded leopard follow-up, there is more chance of being shot by an over-excited client than getting mauled by the leopard itself.

Shortly after first light I, along with Squirrel and my two trackers, returned to the patch of thick bush where we had called off the hunt the previous night. There I found the area was covered with hyena tracks. This was a huge concern. If the hyenas had found the leopard dead during the night, there would be very little left apart from a few bones and torn pieces of his magnificent coat. With my shotgun held at the ready, I bent down and peered into the bush.

Imagine my relief upon seeing the leopard lying on his side stone dead, and, what's more, completely untouched. I was overcome with relief. Not only had the hyenas ignored the carcass, but we had also managed to escape another run-in with an angry, gut-shot leopard!

A considerable amount of jubilation, backslapping, and congratulatory high-fives then ensued. What a lucky break! When all the revelry was over, I bent down and grabbed the leopard by its tail and began to drag it out from under the bush. To my absolute horror, the so-called "dead" leopard suddenly transformed itself into one hundred and seventy pounds of sharp-clawed, open-fanged, saliva-spitting fury!

In an instant I found myself pulled to the ground as though I were little more than a rag doll. The leopard set its dewclaw into the shoulder of my leather jacket and ripped it down the full length of my arm, embedding its claw into my hand in the process. Before the leopard could do any serious damage, Squirrel, an accomplished bird shot, knocked the leopard off me by shooting it with both barrels of his shotgun. In its frustration at having lost its grip on my arm, the big cat sunk its teeth into a sapling in its final act of defiance. It had been a close call, indeed, and I was really lucky to have escaped a serious mauling and even a possible face-lift.

After the dust had settled and my adrenaline levels returned to normal, we carefully pieced the puzzle together. It looked as though the poor leopard

John sporting a "half moon."

A vantage point over the Sengwa River.

had spent most of the night fighting off the hyenas. With the coming of dawn the hyenas had departed, leaving the exhausted leopard to fall into a deep, semiconscious sleep. So deep was his sleep, in fact, that he only woke up when I pulled his tail. All that was left now was the picture taking, so I sent one of the trackers back to tell Royal, my driver, to bring John to the scene.

"Is it the Chiweshu Monster?" was the first thing he asked on seeing that magnificent leopard.

I was honest in my reply, telling him I didn't think it was. Like a spoilt child and much to his shame, he showed his disappointment by begrudgingly having his picture taken. Granted, it was highly unlikely the leopard was the "Chiweshu Monster," but on the other hand, it was one of the bigger cats I had taken in twenty years of professional hunting. I was and still remain disappointed in John's ungrateful and shameful behaviour.

Several days later he shot a fine kudu bull. The occasion also resulted in him becoming a member of the "half-moon" club whereby the recoil of the rifle caused the outer rim of the telescopic sight to whack him above the right eye. This resulted in a deep gash that bled profusely, so deep in fact that it required stitching. As can be imagined, I was not overly sympathetic; in fact, it rather seemed like poetic justice to me.

Protecting the Crown Jewels

Chapter Eighteen

Gabriel, a Mexican client, came out to the Dande with his wife and son for a twenty-one-day double buffalo, elephant, and leopard hunt. Within the first few minutes of meeting Gabriel I realized we were in for a long and difficult hunt. An ethical, fair-chase hunter Gabriel most definitely was not! Hardly had we been introduced before he excitedly told me that he had just completed an amazing white rhino "hunt" in South Africa where he'd shot the new No. 3, record-book-ranked rhino. He explained that the entire hunt had taken only forty-five minutes, from leaving his plush five-star hotel room to taking pictures of himself with the dead, record-ranked rhino.

He also told me the booking agent through whom he had booked the hunt with me had assured him that there was a waterhole near the camp where as many as two hundred elephants came down in the evening to drink. Furthermore, the agent guaranteed that the standard practice was to shoot elephants while taking sundowners at the waterhole each evening. If luck happened to be on his side, he stood a good chance of shooting a bull elephant with over eighty-pound tusks on each side, right there at the waterhole and all from the comfort of an armchair.

Having never heard such exaggerated and unethical nonsense before, I had no option but to level with him right there and then. I explained most carefully that elephant hunting in the Zambezi Valley was conducted only on foot and should be considered very hard going and physically challenging. At most and only after a lot of hard work could he expect a thirty-five pounder–at most. What's more, if he was unhappy with these hard-hitting facts, he was most welcome to get back onto the charter plane, which had delivered him to the valley, and return to Mexico. By doing this, he would still have recourse with the booking agent who had

Gabriel and his elephant bull.

quite obviously pulled the wool over his eyes. Anyhow, after a great deal of muttering and cursing, Gabriel said he and his family would stay.

The first morning found us looking for elephant tracks. Despite my recommendation that she stay behind in camp, Gabriel's wife accompanied us . . . wearing designer shoes and expensive, custom-tailored safari clothes. Tracking elephants through thick and inhospitable *jesse* bush is not advisable for a smartly dressed, carefully manicured, respectable lady. Notwithstanding my advice, she refused to remain in camp. It later transpired she was afraid that the African camp staff would rape her the moment we left!

After a long search we finally found tracks of a mature bull, and we decided to follow it. Once again I recommended that Gabriel's wife stay with the Land Cruiser. She hesitated, took one look at Royal, my driver (who is the ultimate well-mannered gentlemen), and said, "No, I would rather come with you." It was obvious she thought poor old Royal was just waiting to have his way with her the moment we were out of sight.

We had only been tracking a short while when I glanced behind to see how my clients were faring. In doing so, I couldn't help a little chuckle at the elderly Mexicans in their designer safari gear, complete with colonial pith helmets, holding hands as they ducked and weaved through the *jesse*.

As luck would have it, we caught up to the elephant in forty-five minutes, and upon evaluating the bull, I decided Gabriel should shoot it. The decision was based on my assumption that it was unlikely the happy couple was capable or, indeed, prepared to engage in additional tracking in the inhospitable *jesse* bush. I knew they would give up if faced with a strenuous fair-chase stalk.

To his credit, Gabriel shot the bull without hassle, which pleased him no end. He stated categorically that it was the best trophy he had ever taken in his life, primarily because he had had to work so hard for it! I shudder to think how all his other trophies were collected if his best only required an effort of forty-five minutes.

While returning to camp late one evening after an unsuccessful buffalo hunt, the Land Cruiser's headlights picked up a yellow streak dashing across the road. I thought it might be a leopard, and out of curiosity I swung the Land Cruiser off the road in an effort to get a better look at the animal in the headlights. Almost immediately a shot rang out from behind me from the back of the vehicle! It was immediately followed by the ghastly tell-tale growling of a wounded cat.

In a rage I slammed on the brakes and jumped out of the vehicle. Even before my feet touched ground, I was cursing a very excited Mexican. I was furious, firstly for him shooting from the vehicle and then for shooting without my permission. To make matters worse, we were in a Parks and Wildlife safari area where it is illegal to shoot after dark. Such actions could have serious repercussions, to the extent that I could easily lose my hard-earned professional hunter's license. To add to the predicament, I was not even sure the animal in question was indeed a leopard, let alone a male. I should emphasize here that female leopards cannot be hunted for sporting purposes and that there are significant implications and penalties if they are. I had every right to be really annoyed with Gabriel, and I made sure he was aware of it.

Gabriel's son with his father's leopard that was shot under less-than-ideal circumstances.

The only consolation, after following the tracks with the aid of a spotlight, was that the spoor revealed it was a good tom leopard. The bad news, however, was that we found a piece of shattered leg bone, and from the slight scuffmarks to be seen in the dust, we deduced the leopard's left back leg was broken. Following a lightly wounded leopard at night is asking for trouble, so we drove back to camp in stony silence, had a difficult and strained dinner, and an early night. Sleep did not come easily knowing that dawn would bring an unenviably hazardous follow-up for a wounded leopard in thick riverine bush.

The first bird calls after daylight found us on the tracks from where we had left the leopard previously. For back-up I enlisted the help of an English lad by the name of Richard Arnison-Newgas, who was helping out around camp at the time. Richard was a bit of a ladies' man and fresh from the United Kingdom. He was an accomplished bird shooter and always in for an adventure. In the dangerous situation we were about to enter, I was convinced Richard would be a lot more useful than Gabriel, should things go pear-shaped. As it was, Gabriel refused to accompany us, something I was very happy about as he was sure to be more of a liability then an asset! As Richard was new to the game of following wounded leopards, I gave him strict instructions as to what to do should the leopard get hold of any of us.

The tracking was extremely difficult as there was only an occasional drop of blood on the tracks. We noticed that when the leopard was walking, he raised his broken leg so it no longer dragged along the ground. The tracks eventually led us into a dry, narrow riverbed, and we could tell by the clarity of the spoor that we were getting very close. With utmost caution we proceeded very slowly with Morgan and Crispen up front, me following behind, and Richard bringing up the rear.

Suddenly and without a trace of warning, the leopard came flying at us from the riverbank. I managed to hit him at point-blank range, right on the shoulder with a heavy load of pure lead double-zero buckshot pellets. Imagine my horror when I realized they had had absolutely no effect. Immediately, I let go a second round. This one missed the leopard completely. The leopard attacked Morgan, biting him on the leg, before focusing his attention on Richard. As the leopard pounced on Richard, he managed to shoot it on top of the head with a similar load of buckshot. Unbelievably, the pellets had almost no effect on the enraged animal.

Now the fun really began. In a desperate attempt to save himself, Richard fed the leopard his left arm. Trying to get the best advantage to attack the snarling, frenzied beast, the three of us circled the combatants, with Morgan and Crispen hacking away at the incensed cat with their axes while I did my best to get a clear shot in with my .45 handgun. All this chaotic activity was conducted to the sound of Richard's high-pitched screams of *"Shoot it! Shoot it!"*

Eventually, I managed to get in four clear shots with my handgun. These finally killed the leopard . . . but not before the leopard had paid serious attention to poor Richard's lower regions. Rolling the leopard off Richard, I asked the pale-looking Englishman if he was OK. Richard proceeded to give the contents of his trousers a thorough inspection before declaring he was fine, his manhood having survived the ordeal. Whether it was from pure relief or a late reaction, Richard then promptly fainted. Out like a light, he dropped like a sack of potatoes to the ground, ending up right beside the dead leopard.

Upon arrival back at the camp, Richard was taken away on a stretcher while Morgan hobbled around as the result of the vicious bite the leopard had given him. As for Gabriel, the delightful Mexican, well, his only concern was for the leopard. There was, however, a just reward for this thoroughly unpleasant man.

It was discovered after skinning that his leopard's hide contained more holes than spots. There was his initial shot to the left hind leg, eight ax slashes made by both trackers, four bullet holes from my .45 handgun, and two large holes made by the shotgun.

Interestingly, the lead double-zero buckshot pellets from the two shotguns had flattened on impact and not penetrated at all. Regrettably, I did not learn from this experience, and it would take another mauling for me to finally realize just how ineffective lead buckshot pellets are on a leopard. When the penny did finally drop, I changed to nickel-plated buckshot for the initial shot followed by an expanding-type Brenneke slug, should it be necessary. This set-up produced satisfactory results.

As for poor Richard, well, he spent the better part of a week in hospital where he fully recovered. Much to his disappointment for the loss of bragging rights as well as a dent in his pride, his scars healed up to the point where you can hardly recognize them today!

A HEALTHY RESPECT FOR GRAVITY

CHAPTER NINETEEN

After twenty years of hunting big game, my clients often expect me to have a lot of fireside stories as well as a bruised and battered body to back them up. Admittedly, I've had a fair share of them both, but, thankfully, I've more stories than scars. I do have a long, thick scar on my left wrist that is easily visible. This often results in new clients asking what vicious beast I had tangled with. I confess there have been times when I've blown up the story just for fun, but I always come clean in the end and tell them how the incident actually happened. Their inevitable disappointment soon changes to one of amusement when they discover that the scar is actually the result of a rather pathetic accident.

I had been hunting with a Russian client by the name of Victor, who was accompanied by his so-called girlfriend, a common sobriquet used by many Russians to describe newly acquired female friends who accompany them on safaris. These attractive girls possess certain qualities that obviously come at a cost.

Victor's primary hunting objectives were a buffalo and a leopard. My previous safari, which had ended several days earlier, had been a successful leopard hunt, and at that time we had another bait out that had also attracted a leopard. I felt that using this bait would make Victor's hunt too easy, so I told him we needed to shoot a couple of impalas. I told him the impalas were to be used for leopard bait; however, this proved easier said than done. It took Victor twelve shots to bag the impalas.

With the bait eventually in hand, we headed off to Usiwatswa, one of Dande's numerous and beautiful all-year-round springs. This is the spot where the second leopard had been feeding, so it was a good starting point for Victor's quest. It also made sense to hang the bait in the same tree we had used on the previous hunt.

Linda and I with her leopard, Dande, 2003.

The tree in question was an African fig that grew out the side of the riverbank. There was a thick branch growing off to the left side of the trunk, which was where I envisaged the leopard would be sitting as he fed upon the bait. The result would be a perfect side-on position, making for an easy shot. The set-up, as I saw it, would not only give us a clear silhouette of the leopard, should it come in late to feed, but it would also afford us ample cover for an early morning approach into the blind if we needed one.

To hang the bait exactly where I wanted required a lot of climbing and crawling because the branch stretched out a fair way over the riverbank. My tracker, Morgan, was already occupied in dragging the impala guts down the riverbed to leave a scent, so this left Crispen and me to do the bait hanging. I felt guilty about sending the old man up the tree, so I decided to climb it myself.

I got a good footing in the first "V" of the trunk, but I was soon to discover that while Crocs are comfortable shoes in which to walk long distances, they are definitely not designed for tree climbing. The last I remember was of my foot slipping out of the shoe, and the next I recall was sitting on my backside in the dry riverbed while being rained upon, or so it seemed. I sat there for quite some time, concussed and confused. After a while my senses returned, and I realized it was not rain that was drenching me, but my own blood. I raised my left hand to feel what the damage was and to find out where the blood was coming from, and I nearly fainted at the sight of my arm. It was hanging limply at a ninety-degree angle below the elbow.

It appeared I had fallen headfirst out the bait tree as a result of my left foot being caught between the trunk and the branch. In order to protect myself and break the fall, I had thrust out my left hand, which had subsequently broken in two places when it made contact with the ground. This left my head as the next line of defense, resulting in a concussion and a broken nose when I fell headfirst onto the rocks in the riverbed below.

Initially, practical joker Crispen thought it hilariously funny to see his boss fall out the tree. However, his amusement soon changed when he saw the damage that had been caused in the fall. I sent him off at speed to collect the first-aid box from the Land Cruiser. A comedy of errors then ensued. In his haste to help me, Crispen managed to drop the first-aid box, scattering its contents amongst the rocks in the riverbed. While he scrambled to collect and repack its contents, my Russian client who had actually completed three years of medical school pranced around in a hopeless manner while providing little assistance to anyone.

Eventually under my instructions, Crispen and Morgan managed to strap my limp left arm in a splint, which they had hastily fashioned from a mopane tree sapling. I was still groggy from the fall, but my trackers slowly got me to my feet, and, supporting me on both sides, they eventually got me back to camp.

My intention was to get MARS, our Medical Air Rescue Service, to fly in and pick me up. Unfortunately, my fall had occurred in late afternoon, and it was only as darkness fell that we eventually arrived back at main camp. This meant expert medical attention and an air charter evacuation was out of the question.

My face was not a pretty picture. Not only was my nose broken and not in its right place, there were also areas where the skin was badly abraded. Covered in dry blood, I was a real mess. The clean-up process was long and

Linda and her grand old buffalo, Dande, 2003.

painful. Fortunately Claude, our camp manager, was also a professional hunter and quite capable of standing in for me, so I hastily packed a few things, and with Royal in the driving seat, we set off on the long and bumpy road back to Harare. Thanks to a pile of pillows cushioning my arm and some hastily swallowed painkillers, the six-hour trip was bearable.

We eventually arrived in Harare where I was admitted to hospital and my left arm X-rayed. The X-rays were not encouraging: Both my left radius and ulna were cleanly broken below the elbow, which accounted for the acute angle of my arm. More worrying, however, from the orthopedic surgeon's perspective, was my left wrist, which was so badly broken from the fall that some of the wrist's metacarpals were shattered. To repair them would require a bone graft from transplants taken from my hip.

As for my nose, the doctor quickly reset it to its original shape and position with a quick twist of his hand. It sounds like a seemingly effortless procedure, yet it was more painful than anything that had happened thus far, and I nearly wet myself from the agony. Funnily enough, my nose was broken again some two years later by a group of Mexican thugs in an even more embarrassing incident, but that is another story.

I was then moved into a ward to await the operation. There I was confronted with an amazing sight: The ten-bed ward was full, apart from the one assigned to me, and the ward's occupants were all like me, young fellows in their thirties. At a quick glance, it looked as though they all had similar injuries. They, too, were awaiting their turn in the operating theatre. It did not take long for my curiosity to get the better of me, so I asked the young man in the bed next to mine what the story was.

It transpired they were all members of the political party MDC (Movement for Democratic Change) and in opposition to Mugabe's leading party, ZANU PF (Zimbabwe African National Union—Patriotic Front). Earlier that day they had been attending an MDC rally when the police arrived. The brutes on duty decided the meeting was illegal, burst in on the rally, and proceeded to dish out their own form of justice on anyone they could lay their hands on. They set about beating the opposition with rubber truncheons with the intent of teaching them a lesson they would not soon forget. Broken arms and even a broken leg were the result of their dedication to the party. Such is the wonder and effectiveness of African politics.

I remained in the hospital waiting to be operated on far longer than anticipated because there was a severe shortage of orthopedic surgeons, most of whom had left the country in search of greener pastures. The scenario to flee the country was rampant throughout other professions in Zimbabwe as well. As a result there were, at that time, only two in Harare, so they were operating on a priority basis. It transpired that all my newfound political friends were deemed to be of a higher priority than myself. Eventually about a week after my accident I was finally operated upon by Dr. Vera, who did a magnificent job on reconstructing my wrist's metacarpals. Thanks to his professional efforts, my left wrist is now only slightly weaker than my right.

Meanwhile my Russian client, Victor, had continued his hunt with Claude, my camp manager, and trackers Crispen and Morgan. The day after my accident, they managed to haul the impala into the "V" of the tree that

I'd fallen out of, and that same night the impala carcass was hit by a fine leopard tom. The following morning they built a blind only thirty yards from the bait.

This distance is considerably closer than usual, but it was so constructed to compensate for Victor's pathetically dismal shooting ability. By 4 P.M. that afternoon they were comfortably settled in the blind and an hour later, just as the doves flew in for their evening drink, an impala snorted close-by, a sure sign that Mr. Spots was on his way.

Sure enough, a few minutes later a beautiful leopard tom jumped into the "V" of the tree. He was perfectly broadside-on, the ideal position for a quick killing shot on the shoulder, so Claude gave Victor the thumbs-up to go ahead. Victor's rifle barked, and the leopard dropped stone dead out the tree. In fact it landed on the exact spot where I had come to grief two days earlier. Much backslapping, high fives, and congratulations ensued, and in the process Victor's numerous missed shots were forgotten.

Scrambling out the blind, they all clambered down into the riverbed to admire the much-prized leopard. The dead animal was lying on his side, but amazingly there was no hole in his shoulder. This meant he must have been shot on the opposite side. They were thankful to see there was no exit wound to spoil his beautiful skin. When the cat was turned over, everyone became thoroughly confused: There was no bullet hole in that shoulder either! On close inspection, they found a hole in the centre of the leopard's chest. At this point they were thoroughly perplexed because the leopard had been standing perfectly broadside-on the moment Victor had taken his shot.

The answer to the mystery was discovered when Morgan climbed into the tree to drop the bait. (This is a legal requirement.) A very obvious bullet mark on the tree trunk explained what had happened. Victor's bullet had missed the leopard completely. It had struck the right hand side of the "V" in the tree, then ricocheted at a ninety-degree angle, and had then entered the leopard's chest, killing it instantly.

Next came Victor's buffalo hunt. It's somewhat misleading to say it ended successfully, but that's what I shall state. It can be said that Victor managed to shoot the front hoof off the buffalo bull, and that, in turn, so crippled the poor animal that it hindered its get-away. That allowed Victor to barrage the hapless creature with even more poorly placed follow-up shots. Finally taking in all the lead that it could possibly absorb, the unfortunate bull finally expired.

By chance I met Victor with a different "girlfriend" some three years later. On that occasion I was on a shopping trip to Johannesburg. It was late by the time I had crossed over the Beit Bridge border post into South Africa, so I decided to break my journey and spend the night at a very pleasant bed and breakfast on a small game farm.

To my utmost surprise, I bumped into Victor at the bar. He told me that he had come to "hunt" a white rhino in order to complete his Big Five. The so-called rhino hunt had been conducted in a small fenced-off paddock, and despite the convenient set-up, he was either unable to get a shot at the rhino or he was too scared to do so! Whatever the case, he rented a helicopter and shot his rhino from the air.

I thank my lucky stars every day that not all safari clients are like Victor.

******

The recovery process for my broken arm and wrist meant they both remained in a plaster cast for three weeks. I had another hunt booked, however, so with my arm still in plaster, I set off on a leopard and buffalo hunt with Linda Linton, a lawyer from Reno. We had a great hunt, and Linda was successful in collecting both species.

My lasting memory of that hunt was that of a most unpleasant smell coming from inside the cast on my arm. While lifting the vile-smelling "guts bucket" off the back of the Land Cruiser in order to do a drag, my trackers succeeded in dropping it. I was standing too close, and as the bucket hit the ground, its smelly contents flew everywhere, some of the goo landing on my left arm. Before I could wipe it away, the disgusting gunk had trickled down my arm and under the cast. There was nothing I could do to remove it, and for the next two weeks before the cast came off, my arm smelt exactly like what it was, a stinking, two-week-old leopard drag.

Linda's buff hunt was one I remember well. Like most ladies, Linda would only take a shot if she was 100 percent sure of success. At times such reticence can get quite annoying because in Africa one is hardly ever given the perfect situation. There is normally some grass or bush in the way, or the animal is not perfectly broadside. I've learned that one has to take the chances presented. Anyway, we tracked a large herd of buffaloes from a spring early one morning and caught them a few hours later feeding down into an open valley. We quickly maneuvered downwind and crawled up an anthill a few hundred metres ahead of the feeding buffalo.

The buffaloes continued to move down into the valley, and soon they were almost directly below us. We were eagerly looking for a nice old *dagga* boy with hard bosses, but so far we had only seen young bulls. Criton then whistled lightly and drew my attention to an old *dagga* boy whose massive body was covered in mud. He was exactly the buffalo we were after!

The old bull was feeding intently toward us, so I got Linda on the shooting sticks and pointed. Linda did not want to take a frontal shot, which I totally understood, so we waited for him to turn broadside. The atmosphere was electric. Here we were amidst a hundred immense buffaloes with tick birds whirring overhead and buffaloes groaning from all sides!

I was worried that at any second one of the many buffaloes that had already passed us and were downwind would smell us and run off, taking the herd with them. We were willing the old bull, who was now quartering-on, to take one more step, thus exposing a shoulder so that Linda could take a shot. Just as he did, an old cow stepped in front of him, making a shot impossible. Just as we feared, suddenly the buffaloes stopped feeding and their heads shot up in the air. They had smelled the dreaded human smell, and off they thundered into the *jesse* bush, leaving the hunters and trackers sitting dejectedly behind on the anthill.

Linda was in tears thinking she had messed up her chance. I consoled her and told her we would have other opportunities and not to worry. She then said she needed to have a wee, so I gave her the loo paper and off she went down and around the anthill. We were sitting patiently when what do I see but our old *dagga* boy wandering back toward where Linda had disappeared. As the buff got closer and closer, I got more and more worried as there was no sign of Linda. Not only was I worried about Linda's safety, but I also really wanted to have a second chance at shooting this grand old bull.

Eventually, I thought that I had better take action, so I grabbed the shooting sticks and Linda's gun and scuttled down the anthill toward where Linda had disappeared. Meanwhile the buff continued moseying along and feeding. Looking around, I saw Linda squatting. I tried subtly to get her attention, which I eventually did. Whoa, was she not happy to be disturbed by her PH when she had her panties around her ankles! She was about to bollocks me when she realized that there was more to the story!

Quickly cutting short what she set off to do, she pulled her panties and shorts up and hopped over to where I was. I already had the sticks opened and was facing the oncoming old *dagga* boy. Luckily, Linda didn't have time to analyze the shot, and with the buff literally on top of us, she quickly mounted her gun and shot. What a shot it was! That old guy simply dropped in his tracks. What a magnificent bull he was. There was much laughter and relief at how the situation had unfolded.

******

A few years later I was to have my nose rebroken in a brawl. I was at the Safari Club International convention in Reno where we do a lot of our marketing, and one evening after having dinner with clients I joined a couple of professional hunter mates at the famous piano bar in Rum Bullions. It was a great party, but around three o'clock in the morning I decided to call it quits because I still had the last day of the show to attend.

Due to the time difference between Zimbabwe and the United States, I was texting my then-girlfriend (and now wife), Steph, while walking to the elevators. Weaving slightly from the effects of a few too many drinks and with my eyes on my cell phone instead of watching where I was going, I accidently bumped into somebody. I looked up to apologize, but I hardly had said a word before I was greeted by an avalanche of cussing from a Mexican teenager.

There he was at 3 A.M. in the morning with his cap sideways on his head, cheap jewelry around his neck, and his jeans halfway down his backside exposing his grubby underpants! To have this pathetic idiot swearing at me and calling me all sorts of names despite my having tried to apologize made my blood boil. Really, it was too much. Perhaps, it was because he was even shorter than I . . . I don't know, but I'm embarrassed to admit I lost my temper.

Doing so is a rare occurrence for me, but lose it I surely did. I punched him hard in the face and dropped him like a stone. Before I had the chance to congratulate myself for delivering such an impressive knock-out blow, I was set upon by a bunch of equally scruffy Mexican gangbangers. In the one-sided brawl that ensued they managed to break my nose, but luckily for me support arrived in the form of some equally drunken Zimbabwean professional hunters. In no time the Mexicans scattered like the curs they were.

I was hemorrhaging freely from my nose, which left an impressive blood trail all the way back to my hotel room. Once there, I discovered that I had lost the key to my room, so I had to hammer on the door to wake my business partner, Myles, who took one look at me and fell about laughing. At the moment I failed to see the humour, but I have to admit that my bloody face and my nose sitting at a ninety-degree angle to my face could be source of amusement. By convention time the next morning, my nose was swollen to the size of a lemon, and I had two black eyes. I was not a pretty sight. At the end of the day it was not surprising that we had not booked a single hunt the whole day.

One of my previous safari clients who happened to be a surgeon fortunately stopped by our booth for a visit. He asked if he could feel my nose, and to my surprise and before I could protest, he reached out, grabbed the swollen member, and quickly reset it . . . much to the amusement of those who happened to be passing by. How lucky was that! To this day, despite being broken twice, the only thing I suffer from is a slightly crooked nose and a snoring problem.

Sven and Magnus, the Perfect Clients

Chapter Twenty

Having hunted primarily with German and American clients, I was delighted to start a double buffalo and tuskless elephant hunt with two Swedish clients, Sven and Magnus. My limited experience with Swedish clients had led me to believe that although they were invariably good hunters, they put as much emphasis on the nocturnal consumption of alcohol as they did in their pursuit of good trophies.

A hangover is far from helpful when it comes to hunting in the heat and tsetse-fly-infested Zambezi Valley. This is something I can attest to from past experience! So, being something of a lightweight in the drinking department, due mainly to the dreadful hangovers I suffer from even after the slightest overindulgence, I was pleasantly surprised to learn that both men were light drinkers. They each had one or occasionally two glasses of wine before retiring to bed. Hunting hard every day was the main reason they were on a safari, and I respected them for this.

Little did we know at the start of the hunt that we were not destined to have a normal, fourteen-day safari for buffalo and tuskless elephant. That our safari would be commandeered in part by a deranged lion in need of an animal psychologist was something no one could possibly have imagined.

On the opening day of the hunt we set off at first light, and it was not long before we found the tracks of a large herd of buffaloes near the Mukanga River, which is close to the Chewore boundary. As is normal in such situations, we all jumped off the back of the Land Cruiser to see how fresh the tracks were and in which direction they were heading. It normally takes the two trackers, the game scout, and me just a few minutes to figure out the tracks, but on this occasion the buffaloes' tracks were milling around as if the herd was confused, so we had no clear indication in which direction they were heading. The only way to pick up a lead in a case like this is to

A mock charge.

work in a circle until we discover in which direction they were heading. This is what we did, but we had no immediate success with this, so we found ourselves circling farther and farther away from the Land Cruiser.

Morgan and Crispen, the trackers, wandered off close to the Mukanga River while I found myself, together with the game scout, on a ridge about a hundred or so metres from the vehicle. From this elevated vantage point I could see where the buffaloes' tracks were clearly "digging in," suggesting the herd was running.

I called out to the game scout, *"Sei nyati dzirikumanya? Pane shumba kuno."* (Why are the buffaloes running? There must be lions here.)

The words had barely passed my lips when we both heard the low grumble of a lion nearby. I looked up to where the noise was coming from, and there he was, not fifty yards away, lying under a low Terminalia bush. His tail was swishing angrily from side to side, and his piercing yellow eyes were unblinkingly staring into mine! With a gutful of early morning coffee and no rifle, I urgently whispered to the scout, *"Musa manya."* (Don't run.)

With that cynical comment, both of us turned tail and fled.

I can clearly remember the *hur, hur, hur* as the lion charged. The sounds were getting closer and closer, and when I looked round in midstride, he was barely twenty metres away with serious intent in his eyes! Strange as it may seem, I can clearly recall that my only thought at the time was, "What a nice mane he has!" With that pleasant thought, I promptly tripped and fell flat on my face. I knew then that this was definitely the end and what it must feel like to meet the Maker.

As luck would have it, the game scout, who probably was correctly thinking that I was the slower runner, split away from me. The lion promptly charged after him. I looked up just in time to see the scout plunging over the ridge with the lion in hot pursuit. I was convinced I was about to hear a terrified scream coming from the scout as the lion set on him. Instead, I was highly relieved to hear Royal, my driver, pushing down hard on the Land Cruiser's horn and shouting at the top of his voice, accompanied by the equally vocal Sven and Magnus. Luckily for the scout, the Land Cruiser was only about twenty metres away, and all the noise and commotion must have diverted the lion's attention. As a result, instead of sinking his fangs into his intended victim, the lion overshot his target. We are fortunate he did not return to finish the job.

As a result of my fall, most of the skin had been scraped off my knees, and for the rest of the safari, the resulting heavy scabbing made it impossible to bend my legs. This caused much amusement with everyone in camp, and the general consensus was that I looked like a Nazi storm trooper on parade as I frog marched stiff-legged through the bush.

If there is such a thing as a lion psychologist, then this particular lion was in need of a few sessions, for he was to reappear three days later under strange and unusual circumstances. We were following a herd of elephants not far from where we had first encountered the lion, and after a couple of hours' tracking, we caught up to the herd, which was browsing on top of a hill. From a good vantage point, we looked over several cows before finding an old tuskless one that was feeding on some scrub on the

We had to roll Sven's tuskless elephant down the hill.

side of the hill. The wind was blowing steady in our faces, which made for an easy stalk, and we got within about fifteen metres of the unsuspecting cow. Sven then attempted to side brain her, but, unfortunately, it took a couple of shots before she went down for good.

After the usual photo session, we were presented with a recovery problem. The elephant was balanced precariously on the side of the hill, and there was no chance of getting the recovery tractor and trailer anywhere near her. During our discussion on the best way to move the elephant, the trackers mentioned there was an old recovery road at the bottom of the hill and that if we could push the carcass over the side, there was a good chance of it rolling down the hill where the unit would be waiting.

It sounded feasible enough, so after moving a few cumbersome rocks that were in the way and using all available hands, we managed to give the dead cow a mighty heave. Over the edge and down the hill she went, gaining momentum and clearing everything in her path along the way, all this accompanied with much cheering and howls of delight from the trackers. For whatever reason, they always seem to find things like this hugely amusing. As luck would have it, the cow finally came to rest less than a hundred metres from the old recovery road.

By this time Member, the tractor driver, together with the recovery gang were well on their way, having received my message and directions on the radio. Being under a little pressure time-wise, we decided to leave the recovery to the tractor crew and continue hunting as we still had a tuskless elephant and two buffaloes left to hunt and only seven days in which to do it.

The rest of the day proved uneventful, and we had only just settled down to a relaxing dinner when we heard the tractor come racing into camp. I was about to give Member a piece of my mind for driving recklessly when he burst into the dining room looking as though he had seen a ghost. He had a deep cut on his forearm that was bleeding profusely, and only after several attempts to find out what was wrong did we finally get the full story out of him.

He and the crew had arrived at the dead elephant shortly after we'd left, and they immediately commenced the skinning and recovery process. While loading the skin and meat onto the trailer, they heard a lion close-by. This spurred the crew on to greater and speedier efforts.

Suddenly the lion walked out of the bush about ten metres away and promptly jumped onto the trailer where Member and several of the crew were working. The lion immediately gave poor Member a hearty swipe, tearing his entire forearm muscle away from the bone in the process. One can imagine the scene of panic as Member and the crew scrambled to get off the trailer. In the resulting chaos, several staff members suffered injuries ranging from a dislocated toe to a fractured skull, the latter being sustained when the worker in question dived head first into a mopane tree.

By this time Member had jumped onto the tractor, started it, and sped off in a cloud of dust along with two workers who were clinging for dear life onto whatever they could grab. So fast was the tractor going that at the very first corner the hapless workers were dumped unceremoniously into the dirt. Having abandoned the entire crew to their own fates, Member did not slow down until he finally reached the safety of camp.

Wasting no time, we returned to the recovery spot where we found the workers looking highly dejected, all of them huddled miserably around a small fire. Back at camp, a mercy trip was instigated to get the wounded to the closest clinic. Member's wound, like all cat wounds, took ages to heal . . . as did his friendship with the members of the recovery crew. Understandably, they did not appreciate being abandoned and left to the mercy of a deranged lion.

The next day we returned with loaded rifles to retrieve the trailer and carcass, fully expecting a bit of excitement, but the lion was gone. That canny old lion certainly had the last laugh on us, for not only had it consumed a lot of elephant meat, but it had also mauled the trailer's spare tyre beyond repair.

On the morning of the eighth day, we found two *dagga* boy tracks coming from a spring in the Checo Hills. Criton and Crispen took up the tracks that meandered down the course of the spring for a few kilometres before turning into *jesse* bush. I told my Swedish friends that we would catch up to them within the hour because it was now midday and the *dagga* boys would surely be seeking shade from the midday sun somewhere in the *jesse* bush. Sure enough, forty minutes later, Criton suddenly stopped dead in his tracks, and there a short distance away, concealed under a clump of "wait-a-bit" thornbush was a distinct black patch. As we stood watching with bated breath, an ear suddenly flicked.

It soon became obvious that Sven's bull was not mortally wounded, but there was little doubt he had been hit hard. We had not been going all that long when his tracks indicated he had broken away from the other bull. This was a good sign. The wounded bull led us on a long and weary chase, eventually taking us into a strip of thick riverine bush where visibility was down to a few metres. I was uncomfortable with our large group in this inhospitable environment, so I told Magnus, who was only armed with a 7mm—it was his day for plains game—and the scout to wait on top of a large anthill. I said that we would return to collect them after we had killed the wounded bull.

Another hour of very slow and intense tracking followed. We were expecting a charge at any moment, so emotions were high. Every so often we would come across pools of blood where the bull had stopped, turned, and faced us while listening for our approach. That he knew we were following him was obvious, for he kept trotting away before we could get in a shot.

Ultimately it was Criton who discovered something crucial, and he pointed it out on the ground. There the bull's tracks were clearly imprinted on top of ours. The wily old fellow had led us in a circle, and as we stood contemplating the situation, a shot rang out, closely followed by another. We doubled back to the anthill where we'd left Magnus and the game scout.

A large herd of buffaloes in the Mkanga Valley.

Sven's and Magnus's end-of-safari picture.

I was terrified, fully expecting to see a scene of disaster, but, instead, there was Magnus, beaming from ear to ear, standing with one foot on the dead buffalo, which was lying halfway up the anthill.

There was much excited chatter before Magnus explained what had happened. Both he and the game scout had been dozing on the anthill when they heard a noise. It was a buffalo bull trotting down a game trail directly toward them, and they could see blood coming out of its nostrils. At that precise moment, the wounded bull turned and looked back on his trail, and Magnus, being 90 percent sure it was our wounded animal, gave him a snapshot with his 7mm, aiming for the lungs. The buffalo swung round, and on seeing the duo, promptly charged. At point-blank range, Magnus let rip with another round, killing the charging buffalo with a bullet between his eyes.

In the following days Magnus bagged his tuskless elephant with a perfect side brain shot. He also shot an old *dagga* boy after another exciting encounter in thick bush; it was a situation where we had to put the animal down before he harmed us.

At the end of the safari, I toasted the two Swedes who had come as clients and left as friends. It was a toast to honour their impeccable hunting ethics. Throughout the safari Sven and Magnus had stressed it was the experience of true hunting that they wanted. The trophy, as long as it was from an old animal, was of secondary importance to them. What a pleasure it would be for us professional hunters to have safari clients who only espoused this sort of philosophy.

This philosophy is especially important in regards to buffaloes and should most certainly be the main criterion in hunting them. Unfortunately, it is not the case. Unlike Sven and Magnus, far too many American clients arrive in camp brainwashed by the Safari Club International's scoring system and record book. They insist on shooting young buffalo bulls that score better because the tips of these animals' horns have not yet had time to wear down. It is the measurement of a buffalo's horn tip that provides the extra points in the so-called "book." That these young animals still have soft bosses that have gained little girth is of no consequence just as long as the trophy makes the "book." In essence, these so-called trophies look little better than a glorified wildebeest.

More importantly, and of concern, is that most of the younger bulls that are shot as "record-book"-qualifying trophies are still of a prebreeding age. The continual removal from the gene pool of better-than-average, trophy-size bulls before they have the opportunity to breed will, over time, inevitably lead to the gradual decline in the buffalo population and in trophy quality.

Safari Club International urgently needs to rethink its buffalo-measuring system, and in so doing, it should place greater emphasis on a buffalo's boss. A suggestion that would encourage shooting older bulls would be to measure the skulls after they are boiled and to then officially record the widest point. This would promote the shooting of old bulls that are past breeding age and would not disturb the breeding herds.

Race Against a Dead Lion

Chapter Twenty-One

I was on a lion hunt with a Frenchman by the name of Guy, who was employed by a Nigerian oil company. We had been baiting for four days without success, so I decided to take a drive down to the far western corner of Dande to see if there had been any lion movement into the area from the adjoining Chewore Safari Area.

The drive proved uneventful until we turned a sharp corner and literally bumped into two big lions lying in the middle of the road. We came to a screeching halt in a cloud of dust just as they loped off into the tall grass. From the brief look I managed to get at them, one seemed to be very respectable; he was typical of a Zambezi Valley lion and had a reasonable mane. He was certainly old enough to be hunted, so in a matter of minutes we were kitted out and ready for the hunt.

The tracking was initially very tricky, but as I had come to expect, Crispen and Morgan worked their magic, and we managed to keep up a fair pace on the tracks of the fast-moving lions until at last we bumped into them at the base of a steep, grassy hill. Unfortunately, there was not enough time to get a shot at the bigger of the two because his lesser attractive and maneless partner was standing in front of him. The two lions then parted company, with the maneless animal heading down the valley while the bigger lion continued up the grassy hill.

As the lion climbed steadily up the hill, we followed closely behind. We managed to keep him in sight pretty much all the time, hoping he would stop and look back to give us the opportunity of a shot. Instead, he continued to climb, and as he got near the top of the hill, I quickly set up the shooting sticks and got Guy into position. I advised Guy to be ready, for at any moment I expected the lion to stop at the crest of the hill and look back at us before disappearing down

Carrying out a 450-pound lion from the Dande. That's a lot of lion!

the other side. This would be the only chance Guy would have of getting in a decent shot.

Just as I had anticipated, when the old lion reached the top of the hill, he stopped and took a quick look back at his pursuers. This was the opportunity Guy had been waiting for, and despite the difficulty of a forty-five-degree-angle shot, he took careful aim and fired. His shot hit the lion perfectly behind the shoulders. The incensed lion let out a mighty roar and immediately charged straight down the hill toward us.

Crispen who had been up front tracking, took one look at the rampaging lion coming straight at him. *"Bwana iri kuwuya!"* he screamed at me in Shona. ("Bwana, he's coming!") And with that, the old tracker set off down the hill like a sprightly teenager.

Both Guy and I fired at the lion at the same time. One of our bullets, I don't know which, missed the lion completely, but the other one, because of the acute upward angle, went through the lion's front paw and into his face. The heavy bullet continued its path through the lion's head and into the neck region, smashing his spine and killing him in the process. Due to the extreme angle and the speed at which he was coming down the slope, the dead lion gathered momentum, and at an ever-increasing pace came cartwheeling head over heels right past us.

Poor Crispen had thought his youthful sprinting efforts had put sufficient distance between himself and the charging lion was now resting with his hands on his knees, catching his breath. His recovery period was to be short-lived. Interrupted by the noise above, he turned to look upward only to find the lion cartwheeling straight at him. Usain Bolt, the Olympic one-hundred-metre champion and the world's fastest man would have been left stone cold out of the starting block had he been racing against Crispen at that moment. Despite the howls of laughter from the rest of the group, Crispen did not stop running until he was safely at the bottom of the hill.

It took a great deal of persuasion from the rest of us to get him to come back up again to assist us in carrying the lion's heavy carcass. To crown it all, much to the old boy's embarrassment but to the amusement of the others, poor Crispen had actually wet his pants.

******

Crispen was very much the showman; he loved nothing better than playing to an audience. There were, however, occasions when his audacity got the better of him. On one such occasion we were driving around Dande looking for elephant tracks. Since we were on a multiple elephant hunt, I had both tracking teams engaged: Crispen and Morgan were the "A" team; Criton and Tino were the "B" team. Also along were a game scout and Ian, my cameraman. The whole lot was on the Land Cruiser at the same time.

As we turned a bend, we came upon a pride of lions that had recently killed a buffalo right on the side of the road. Understandably, we stopped to have a look at the pride and to get some video footage. Crispen then decided to get off the Land Cruiser and relieve himself. Knowing him as I do, I realized the bravado was merely an attention-seeking act, for although he was a brilliant tracker, bravery was definitely not one of

Crispen's stronger points. Making sure everyone's attention was focused on him while in the act, Crispen deliberately positioned himself between the Land Cruiser and the feeding lions. It was as though he was saying out loud, "Look all of you, see how brave and macho I am."

This was too good an opportunity to miss, so I signaled Ian on the back of the Land Cruiser to get his camera rolling, then I let out the Land Cruiser's clutch and put my foot down on the accelerator. Crispen's reaction was priceless. In an instant his bravado evaporated, and in midstream, as the saying might go, with all still exposed, he only just managed to catch up to the departing Land Cruiser. There was much hilarity from the rest of the crew in the back.

Crispen and the Hornbill

Chapter Twenty-Two

J. C. Bunn and his good friend Roger came to Dande on a hunting trip in 2003. While both turned out to be good hunters, their goals on this trip were quite different. J.C. intended to shoot a big-mane lion while Roger came along to collect exotic bird species for his taxidermy business.

The occasion turned out to be one of those textbook hunts. During the first three days we managed to shoot two buffalo cows and a zebra, most of which we used for six baits for the lion. We subsequently had a total of six hits on the baits, all of them from male lions. There was one buffalo bait that had us extremely interested.

We had placed this bait in a stunning spot on the bank of the Mkanga River and were pleasantly surprised to discover two big males had been feeding on it. One of the lions, or possibly both, had left strands of sixteen-inch-long mane hair that was blond at the roots, turned red in the middle, and then became pure black at the tip. It had all the markers of an extremely desirable mane. So we built our blind on the side of a hill that was opposite the river and replenished the bait. The site was approximately sixty yards from our blind.

By four o'clock that afternoon we were inside the blind and waiting patiently. Sitting quietly in a blind bores most people to distraction. Personally, I enjoy the forced silence and solitude, for it gives me time to absorb the sounds of the African bush as late afternoon changes to dusk. On that particular afternoon we had an entertaining wait thanks to a small pool of water in the riverbed just a few feet away from the bait.

We had arrived that afternoon at a time when daylight in Africa is at its most impressive. Photographers call it the "golden hour." Just after our arrival, a delicate bushbuck doe accompanied by a troop of rowdy baboons made their way tentatively down to the water. After quenching her thirst, the bushbuck turned and scampered away to the safety of the thick riverine bush along the bank. By five o'clock, laughing doves began to fly in, settling down at the water's edge to drink. They were followed by their larger cousins, the red-eyed turtle doves, and then when the doves were finished and right on cue, we were greeted by the endearing sound of the double-banded sandgrouse.

The sandgrouse had jetted in from all directions, landing on the river's sand and *chuck chucking* their way down to the edge of the pool for their evening drink and bodily submersion into the water. They carry the precious fluid in their body feathers back to their chicks waiting patiently in an open nest far off on some rocky ridge. Witnessing this serene and special occasion from the safety of a blind makes me feel like an unwanted gatecrasher, a peeping tom, infringing on an occasion not meant to be viewed by man.

Suddenly the tranquility of the early evening was disrupted by a sharp bark from the recently departed bushbuck. A lion was on its way! Sure enough, some five minutes later, there swaggered toward centre stage a magnificent cat of such brute power and arrogance that he took my breath away. Down the sandy bed of the Mkanga River he came, and what a beautiful specimen he was! Big, dark, powerful, and proud, he had the best mane of any lion that I have ever seen in the Zambezi Valley.

He stood not thirty yards away, in the middle of the riverbed, between the blind and the bait. With the last of the evening light shining down on his magnificent frame, he stood as though he had the power to control the world itself. With his head held high, he sniffed at the bait, and it was as though his body language said, "I am king of the jungle, and there is no one out there who can challenge me."

"Take him, J.C.," I whispered urgently.

"Shouldn't we see what the other one is like?" he replied in an excited voice.

"Listen, J.C.," I responded insistently. "In thirteen years of hunting I've never seen a finer-looking lion than this one. I suggest you take your chance NOW!"

J.C. shot him through the shoulders. The lion turned and ran up the bank and, after letting out a throbbing roar, sank down under the bait tree and died. Until that point in my hunting career there had not been many times when I regretted shooting an animal, but on that occasion I

J.C. (left) and Roger with Roger's amazing lion.

most surely did. I shall never forget that lion and what a glorious sight he made, standing so proudly in the riverbed during the last moments of day. The vision of his magnificence haunts me to this day. Since that time I have experienced similar feelings, especially where lions are concerned.

So J.C. had a lion that would be the dream of any trophy hunter, and I had a happy client. Even happier were the trackers now that the quarry was safely in the back of the Land Cruiser.

Anyway, with the main trophy "in the salt" as we say, we turned our attention to what are commonly referred to as the "rats and mice." Without being derogatory, these are the minor or smaller animals like duikers and grysbok that one only makes an effort to hunt when one has shot all the main trophies. At this point, Roger began to take an active role in the safari.

Armed with my 12-bore Beretta shotgun, Roger would excitedly knock on the Land Cruiser's roof whenever he saw a bird that took his fancy. They were all considered "trophies" and destined for his taxidermy shop. So off he would go, accompanied by my old tracker Crispen, who was more than happy with the arrangement.

Crispen's advanced age as well as the loss of his front teeth meant that soft bird meat featured high in his diet. Unfortunately for Crispen, Roger was a poor shot. Time and again we would see them both walking dejectedly back to the vehicle, with Crispen shaking his head sadly and Roger, with shoulders slumped and eyes downcast, telling us he had missed yet another sitting duck.

Upon hearing J.C. and I taunting Roger mercilessly over his poor performance, Crispen decided that in view of his seniority in the hunting party it was his right to join in the banter. The finer points of this type of leg pulling were lost on the old tracker, however, and I can only say that I'm glad that Roger and Crispen spoke different languages.

Over breakfast on the last day of the safari, Roger decided he had had enough of Crispen's teasing and hatched a plan to get even. With great care he removed the pellets from a shotgun shell and then resealed it. Making sure Crispen wasn't around, Roger told us exactly what he intended to do. The stage was set for a hilarious morning.

After breakfast we set off, and we'd not gone very far when we spotted a hornbill sitting in a baobab tree twenty yards off the road. Pulling over to the side, I told Crispen that after giving Roger such a hard time, he'd better show him how to shoot. Roger handed Crispen the shotgun loaded with the empty cartridge.

Approaching the tree with great caution, Crispen raised the shotgun and carefully took aim. We all waited in anticipation as the seconds ticked by. I wondered if Crispen had actually seen the bird through his cataract-blurred vision. All six of us on the vehicle expected to hear the shotgun fire and watch the hornbill fly away. We were all set to give him grief for missing such an easy shot when suddenly there was a loud bang, and the broad smiles on our faces turned to looks of amazement, for out of the baobab tumbled the hornbill, falling flat onto the deck.

Incredible as it sounds, the bird had been hit on the head and killed instantly by the plastic spacer wad in the shell. Arrogantly, Crispen walked nonchalantly up to the baobab, picked up the dead hornbill, and brought it back to the Land Cruiser. He then dropped it in the back and gave an open-mouthed Roger a look that quite plainly said, "That's how you do it, chum!"

To his credit Roger saw the funny side of the incident, and at one stage I thought he might wet himself he was laughing so hard. He graciously accepted a final day of Crispen's taunts that were, under the circumstances, particularly severe. After all, the old fellow's spirits were riding high after such a highly successful hornbill hunt!

DANGERS ON LAND AND WATER

CHAPTER TWENTY-THREE

One of the main advantages of hunting in the northern blocks of the Zambezi Valley is the river itself. To wind up a successful safari with a few days of relaxation and fishing on this impressive river can be regarded as a fitting end. Such was the case with the Swallow family from Louisiana.

The Swallows and Dean, Lance, and I had been hunting in the Dande. We had recently completed a successful three-on-three hunt where Father and his two sons had each shot a buffalo bull as well as a variety of plains-game species. Since we had time to spare, we decided to go down to the Zambezi and spend a few days catching fish and having a good time in general.

The Swallow boys, John and Dave, were roughly our age. It was obvious that they were in the right mood for a party; in fact, they kept telling us that "the boys from the South," as they referred to themselves, would show us Zimbabwean hillbillies just how to drink.

On the Zambian side of the Zambezi and a short distance upstream from Masau, the camp we were occupying, lived an interesting, larger-than-life person by the name of Hugo. Hugo was well known to all and sundry for his all-night beer-drinking parties, commonly referred to as "benders." Hugo had a hard-and-fast rule that all visitors to his camp were required to obey. It went something like this: Regardless of the amount of alcohol you took into his camp, Hugo would match it, and his visitors were not allowed to leave the camp until it was all finished. In some instances this might require only a few hours of "dopping" as the locals call it, while on other occasions, the revelry was known to last a couple of days.

Hugo was a typical example of the amazing oddball characters that you only find in the far-flung and inhospitable corners of Africa, far from the normality of the civilized world. Of staunch Afrikaner stock, Hugo surprised all when at the ripe old age of sixty he abandoned Tiki, his wife of many years, bleached his hair, and remarried a local maiden from Lusaka.

Despite being warned of the dangers of what they were letting themselves in for, the Louisiana boys insisted on paying Hugo a visit. Being well bred and raised as "good old Southern boys," they didn't want to pitch up at Hugo's camp empty-handed. Ironically, this turned out to be their downfall. Despite our impromptu arrival, we were warmly welcomed by Hugo, his son Valdo, and their four yapping Jack Russell terriers.

Soon the party was in full swing, and by all intent our two Southern boys were making a good account of themselves, knocking back the beers as though they were about to die of thirst. At the same time they insisted on preparing a traditional guinea fowl "gumbo" from the brace of birds we had shot a few days earlier. To be honest, I was not impressed with their culinary skills, but thanks to copious amounts of alcohol, the offerings proved edible.

As already mentioned, Hugo was of solid Afrikaner stock, and when he discovered my middle name is Durnford, the result of a direct relationship to Lt. Col. Anthony William Durnford of Anglo-Boer War fame, he went off the rails. He acted as though I was personally responsible for sending his relatives to die in the pitiful and inhumane concentration camps that the British army established in a last-ditched attempt to suppress the Boers.

In Hugo's alcohol-fueled opinion, I, like every other English-speaking African of Caucasian ancestry, was simply a bloody *"rooi neck." Rooi neck* means red neck and it is the term the Afrikaners gave English servicemen during the three-year Anglo-Boer War because the necks of English soldiers became sunburnt in the African sun.

The ability to forgive and forget is not a character trait of most Afrikaners; in fact, many still hate the British with a passion—so much so as to imply the First and Second Boer Wars ended last week instead of a hundred and ten years ago. With a copious amount of alcohol added to these sentiments, the situation can all too quickly get out of control.

Since Hugo's camp was in Zambia, we were actually illegal visitors. Given our illegal status and the fact that he was also well known for his fiery

A view of the beautiful Zambezi River from the Dande North Safari Area.

temper, I resolved not to get involved in a heated political debate. Instead I decided to move to the fire to chat to Valdo. I had heard him talking about two beautiful Swedish teachers who had recently been posted to a local school only a short distance upriver, so I decided to see what he knew.

By the time I arrived at the campfire, our Southern boys, Dave and John, were looking decidedly the worse for wear. That they could not keep up with the hard-drinking Africans was becoming increasingly obvious, and it was not long before the ever-faithful barman had to be called over to carry the Louisiana lads off to bed.

Inevitably the fireside talk turned to the blonde Swedish teachers, who in our inebriated opinion were sex-starved nymphomaniacs just waiting to be swooped upon by young, good-looking, rugged, and suntanned, testosterone-oozing Zimbabwean professional hunters. For what other reason, we debated, should they want to come to such a lonely, isolated, malaria-infested part of Africa, if it wasn't for the likes of us?

After much discussion, a plan of attack to rescue the lonely maidens was hatched. It was decided that as I knew that part of the Zambezi River better than anyone present, it would be fitting for me to navigate the four kilometres up the river in the darkness, through the hippo-and-crocodile-infested Mupata Gorge to the place where the local school was situated. It was also decided that Valdo, whose nose had not been broken on two occasions and as a result was deemed better looking than me, would turn on the charm. It fell upon his shoulders to persuade the Swedish maidens to return with us to our camp. In our drunken state, the plan seemed infallible.

Packing a few bottles of Zambian beer into a cooler box, we set off for the jetty where our boat was moored. Unfortunately, a glitch to our plan immediately presented itself. To get to the jetty where our boat was moored required negotiating a steep flight of steps that descended several metres to the river's edge. On our way down, I stumbled into Valdo and knocked him into the banister. To prevent himself from falling over the side, he grabbed onto me, and the two of us tumbled down the rest of the stairs in a tangle of waving arms and kicking legs . . . straight into the cold and dark river five metres below.

Infused in my alcohol-muddled brain as I fell through the air was a vision of undigested human remains recovered from crocodiles my clients had shot over the years. Suddenly, a dunking in the Zambezi in the dead of night no longer seemed such a good idea. I realized it was the very last place any sane or sensible person would ever want to be. Just before I hit the water, my mind became perfectly clear, and the only thought I had was to get the hell out of there, and pronto!

Valdo and I hit the water together, making quite an impressive splash, noisy enough to have advertised our presence to every self-respecting crocodile within a mile. When I tried to surface, I found I was beneath the jetty and still under water. Unable to breathe, I dived again and for a second time tried to surface, only to hit my head on what I presumed was the bottom of one of the boats. My situation was fast becoming serious. My third attempt also failed, and I realized at that moment I was going to drown.

Amazingly, I felt no fear at all, but the bizarre thought of "what a stupid way to die" flashed through my mind. I gave it one last attempt to clear the jetty and boats, only to bang my head again. It was at this point that I gave up the effort and swallowed a large mouthful of water. The next thing I remember was my apprentice pulling me out the river by my hair. After vomiting copious amounts of water, I found my partner in crime, Valdo, also lying on the jetty. Valdo, however, was looking far worse than me, for he had sustained a broken thumb and his nose was badly swollen. I suspected that he, too, was now a candidate for the "broken-nose club."

It was at this stage we decided to postpone our search for the Swedish girls and, instead, have a final nightcap beside the fire. In Zimbabwe, such a drink is known as an ABF, an Absolutely Bloody Final drink. Thus ended an entertaining night! Valdo, however, stayed on for yet another drink, this one known as an FTC or F--- the Consequences drink, which probably explained Valdo's total absence the next day.

We needed to be up the following morning for an early start in order to get the two sorry-looking and hung-over Southerners back to their father. They were due to head back to America, and to do that, they first had to catch their charter flight out of the "valley." I was scheduled to start prebaiting for a leopard hunt that was due to start in a few days. Feeling pretty awful, the result of a monstrous hangover, I said good-bye to my Louisiana friends and having seen them safely on board the charter plane to Harare, I set off in search of some impala to hang as leopard baits.

Had I been clear-headed, shooting a few impalas would have been a breeze, but due to my hangover, it took a few attempts before I finally managed to secure a nice ram that would be big enough for two baits. Having cut the ram in half, I carried a portion down into a gorge where I knew a big, old tom leopard regularly frequented. Having hung the bait, I began the long climb out. My chest was wheezing like that of a fifty-a-day smoker, and I was forced to take several breaks to regain my breath. Finally and much to my relief, I made it to the Land Cruiser.

I was concerned about my wheezing chest, so right there and then I phoned my doctor via a satellite phone that is always on standby in all our vehicles, just for this sort of situation. I explained the previous night's escapades, my near drowning, and the fact that I had guzzled a fair amount of water. The doctor told me in no uncertain fashion to get out of the valley immediately and to get my sorry self to the nearest hospital as soon as possible.

After a seven-hour drive and a chest X-ray, I lay in the hospital bed feeling a lot better. So much so that I expected the doctor to tell me the scare was only a false alarm and that I could head back to the Dande in time for the arrival of my next client. Doctor Stack thought otherwise. He took one look at my X-ray and promptly stated that I must have been seriously drunk at the time of the incident. I was amazed at how quickly he had assessed this, and I confirmed his suspicions. Out of curiosity I asked him how he knew.

"Buzz," he told me. "When a drowning person swallows water in an upright position most of it goes into his right lung as that is the way the trachea is formed, the right lung's entry being higher than that of the left. In your case, however, 60 percent of the water you swallowed is in your left lung! This means that you were upside when you swallowed the water. What you thought was the jetty and boats was, in fact, the bottom of the river. You must have been so drunk that you didn't know the top from the bottom! You were like a deep-diving Rapala fishing lure, continuously hitting the bottom; it was only when you gave up and resigned yourself to meeting your Maker that you floated to the surface."

The result of this *rooi neck's* visit to Hugo's camp was three days in intensive care. I was on a drip and given a hefty dose of antibiotics as Doctor Stack was concerned I might be getting secondary pneumonia! Not one to lie around being idle, I could not get out of hospital fast enough, but my misfortunes were far from over.

On my trip down to the Dande, I stopped on a newly cut verge of the road to take a toilet break. As I stepped off the Land Cruiser, a needle-sharp, newly cut piece of thatching grass pierced my calf muscle. Initially it was not painful, provided I stood upright and perfectly still, but the pain became excruciating when I tried to walk. Luckily Crispen was with me, so I asked him to pull out the bit of grass as it had penetrated my leg at an angle I myself could not reach.

Crispen was about seventy years old at the time, and his eyesight was failing. Instead of pulling out the entire piece of grass, he managed to break it off, leaving a sizable portion embedded in my leg. Our lone option was to try to cut it out, but the only knife I had on hand was blunt and had last been used to skin a hyena. In the end I had no choice but to drive to the closest clinic in the farming village of Mvurwi.

The place was deserted with only one nurse on duty. She took one look at my problem and said that I would have to get the resident doctor to help me. She told me the doctor could be found at the local bar where he was watching the World Cup (football). The bar was packed shoulder to shoulder as Cameroon, the African favourite team was playing. The doctor was happy to help, but only at half-time; in the meantime he offered me a beer.

When half-time came, the doctor was in a jovial mood because Cameroon was ahead of England. His consumption of several scuds (local Zimbabwe beer sold in paper cartons) during the first half contributed significantly to his happy frame of mind. Together we returned to the clinic, where in spite of his happy state, he did a really good job of cutting out the offending piece of grass. When the procedure was complete, I asked him what I owed. He slapped me on the back and asked for a U.S. dollar, enough to buy another scud. But I paid him with interest, and having wished Cameroon the very best of luck, I gratefully went on my way.

I arrived back in camp to find my client David already there. We immediately set off to check baits and were pleasantly surprised to find a leopard was feeding on the bait I had hung in the remote gorge. To make the situation more interesting, a lion and lioness had also visited the bait sometime during the previous night. Close inspection revealed several long black mane hairs! They were from a lion that most definitely needed further investigating.

Suddenly our leopard hunt had evolved into an upgraded lion hunt. Such occasions need a lot more bait, so with some difficulty we manhandled and dragged half a buffalo carcass down into the gorge. The effort this required made me realize that if Lady Luck should smile favourably upon us and we were successful in bagging the lion, we would have to skin the animal right there. A big lion can weigh close to five hundred pounds, and to carry this weight out of the gorge—more than likely in total darkness—without dropping, dragging, and damaging its hide would have been an impossibility. Being ever optimistic, I got Royal, my driver-cum skinner, to wait within radio-calling distance with skinning knives and gas lamps, just in case.

We chose the site of our blind with considerable care. We placed it under a large tree, on the side of the gorge, and facing the prevailing wind.

We then built a secure blind, and by 4 P.M. that afternoon we were settled in, full of expectation for the chance of getting a look at the lion.

I love being forced to sit absolutely motionless for hours on end, for it enables me to test my senses to the limit and, at the same time, appreciate the beautiful sounds, sights, and even smells of the African bush. Baits are often hung close to a water source. The opportunity to watch unobserved all the activity around a waterhole is a most rewarding experience. This is something hunters of other species rarely get the opportunity to experience. It's a shame because they miss much of the smaller, yet just as fascinating forms of life Africa has to offer.

The harsh afternoon light slowly began to soften and as we watched, a shy and cautious bushbuck ewe came cautiously down to the water to drink. She was closely followed by a family of warthogs strutting toward the hole

Dave's lion went down, let out a deep guttural growl, and rolled over dead, Dande.

with their tails held high. All the while the various species of doves began settling in the trees around this oasis. A single dove eventually flew down to the water's edge to drink. It became the signal that the coast was clear, and for the next half-hour wave upon wave of common laughing doves flew in en masse. Eventually the stream of doves slowed down, and this left the stragglers to come in singly or in pairs, accompanied by their bigger cousins, the large Cape turtle doves.

It was at this precise moment there appeared at the base of the tree, as if by magic, the most beautiful leopard. In whispers we discussed whether we should take it or wait for the lion. I told Dave that in my experience, once a leopard is on the bait and confident with the surroundings, it will remain there for some time. We decided to wait awhile for the arrival of the lions, and it did not take long!

While we sat watching the beautiful leopard hungrily eating the bait, I could not help wondering if we were missing a golden opportunity. It was while my thoughts were focused on this dilemma that I heard a tree break close behind the blind. I was startled by the noise, but having heard elephants earlier on in the evening, I took a quick look behind the blind just to make sure. The very last thing we wanted at that tense point was for an elephant herd to think our blind, the only green bush in the area, was a tasty evening snack.

Luckily there were no elephants in sight, so we refocused our attention on the bait. At that precise moment, the leopard stopped eating. Seconds later, he launched himself straight out the tree, and with a defiant grunt disappeared up the opposite side of the gorge. Only the pending arrival of lions would have caused such a reaction, and so it was.

The light was fading fast when a rather thin lioness and an absolutely stunning lion wandered into view. As the two sniffed around the base of the tree smelling the recently departed leopard, we could see the reason why the lioness was so thin. Her right front paw was missing, more than likely from being caught in a wire snare or a gin trap. The view of the two of them standing at the base of the tree, with their heads raised high while smelling the bait gave me the impression that they were, indeed, the rightful rulers of that small piece of Africa.

A quick look through my binocular in the fading light was all it took to confirm the lion was indeed a "shooter." He had a big body and a good, dark mane that covered his ears and the front of his chest. I gave Dave the thumbs up, and he took careful aim at the magnificent creature with his .375 Holland & Holland. At the sound of the shot, the lion somersaulted high in the air and bit at its front leg as it absorbed the full shock of the 300-grain, Swift A-Frame bullet. This was a sure sign of a good, solid hit. The lion went down, let out a deep guttural growl, and rolled over dead.

There was much excitement in the blind as we impatiently waited for Royal and the two trackers to arrive. After about twenty minutes we could see the snaking lights from their torches as they slowly made their way down the gorge. There was much backslapping and excitement from Royal and the trackers as we examined the lion, a beautiful specimen with a very respectable mane. It was most definitely a well-earned trophy and one to be proud of. Our decision to pass up on the leopard turned out to be the correct one.

The gas lamp was set up in the bait tree. Its light was sufficient for Royal to start skinning the lion, for, as I said before, there was no way we could carry the entire five-hundred-pound carcass out the gorge and back to the Land Cruiser. We all remained anxious while Royal carried out his handiwork because we knew the three-legged lioness was out there somewhere, lurking in the shadows just out of the range of the gas lamp. That she was probably enraged was a forgone conclusion.

As a result, tensions were running high. It was not surprising, therefore, that we got the fright of our lives when we heard from the direction of the blind, an almighty crack followed by the sound of a falling tree. We were a happy bunch when Royal finally had the lion skinned and the hide wrapped in a bundle, and it was with much relief that we made haste to climb out the gorge.

Throughout Africa, the successful collection of a trophy lion is always a joyous occasion, and we made the most of ours. The whiskey flowed freely to the accompaniment of songs from the compound where the team was also partying, thanks to the two crates of beer that Dave had given them. It was only in the wee hours of the morning that we finally decided to call it a day and hit the sack.

All too soon my ever-smiling waiter woke me with his usual "Morning boss" and a cup of tea. I have to say that it did little to relieve my headache. The camp cook had prepared a quick breakfast of scrambled eggs, bacon, and tomatoes, so we were soon off to drop the bait out of the tree and disassemble the blind, a legal requirement.

The walk down into the gorge seemed particularly difficult that morning; no doubt the previous evening's celebrations had something to do with it. When we arrived at the blind, we became instantly sober, for it had been completely flattened by a huge acacia tree that had fallen directly on top of it. The metal camp chair in which Dave had been sitting was completely destroyed. It had taken the brunt of the huge trunk and was mangled beyond recognition.

This is when reality set in. Had the lion not come in at all or had its arrival been an hour later, we would not have carried a beautiful trophy lion out the gorge; instead, we would have carried out a badly crushed and more than likely deceased Dave. For ages we stood around in awe wondering about the probabilities.

Tracker Crispen was never one to sit still for too long, so he went to investigate why the tree had fallen. He returned happily munching on something, which I presumed was a piece of biltong he had brought from camp. Closer inspection revealed he was happily eating live white borer grubs, culprits of the falling tree.

Dave asked to see what Crispen was munching, by which time the tracker's gray beard was covered in a white mess of goo. The sight was too much for Dave, and he promptly disappeared into the bush. From where we waited, we all heard him losing the tasty breakfast Cook had so lovingly prepared.

Hippos and Crocs

Chapter Twenty-Four

After the elephant and white rhino, the hippopotamus is the third largest mammal in Africa. Its sheer size seems to appeal to the sport hunter. Hippos spend most of the day resting in water, be it a lake or a river, but in the evening they leave the safety of the water and move inland to graze. In cases where overgrazing has taken place, a hippo will travel long distances in search of food, but in areas where they are persecuted by hunters or poachers, they only leave their safe water havens in complete darkness and return at the first sign of dawn. At times they will find shallow sandbars where they can bask in the sun, and only on rare occasions will they venture inland to feed during the day.

As with their buffalo counterparts, old hippo bulls often seek a lone, solitary life. To do so they will find an isolated pan to call home. This pan could well be situated many miles away from the main body of water.

There are three methods for hunting hippos. The most common method is shooting an animal out of a pod when it is still in the water. However, this method is by far the least exciting; in fact, it's more of a sniping exercise than a hunt. Essentially this entails finding a pod within shooting distance and then getting into position to take the shot.

This can be harder than one might think because hippos have excellent eyesight and a great sense of smell. The flow of the river is also a major consideration. If the current is too fast, there is always the likelihood of the hippo's carcass being carried a long way downstream and eventually floating ashore a long way off.

Worse still is the possibility of the carcass floating out of the concession's boundary. This happened to me on one occasion, and when we finally located the carcass, it had washed up inside Mozambique, some twenty kilometres from where the hippo had been shot. The locals had butchered and feasted upon our carcass, and to add insult to injury, we were obliged to purchase the tusks back from them!

Having maneuvered into a suitable shooting position, the hunter's next move is to select a bull from the pod. As a general rule one looks for sheer size as well as a "Roman nose." The tusk bulges, the large humps that protrude from just under the skin next to the tusks, are also an indication of size. If there happens to be an animal noticeably larger than the rest of the pod, then there's no problem, but distinguishing the difference between an average bull and a big cow is extremely difficult. I am yet to be convinced that anyone has mastered the difference.

A good friend of mine, Ian Gibson, who was tragically killed by an elephant recently, was based on the Zambezi for twenty-odd years and had more experience in hunting hippos than anyone I know. When I asked him how he told the difference between the sexes, he said it was simple: "The bulls have pink around the eyes while the cows have brown!"

After selecting a bull, the hunter needs to position himself for a brain shot. This shot is essential, for a successful brain shot will kill the hippo instantly, and it will sink without movement. Should the hippo be shot in the lungs or heart, the effect is not immediate, and the hippo will rush for deeper water where the usually strong current can carry the carcass away.

The hunter has a couple of options when placing a shot to the hippo's brain: the side-on brain shot or the frontal brain shot. I feel the side-on shot is preferable because the base of the ear makes an easy target. Then there's the frontal brain shot. When placing this shot, point directly between the eyes and at the tip of the inverted "V" created by the bulging eye sockets.

Once you've shot the hippo in the brain, from then on it is simply a matter of waiting for the carcass to float. This occurs when the contents of the gut ferment and the resulting gasses in the stomach expand, forcing the carcass to rise to the surface. The later you shoot in the day, the longer it takes for the carcass to float. This is due to the increased amount of food digested and subsequently excreted.

If a hippo is shot around eight in the morning, it will take an hour or two for the carcass to surface, depending on whether it is summer or winter.

A pod of hippos in the Zambezi River.

The warmer the water, the faster the gas production and the quicker the carcass will float. As a general rule, hippo hunting is a morning activity. Hunting a hippo later in the day could result in the carcass surfacing after dark, which could mean losing your trophy.

The second method of hunting hippos is far more exciting, for it involves stalking a hippo on land. Care should be taken in selecting an area where the hippos have experienced little hunting or poaching pressure. In such areas they love to come out of the water, either to bask in the sunshine or take the opportunity to graze on the riverbanks. Any hippo seen out of the water on its own is more than likely to be a bull.

Careful stalking is essential. Unnecessary movement should be restricted, and binoculars used to study the waterline. A careful approach should be planned, using whatever cover is available until you are within a suitable shooting distance. Some areas, like Lake Kariba for example, may require a long stalk over open, flat ground. As can be imagined in this situation, the stalk is an intense, exciting affair with stealthy movements and a lot of crawling.

Jeff and his "already dead hippo" from Chewore North.

Trev (left) and Allan next to the hippo that was shot in jesse *bush at close quarters —a dangerous affair, Dande, 2016.*

There have been times when I've stalked a hippo on land that I've made use of a blind. The blind I'm talking about is mobile. When the hippo looks in our direction, we stop and hide behind the blind. As soon as it starts grazing again, we resume the stalk. It is amazing how effective this method can be.

There is another reason why hippo bulls come out of the water during daytime. Territorial fights between rival bulls for dominance are common amongst hippos. Such fights can cause serious injuries, such as deep cuts and puncture wounds that can sometimes be fatal. When in the water, fish take advantage of the open wounds for an easy meal. This irritates the injured animal, and as a result, such bulls often spend a lot more time out of the water than normal.

Such instances can offer the hunter a good shooting opportunity. A brain shot is essential if you are shooting a hippo that is standing next to flowing water. Hippos are neither particularly tough nor tenacious. Heart or lung shots, with a suitably large-calibre rifle and good solid rounds of ammunition can be an effective option if the hippo is some distance from water.

On one occasion we spotted a bull that had beached himself on the banks of the Zambezi River. The hippo was a magnificent specimen, an ancient bull with numerous old and freshly made scars. After checking the wind direction, we made a long and cautions approach that entailed a lot of rear-end shuffling to get my client, Jeff, into a good shooting position. From a steady rest Jeff put two shots into the hippo. It never moved, so we assumed Jeff had effectively brained the bull with his first shot. The customary congratulations were made and everything looked fine until we rolled the bull over. To our amazement we discovered he was stiff with rigor mortis. Closer inspection revealed that the hippo had been dead for a few days. It was little wonder the old fellow never moved when he was shot!

The third and most exciting type of hippo hunting lies in seeking out old and solitary bulls that have found sanctuary away from the pod. These bulls will often be found in a pan or a gully that holds permanent water replenished annually during the rains. As the dry season approaches and evaporation takes place, the water level in these pans drops to a point where at times there is barely enough there for the hippo to submerge itself.

Such bulls are often grumpy and aggressive. They also become very possessive of their pans and are liable to charge when approached. With little warning, they come at you with incredible speed, often creating a bow wave in front of them as they charge. They emerge from the water with their impressive jaws snapping and their heads swinging from side to side, and all the while their beady little eyes never leave you. In such instances only a brain shot will work. If it doesn't, you stand a good chance of being bitten in half.

A heavy-calibre rifle with a good-quality softnose bullet is essential. The skin on top of a hippo's head is thin and so is the skull surrounding the brain. This makes expanding bullets a lot more effective than solids for brain shots on hippos.

Some blocks in the Selous Game Reserve are probably the best areas to find these solitary animals. The Charara Safari Area on Lake Kariba also offers good opportunities for hunting lone hippo bulls as there are many inland pans that the old bulls seem to fancy.

Occasionally you'll find the tracks of an old bull that has recently left his pan and not returned. If the spoor is fresh enough, the hunt is on! This is my favourite type of hippo hunting as it entails tracking the animal, which will either have moved to a new pan, be in transit, or resting in the *jesse* bush. In this instance a very cautious approach is necessary in order to get in a telling shot.

Hippos kill more people in Africa than any other animal. Most of the victims are local fishermen who get knocked out of their canoes where they either drown or are subsequently bitten by a hippo or eaten by crocodiles as they try to make it back to land. Thankfully, I have only had one incident of being attacked by a hippo while I was on a canoe. It is a terrifying experience and one that I never want to repeat.

Crocodiles

Crocodile hunting must be one of the most underrated hunts around. These one-ton killers have been on planet Earth since the time of the dinosaurs, and since the end of the Mesozoic Era they have changed very little. Crocodiles are the ultimate killing machines, blessed with senses second to none. They are so in tune with nature that even the chirp of a bird is enough to scare the cunning creature back into the water. A five-metre crocodile will be seventy years or older, and one can almost guarantee

Werner Müller and his big fifteen-foot croc from Dande North.

Croc showing the two perfect killing shots.

that if you are lucky enough to shoot one this big, it's been a man-eater at some point in its long life. There are two ways to hunt crocodiles; both are exciting and each has its own merits.

The first method is to find a crocodile that is out of water. Being cold-blooded, a croc needs to raise its body temperature, especially during the colder months, It does this by basking in the sun. When a croc reaches its optimum body temperature, which is 37 degrees Celsius, it opens its jaws. Its mouth is full of tiny blood vessels that lie close to the surface, and by opening its mouth and allowing the wind to pass through, it is able to regulate its body's temperature.

A very careful approach is needed in order to get within shooting distance of a basking croc. This is a lot more difficult than one would expect. As I have already mentioned, the crocodile is a great survivor with amazingly fine-tuned senses. Although I have shot many crocodiles by stalking, one should be prepared to accept the difficulties and realize that the effort might well end in failure.

My modus operandi is to look for a big crocodile and then find its preferred basking place. Even if this means chasing it away, I will then erect a blind within a reasonable shooting distance to where it prefers to lie. Once the blind is built, I clear a pathway that will give me a hidden approach, a procedure that is similar to preparing a leopard blind. After closing the shooting holes in the blind, I stay away from the spot for a few days. After this it is a matter of waiting for the croc to return. Careful daily observation from a boat at a distance will reveal when the croc has returned to its favourite spot. If the croc is there, I then beach the boat well out of sight and make a careful approach to our path and then into the blind. Then all that is left is to hope we will get the opportunity of a shot.

The second method of hunting crocs is to set a bait. This is an extremely exciting method as one gets to experience a croc's raw power and primeval habits, habits that have remained unchanged for millennia as it feeds on the bait. Selecting the right baiting site is important. First of all, one needs to have seen a trophy croc within the general area. Then careful consideration must be given to erecting a blind that is downwind and no more than one hundred yards shooting distance away. The reason for this is simple: There are only two shots possible on the croc and both are at very small targets.

The first option is the brain shot. When broadside-on, the shot should be placed below the "horns," the little rises behind the eyes. These projections are, in fact, the crocodile's ear ridges. The brain itself is smaller than a golf ball. When hit by the right type of bullet (a quality expanding one), the top of the head including the brain explodes, instantly killing the crocodile.

The second option is intended to break the spine and paralyze the crocodile. When the crocodile is broadside-on, the hunter should aim for the end of the "smile," in other words, where the rear end of the jaw joins the bulge in the neck. If the bullet is well-placed, the spine will be severed at the base of the skull, paralyzing the reptile. The croc can then be approached and killed.

If the croc is dispatched by a heart shot, it will take a long time to die. This has something to do with a crocodile's ability to slow down the rate of its heartbeat, especially during the winter months.

In my opinion a trophy crocodile is one that exceeds thirteen feet in length. The difference between a thirteen-foot specimen and one of fifteen feet is incredible. The additional two feet of length represents an exponential increase in body mass, especially around the stomach area, and, in many instances, a fifteen-foot croc will weigh twice as much as its thirteen-foot counterpart.

On opening the carcass of the croc, we discovered the torso, head, arm, and a leg of a man.

I have hunted a lot of crocodiles on the north bank of Lake Cahora Bassa. There are numerous small grassy islands in this area, all of which offer protection to crocodiles during the breeding season, so much so that the area is a mecca for the reptiles. The crocs in the lake are huge and many are man-eaters. In one year alone more than one hundred people were reported killed by the reptiles in this area.

While hunting in that vicinity one day, we were surprised to see a young American in a kayak. We later found out he was kayaking from the source of the Zambezi River in Zambia, all the way to the ocean in Mozambique. We informed him that the stretch of river in which we were operating was highly dangerous and most unsuitable for kayaking. In fact, we even offered to take him by boat to the beginning of Lake Cahora Bassa itself from where he could at least continue his journey in safer, open water.

He refused our offer, so we said good-bye and wished him well on the rest of his journey. Ten kilometres downstream he was knocked out of his kayak. Luckily on this occasion he was not attacked, but in spite of this incident and of our warning, he stupidly continued his journey. He was attacked and eaten by crocodiles a few kilometres farther downstream.

Every client who shoots a crocodile wants to see the contents of its stomach. This stems from a morbid fascination to see what it has eaten. Over the years we have found many interesting things. These have included pangolins, porcupines, motor vehicle number plates, and even shoes. Smooth stones are always found inside the stomach. They help give the crocodile ballast by weighing it down and keeping it steady.

We also make a point of publicly removing the gall bladder from the liver and throwing it in the river. The fluid in the gall bladder is deadly poisonous and is reputedly used for murder in Africa. The fluid is left in the sun to evaporate and the residue is a white chalky substance that has no smell, is tasteless, but if swallowed, is lethal.

On one particular hunt our tracker's son, a fisherman, was reported missing. Two days later we killed a monster fifteen-foot crocodile that from the sheer size of its stomach appeared to have eaten something large. On opening the carcass we discovered the torso, head, and a leg of a man. The acid in the croc's digestive system had removed all the skin's pigmentation, but on closer inspection our tracker confirmed the body was, indeed, that of his son. In true African style the man took two days off to give his son a decent burial and then came straight back to work.

Some of the best crocodile hunting I have experienced was in the top end of Lake Cahora Bassa in September when the crocs were mating. During this time the big females would also start laying their eggs on the high sandbanks; the females would then lie on top of the eggs during the day to protect them from the many threats made by birds of prey, monitor lizards, and a number of other scavengers. Often you would get the fright of your life when a massive fourteen-foot crocodile that has been disturbed by the boat would get such a fright that it would nearly land up beside you in its desperate attempt to get back into the water.

Paul Macmier shot this massive croc in Cabora Bassa, Mozambique.

During this time you could also see the dominant males swimming beside the big females then watch them slowly glide on top of the receptive females that are ready for mating. As ironic as this may seem, watching this mating process in the early morning in quiet channels of the Zambezi River with mist rising off the warm water is in itself strangely romantic!

The crocodile is the ultimate survivor and a worthy trophy. To hunt one of these dinosaur-age creatures ethically in a lake or river system is to embark on a hunt that will truly be memorable.

Michelle's Introduction to Africa

Chapter Twenty-Five

Early in 2005 I received an email with the simple title, "Are you the Buzz?" I was about to delete it as spam when, fortunately, on second thought, I opened it to discover I had a half-sister by the name of Michelle living in Denmark.

Apparently, several years before my father met my mother, he fell in love with a Danish girl while on a skiing trip in Europe. They got married and had a baby daughter whom they named Michelle. Unfortunately, the relationship ended when Michelle's mother decided she'd rather live in Denmark than the wilds of Kenya. At that time my father was training to be a professional hunter with the well-known safari company, Kerr & Downey, under the expert eye of the legendary hunter John Kingsley-Heath.

So there I was, thirty-three years after she was born, organizing a trip for my half-sister to come and meet me in Zimbabwe and spend a couple of weeks with us over the Christmas holidays. While sitting at the airport waiting for her arrival, I became a little apprehensive. A friend of mine also happened to be at the airport and was waiting for a relative on board the same plane. During the course of our conversation he asked me what Michelle was like.

"I have no idea," I replied. "I don't even know what she looks like!"

While waiting, I wondered, somewhat nervously, if I would even recognize her. I happen to be the shortest member in the family. My late father was in excess of six feet, and my brother Ross stands six feet, two inches tall. Aware that her mother is Danish, I imagined Michelle to be a tall, strikingly beautiful blonde with typical Scandinavian features.

Sure enough, as the passengers began to appear, here she came, strolling out the exit, the tall beautiful blonde beauty of my imagination. To my disbelief, as I approached her expectantly, she took no notice and walked straight past me without a glimpse of recognition. However, right on her heels appeared a short, dark-haired woman who immediately rushed up and enthusiastically threw her arms around me. My *little* half-sister had finally arrived. Evidently, she had watched one of my videos and had instantly recognized me. Michelle and I hit it off right from the start.

Zoe, Jesse, and I visit Dad's memorial in Nyanga, 2015.

After spending two days in Harare, we set off to Nyanga, a three-hour drive from Harare. Nyanga is a beautiful mountainous region in the eastern highlands of Zimbabwe. The main reason Michelle wanted to visit that part of the country was to see where our father had lost his life. He died tragically in a hang glider accident in September 1974 at the young age of thirty-three, which ironically is my age as I write these notes. The experience was an emotional one, but it cemented our brother-sister relationship.

After our emotional Nyanga experience, I decided to take Michelle, along with my girlfriend, Steph, and my apprentice-hunter, Guy, on a five-day canoe safari down the Zambezi River from Mana Pools to Kanyemba. I had decided on this particular safari because Mana Pools is one of Zimbabwe's great wildlife parks. This was where I knew Michelle would have the finest game viewing and photographic opportunities, especially during the Mana Pools section of the canoeing trip.

From Mana we would then canoe past the Sapi Safari Area, Chewore North, and into the Dande communal area, all of which are familiar territories to me. I had spent the better part of the previous twelve years hunting in these areas and very much wanted to share some of my past life with my newfound sister. On the completion of our canoeing trip, the plan was to spend Christmas at Tiger Odyssey, a fishing camp I had recently purchased, which is on the banks of the Zambezi at the confluence of the Luangwa River.

After a back-breaking five-hour drive, we met up with our canoe guide "Bono" at the Nyakasikana gate, the entrance to Mana Pools. We transferred our baggage into the Land Cruiser and sent Royal, my driver, on his way. He would meet us later at Tiger Odyssey to resupply us with food and drinks for the Christmas holidays. Having only just completed a full hunting season with all the responsibilities involved, it was a wonderful feeling to open a cold beer and relax, knowing that I was the guest this time and that the responsibility for a successful canoe safari lay upon someone else's shoulders.

It was a most enjoyable trip from Nyakasikana gate, through Mana, and on to the starting point of the canoe safari. We saw elephants, buffaloes, impalas, waterbucks, and, in fact, all the species common to the area. The floodplain of Mana Pools is one of the most beautiful sights in the Zambezi Valley, and it was a joy to witness Michelle's reaction to this Garden of Eden. Her appreciation made me realize just how much we take our beautiful country for granted.

At the starting point, we off-loaded the canoes from their trailer and packed them for our five-day trip. As we pushed them into the water, I noticed that Michelle was looking a trifle nervous, but I told her all would be well. For the first day she would be with Bono in the lead canoe, by which time she would be over her fear of the unknown and would begin to relax.

Prior to setting off, Bono gave us the usual ten-minute safety talk, the do's and dont's of participating in a canoe safari. Then it was cast-off time, with Michelle and Bono in the lead, Steph and I following them, and bringing up the rear came Guy with a learner guide in the canoe that was laden with beer and an assortment of drinks.

A hundred metres from our starting point an old hippo bull was grazing on one of the many islands in that part of the river. As we got closer to him, I took out my video camera, asked Steph not to rock the canoe, and started filming the old fellow. I can remember thinking what great footage I was getting as he took off, plodding down the bank and into the shallow water.

Elephant bull on the road into Mana Pools National Park.

Initially, the hippo was running parallel to our line of travel, but suddenly he turned and came charging toward us. It was obvious that his intent was to cause harm, for he was chomping at the water with his massive jaws as he drew closer. Suddenly, in addition to the hippo, Bono and Michelle's canoe appeared in my video's viewfinder, and I realized then, with horror, that things were not looking good.

Astonished at this sudden turn of events, I could not believe what was happening before my eyes. Bono was standing up in his canoe, screaming wildly and beating the water with his paddle in an attempt to scare the hippo off. It was clear his efforts were having little effect. The huge animal hit the canoe literally seconds after both Michelle and Bono had leapt into the water. They both then waded frantically through the shallows to the safety of the bank.

Not satisfied with the destruction it had inflicted upon the first canoe, the hippo then turned and came charging toward us. I shouted at Steph, who was up front, to get to the back. In scrambling backward, she nearly turned the canoe over, but thankfully at the last moment and for whatever reason, the hippo veered off and swam past us barely an arm's length away. I can still see the water cascading over his massive, scarred back.

As his head drew level with me, Steph hit him on the backside with her paddle. This infuriated him, and he turned his attention on our canoe. I saw his huge front lip come over the top of our canoe, and then there was an awful crunching sound. The fibre-glass canoe simply crumbled in his massive jaws. I distinctly felt the abrasive hairs of his nostrils and lips touching my thigh. He was far too close, so at that point, I decided the water was a far safer place to be and I leapt into the river. Thank heaven when I surfaced Steph was beside me, and better still, the canoe was between us and the irate hippo.

Satisfied with the scuttling of our canoe, the hippo then turned and headed for the third one, by which time Guy and his companion had made it to the bank and had already drawn the canoe halfway out of the water. This did not deter the animal in the slightest, and he launched his attack on the rear part of the canoe that was still in the water. While this was going on, I was desperately trying to salvage whatever equipment I could from the river. As I turned to see what was going on, I was just in time to watch our precious supply of beer being thrown into the air as the hippo decimated the canoe.

When I finally made it to the bank, I found Michelle sobbing hysterically. She later told me that the last view she had of her newfound brother was one of the hippo's jaws closing around him. She was convinced at that moment I had departed for greener pastures. Turning away from the scene of destruction, she had proceeded to run up the bank, straight into two *dagga* boy buffaloes that were grazing peacefully on the top. As a result of all the mayhem, it's no wonder I found my sister suffering from shock.

Once we had regained our wits and calmed down, we recovered what we could and walked the hundred-odd metres back to the Land Cruiser.

Do NOT get in the path of a charging hippo!

This is one of the three canoes bitten through by Mr. Hippo.

We reloaded all three of the disfigured canoes back onto the trailer; we then decided to head straight to Tiger Odyssey. None of us was particularly keen to get into another canoe, despite the kind offer from the canoeing company who assured us that they had new canoes available for us to resume our holiday. In retrospect, we did achieve something from that somewhat unpleasant experience. It was the distinction of partaking in the shortest canoeing safari in the history of the Zambezi River—exactly seven minutes' duration.

But all's well that ends well, and Michelle and I spent a wonderful Christmas in the Mupata Gorge eating turkey, drinking champagne, and celebrating with Christmas crackers. Other than our group, there was not another person on the river to disturb the tranquility of what must surely be one of the most beautiful places on earth. It is at special moments like this that one realizes why we live in Africa.

NORBERT HANSEN

CHAPTER TWENTY-SIX

To be recognized and stand out as a professional hunter by the many operators working in Africa, you need to corner a specific field of the market, be it elephant, buffalo, lion, leopard, or even the many plains-game species of which Africa abounds. My particular niche was fueled by my passion for elephants.

Early on I realized there was a market for hunting tuskless cows, which in those days were considered by most operators as unmarketable trophies. Their reluctance to shoot tuskless elephants stemmed from a lack of interest shown by their clients. As a result, I saw a distinct opportunity in the market, and I took it. I made full use of the preconceived notions on the part of both operators and clients to gain valuable experience by hunting as many tuskless elephants as I could. Clients like Norbert Hansen helped me take advantage of the situation by promoting my name, and it's thanks to him and my other clients that my business took off.

Unlike today where a single tuskless cow requires seven-to-ten days of hunting, back then I could purchase a seven-day tag for a tuskless cow and the operators would tell me I could shoot as many as I was able to within that seven-day period. I developed what I called my "ultimate teams": These consisted of two sets of trackers, each carrying a radio and each accompanied by a driver. This arrangement allowed me to focus the hunts in different areas and that often resulted in multiple kills within the seven-day period.

Much to the annoyance of the operators, I showed them that they were on the losing end of a financial deal when at the end of the seven-day period I handed them the paperwork claiming a kill of five or more elephants in that limited period. Initially they thought that, at most, I would succeed in killing only two or three. The operators who had not appreciated the value of these animals soon changed their minds. On one particular hunt,

Norbert with one of his many tuskless elephants.

Norbert and I killed eight tuskless cows in a seven-day-hunting spree in the Dande South and East areas.

Over the many years that Norbert and I hunted together, we must have shot close to thirty elephants. Most of these were tuskless, but there were a few cows with tusks and the odd "problem-animal" bull. I met Norbert originally through Makoni, my mentor. Norbert had hunted with Makoni the year before I qualified. On that occasion he shot a cow from about fifty yards. It was a heart-lung shot, but, nevertheless, he enjoyed the experience. He also shot a cow with a frontal brain shot. From that day on Norbert was hooked on close-quarter elephant hunting.

Thanks to Norbert I developed my elephant hunting techniques, and they held me in good stead for a number of years. I started off by shooting unsuspecting elephants at sixty yards using the heart-and-lung shot. We then progressed by getting much closer, thirty yards or so, before executing a side-on brain shot. My final and most successful method was to get as close as possible—to the point where the elephant becomes aware of your presence and turns to face you. As it turns, we move in even closer, say fifteen yards, before executing a frontal brain shot as the huge animal looks down on you. It was this type of hunting that Norbert loved.

Norbert hailed from Cologne in Germany. He was an engineer for Philips and a fanatical ammunition reloader. I must admit his constant ramblings about reloading cartridges bored me to death, but in saying that, it was Norbert who designed the first flat-nose solid bullet. He called it Norbert's Super Penetrator. As you can imagine, this made him wide open to all sorts of jokes, some of which he just didn't understand. In spite of his competency in the English language, invariably some things were just lost on him, especially the one when I asked him how Norbert's Super Penetrator was holding out!

Jokes aside though, the vast majority of solid bullets now have a flat nose, and credit must go to Norbert for this. He designed the projectile after reading about the Russian K-141 Kursk submarine that was lost with all hands on deck when it sank in the Barents Sea on 12 August 2000. The submarine was armed with flat-nose torpedoes that outperformed other Western designs in stability, penetration, and distance. The concept for this design was based on the assumption that the flat nose caused an air or moisture bubble around the projectile, and this resulted in less resistance in its travel path to the intended target and, thus, resulted in greater penetration. For angled-brain shots on elephants, better and straighter penetration is a considerable advantage.

Norbert was well known for being overly careful with his money. The first year he developed the "Super Penetrator," he only brought three cartridges to test in the field. We used the first cartridge on an improvised range, the second cartridge Norbert lost in the grass, and the final one he used to side-brain an elephant cow. He was highly excited when we discovered the bullet had exited the cow's brain.

I was less impressed, however, and I told him that any solid-nose bullet would exit the relatively small head of an elephant cow that had been shot through the brain from the side. Anyway, time has since proved that his bullets were, indeed, superior to the other round-nose solids of that period.

Norbert wasn't just overly careful with his money—he was parsimonious to his core. Not only was it typical of him to bring only three rounds of

Norbert and I lean against a PAC bull that Norbert shot early in the season.

ammunition to test, but also, in true Norbert fashion, the first gratuity I received from him was a complimentary sewing kit that he had been given on the Lufthansa flight out to Africa! While I would be lying if I said I did not appreciate a tip, I was never overly concerned about them. It most certainly did not affect the effort I put into a hunt.

On the other hand, I did care that my team received a decent tip at the end of each hunt, so in Norbert's case, I would have to ask him to dig deep into his pockets when he gave my staff tips. I had to ask him to give the trackers and driver $100 each! With tears in his eyes at having to part with his money, Norbie (as he was affectionately known) would grudgingly pull out a few $100 bills and hand them out to the guys.

Norbert was the first client of mine to bring out a Blazer rifle, which he loved. In those days Blazer was a much-scorned weapon because of its extreme unconventionality. When reloading a Blazer, the bolt was drawn straight back rather than using the "up-and-back" action of a conventional rifle. In Norbert's day, the largest calibre rifle built by Blazer was the .375 H&H, but being an engineer and fantastic with his hands, he had fitted a .458 Lott barrel to his Blazer rifle, and it was with this unconventional weapon that Norbert became an accomplished elephant hunter. Norbert became so proficient with his Blazer that to this day I have yet to meet anyone with a normal bolt-action or double-barrel weapon who could get three rounds off as fast as he could.

Norbert insisted on using a shooting stick. I am not a great fan of shooting sticks, especially when it comes to hunting elephants because they take ages—relatively speaking—to set up. Instead of focusing on the target, which more than likely was only twenty odd yards away, I would invariably be setting up the "sticks" to the correct height. In essence, rather than messing about with the "sticks," I felt my attention should rather have been focused on the elephant, just in case things got out of hand. To be fair, when Norbert did pull the trigger, the elephant invariably went down without a hassle. In fact, out of the thirty-odd elephants we shot together, there were only two that required more than one shot. This is an amazing record for anyone!

On one of our hunts together, he brought out a .500 barrel to see how it would perform on an elephant. We set off following the tracks of some elephants early one morning and caught up with the herd a few hours later. Having found a suitable tuskless cow, we commenced our final approach. As usual Norbert reminded me, as he did on every approach, that he did not want me to shoot unless it became life threatening. Anyway, the cow gave Norbert the opportunity for a frontal brain shot from about twenty yards.

When he eventually pulled the trigger, the additional recoil of the .500 sent the telescopic sight crashing back onto his glasses, shattering the right eyepiece in the process. It should be mentioned here that Norbert's glasses were as thick as Coke-bottle bottoms. The result was a nasty, deep cut above his eye that bled profusely. The elephant was knocked straight down by the .500 bullet, but it got up again. Knowing that Norbert would be unhappy if I shot the wounded animal, I quickly found the unbroken eyepiece and held it in front of his shooting eye so that he could finish off the cow, which he did, in spite of blood spurting all over the place.

Being tight-fisted, Norbert had only brought one pair of glasses, and we still had a number of elephants to shoot. We needed to come up with an innovative solution that would allow him to continue hunting. We eventually solved the problem by sticking the broken pieces of his glasses together with duct tape and copious amounts of super glue.

Norbert (left) and a "sheepish" Doug with PAC lion.

There was no one who liked a bargain more than Norbie, and without fail every year he would inquire about any problem animals that needed to be controlled. In those days a client was permitted to accompany the operator without having to pay a cent. Norbie managed to bag several problem animals throughout his hunting career, and in this regard he was remarkably lucky. I say he was lucky, for his trips invariably coincided with a report about some problem animal within that council's jurisdiction. I have never, unlike many others, fabricated PAC animals to fit a client's needs, and I have only ever shot the genuinely problematic ones. It is for this reason that Norbert was so lucky.

On one particular trip we received a message informing us there was a lion with a broken front leg near one of the villages. As the lion was in distress and a potential threat to the villagers, we were asked to put the poor beast out of its misery if we came across it. This was music to Norbert's ears, so we actively sought out and tracked the lion.

On that particular hunt was a friend of mine, Doug Hidden. Doug had joined me as an apprentice to get some experience hunting elephants. We picked up the lion's tracks along the road that morning, and the spoor revealed that the lion was dragging a front foot. They were clearly the tracks of the wounded animal we sought. Knowing only too well how Norbert felt about backup shots, I told him that neither of us would intervene unless a dangerous situation developed.

With his broken leg, the lion did not go very far, and we heard him growling from a nearby patch of tall grass. I got Norbie on the sticks and moved off to his right while Doug positioned himself on the left side. Suddenly the lion appeared out the grass. Norbie had a clear shot, and I told him to take it. I also raised my .416 rifle and had the lion in my sights just in case things turned nasty. There was an explosion, and I saw the lion take the hit. The beast swung around and made a somewhat awkward charge, but a charge nonetheless, so I fired and put him down with a brain shot. Knowing that Norbert would be unhappy about my interference, I attempted to pacify him.

"Well done, Norbert," I exclaimed. "Your first shot was excellent. The lion was dead on his feet without knowing it."

"But I haven't had a shot yet!" replied an indignant Norbert.

I looked over at Doug and saw him ejecting an empty cartridge. He was looking very sheepish. That was the last time Norbert allowed an apprentice hunter on any of our hunts!

On my final hunt with Norbert we went to an area called Nyamuswa, which is near Karoi in the northwest of Zimbabwe and only three hours from Harare. It is a privately owned area that has a lot of elephants. We shot a couple of trophy bulls there every year as well as conducting problem animal hunts. There were great numbers of problem animals in the area as the place was surrounded by villages. Toward the end of summer, numerous elephants, mainly bulls, came up from Gache Gache on the shores of Lake Kariba to raid the natives' maize fields.

Norbert was successful in getting his final elephant at Nyamuswa; this occurred on the third day of his hunt. Being solely an elephant hunter and not interested in anything else, I was dreading the remaining seven days as I am not a person who can sit around doing nothing.

The area, before the economic crash that was brought about by Mugabe's idiotic land-reform program, was a successful photographic area. With the

Norbert and a perfectly side brained tuskless cow.

downfall of the photographic industry, the occupants turned to hunting in order to survive. So we took on their small quota of animals.

One of the activities the owners of Nyamuswa offered was horseback riding on a few old "plodders" on a wonderful trail. As the horses were still there, I ended up riding every afternoon and despite my aversion to horses, I have to say I enjoyed the experience very much. One morning to my abject horror, Norbert decided to join me. Considering his age, lack of mobility, and the fact that the trails were over large kopjes and across streams, I was somewhat concerned he might fall and injure himself.

He insisted, however, so we saddled two horses. That's when we came to a screeching halt. It was just too difficult to get him into the saddle. So we loaded him into the back of the Land Cruiser, reversed the vehicle up to the poor horse, and by degrees got Norbie mounted. The process involved a great deal of flatulence, a problem Norbie suffered from whenever he exerted himself. Finally we were off. We had one small mishap en route when a branch whipped off his glasses, rendering him instantly blind. This happened on the edge of a rocky crevice. Disaster was averted when we retrieved his glasses, thankfully before the horse bolted!

Our plan was to go for an early morning ride and to end at a beautiful dam where Justin, my cameraman, would meet us with a tasty cooked breakfast. I was very relieved when we arrived at the Land Cruiser without mishap and to the smell of fried eggs and bacon.

I instructed Justin to reverse the Land Cruiser so that Norbie could dismount into the back. This he did, and I thought we were home free when I saw Norbie fall off the vehicle straight onto his back, accompanied by a great deal of swearing and cursing in German. Thankfully, there was no serious injury, unlike the following night. . . .

As was customary with Norbert on the last night of a safari, each of us would have a bottle of red wine with our dinner. Mukuyu is the wine from a local distiller and it tastes really awful. Norbert, however, insisted we drink the ghastly stuff. After dinner we all went to sit by the campfire. When we had drunk all the wine, Norbert got up to go to bed. I could see he was a little wobbly, so I took him by the shoulder and led him to his tent.

While I was unzipping the flaps, he overbalanced and fell forward, hitting his head on one of the gum poles that supported the thatched roof over the tent. I turned around to see him lying on the ground at an awkward angle. His eyes were wide open, and as I could get no response, I thought he was dead. With all my first-aid courses temporarily forgotten, I poked him in the eye to see if there was a reaction.

Thankfully and much to my relief, Norbie blinked a few times and then slowly sat up. To my untrained eye he was clearly concussed, and after I got him up and into bed he looked at me and wanted to know who I was. He did seem to know he was elephant hunting, for he asked me if he had been trampled by one! I decided not to panic and to let poor old Norbie sleep it off, hoping he'd be fine in the morning. Indeed he was, for other than a slight battle to walk normally, he appeared to be fine.

In retrospect I think Norbert had had a minor stoke that night. Perhaps it's just as well that it was our last safari together. I had great times with him, and we shared many amazing experiences. Only in the pursuit of hunting big game, in his case the elephant, could have brought together two such different types of people.

IKE AND KATE

CHAPTER TWENTY-SEVEN

Getting to meet and become long-lasting friends with many different and interesting people is one of the bonuses of being a professional hunter. During my twenty-five years in the business, I've had the opportunity to meet hundreds of clients, but if I were asked who had impressed me the most, I would say without hesitation it was Ike and Kazakue, or Kate as she was known to non-Japanese speakers. This unique Asian couple made a huge impression on me, and I'm the first to admit that without them I would not be where I am today. Here then is their story:

I met Ike and Kate under unusual circumstances. I had just completed my first elephant-hunting DVD and was on a visit to Atlanta to work on the

Kate and her elephant.

Ike and Kate with Ike's elephant bull.

second one when I received an unexpected call from Ike. Somehow he had heard I was in the United States, so he had tracked down my contact number and phoned me. He explained that he had booked an elephant hunt in Zimbabwe for later in the year, but after watching my first video he was so impressed that he wanted to know if he could book a hunt with me.

No right-minded professional hunter ignores opportunities like that, so I told him I was available. Upon hearing this, he canceled the hunt he had already booked, even though it meant losing his deposit. That alone equated to the hunt's daily rate. This did not affect me, though, and I was more than happy to have an elephant hunt booked for later in the year. All it took, moreover, was a telephone call and an email. Believe me, selling expensive hunts do not come easier than that.

Ike and his charming wife, Kate, flew into Harare a couple of months later. I collected them at the airport in my Land Cruiser that I had already loaded, so we were ready to go to the Makuti Safari Area, which is situated along the Zambezi Escarpment.

The cabs of the older model Land Cruisers are not the biggest, by any means. When fully kitted out with reference books on the dashboard, a torch or two, water bottles, binoculars, a couple of ammo belts, and maybe a jacket or two, there is not much extra room left over. Two normal-size

Ike, Kate, Steph, and I are all smiles over this stunning 40-inch dagga *boy from Makuti.*

people fit into the cab with little space to spare, but Ike and Kate, like most of their Asian counterparts, were tiny, and the three of us fitted into the packed cab with ease.

I stopped briefly at my house in Harare because my clients wanted to take a shower before commencing the long trip to Makuti. Just as we were about to set off, Royal, my driver, who had featured on the first DVD, drove into the yard. Ike and Kate immediately recognized him and enthusiastically shook his hand, saying that they had seen him on the video.

Anyway, we were soon on our way and to keep an element of conversation going, I was telling Ike and Kate about Royal and the fact that he was infected with the HIV virus. There was a moment of silence while Ike and his wife stared at each other in shock. They exchanged a short conversation in Japanese then Kate went frantically through her carry-on bag and drew out a box of wet disinfectant wipes. They then enthusiastically set about wiping their hands with the tissues.

The five-hour trip that followed was most interesting. The reason for this was a three-way conversation we had, for Kate spoke no English at all despite having lived in New York for seventeen years. Ike dutifully translated everything we spoke about back into Japanese for Kate's benefit. It was during that long trip that I learned about their amazing life, which included one of the most touching love stories I have ever heard. In fact I have often tried to persuade Ike to write about it, for it is so poignant that I believe it has the potential to become a bestseller. I could never do justice to the story, I'm afraid, but as Ike's not prepared to write about it, then I will, because I feel it is a story that needs to be told.

Both Ike and Kate were born in Japan just before the onset of the Second World War. Japan's surrender to the Allies at the end of hostilities six years later was to result in both Ike and Kate experiencing trying times. Life in Japan during the postwar period was particularly hard. There were few medical facilities in that decimated, war-torn country, and as a result, hypodermic needles had to be shared when vaccinations were given. The result was that both Kate and Ike contracted Hepatitis C.

Ike and Kate grew up in a small Japanese town where they were playmates from the time they could walk. They attended the same junior and secondary schools, and eventually as they matured, fell madly in love. Ike told me he had always anticipated marrying Kate at some stage, but it was not to be. One day during the latter part of their secondary-school years, he returned home in tears. When his mother asked him what was wrong, he told her that Kate was to be married off to a wealthy and prominent businessman. While obviously sympathetic toward her son, Ike's mother explained that in Ike and Kate's case, this was the way it would always be as she belonged to a higher social class.

Ike could never accept the situation, so the following year after he'd finished school, he packed his bags and left for New York. In the Big Apple he made and lost two fortunes in both the material and construction business. During this time he kept in contact with Kate through letters, then faxes, and finally emails.

Realizing that cultural differences had dealt him a rough blow, Ike eventually met and married a local girl, not for love, he confessed, but because she looked like Kate. The marriage produced a son who, like his father, was to become a hugely successful businessman. In many cases loveless relationships do not last forever, and this was what happened with Ike's first marriage. It ended in divorce.

Over the years he would take the occasional trip back to Tokyo where he and Kate would meet secretly. Kate, now the mother of two daughters, was similarly unhappy with her tycoon husband. Eventually when he turned sixty, Ike sent Kate an email telling her he would be arriving in Tokyo the following morning. He told her he had bought two return tickets for the same day, and if she so desired they would return to the United States together. If she wanted to leave with him, he told her that she should meet him at the airport with only her handbag and passport.

Kate did what, at that time, in Japanese society was unthinkable. She abandoned her husband and the daughters she deeply loved and absconded with Ike to New York. For a Japanese wife to leave her husband for another man brings great dishonour to the family, and this was the case with Kate. Her family immediately disowned her. To save face they spread a rumour

Everyone is happy that Kate finally got her dagga *boy, Makuti.*

that she had been admitted to a mental institution, which was why she was never seen.

It was not long before Kate began to miss her beloved daughters, but she was too afraid to return to Tokyo. If the truth of her whereabouts ever got out, it was not inconceivable that her jealous husband would have her assassinated rather than face public embarrassment. To this day, one of her daughters refuses to acknowledge her mother while the other one has rekindled their relationship.

Ike was the most excitable hunter I've ever experienced. He simply loved every second he spent in the field. On our first safari we tracked an old *dagga* boy and eventually caught up with him while he was feeding in our direction. It was a perfect ambush, with the bull totally unaware of our presence as he slowly came toward us.

In a whisper I suggested that Kate should shoot the old bull. While Ike agreed with my suggestion, Kate, understandably, was slightly apprehensive as this was her first crack at a dangerous-game animal. It was, however, a perfect situation and one that would afford her the opportunity of an easy shot. The old *dagga* bull continued to give us plenty of time to set things up in a relaxed and confident manner. The circumstances couldn't be better.

I made sure the correct cartridge was chambered into Kate's rifle, adjusted the scope to the most suitable setting, and then got her comfortably settled on the portable tripod. Then we waited while the bull came ever closer. When he was only twenty yards away and still feeding contentedly, blissfully unaware of our presence, I told her to shoot. With my fingers jammed in my ears, I waited for the report of the rifle, but it never came. The bull continued to feed closer and still closer.

Wondering why she hadn't fired, I glanced at Kate. In looking at her closely, I saw that she appeared to be calm, her emotions under control, and more importantly her finger was turning a shade paler as she squeezed the trigger. Moments before her shot rang out, there was a huge bang on my left. I swung round to find Ike, grinning like a Cheshire cat.

"That was Kate's buffalo, Ike!" I said sternly.

Looking guilty, he apologized for being impulsive but added he just could not help himself. He said that the situation had been too perfect to

Ike and I are two contented hunters after a marathon tracking session for this stunning lion.

let the bull escape. With the old *dagga* boy unaware of our presence and almost on top of us, he felt he had to shoot. "Kate can shoot the next one," he added sheepishly. This she did, too, when a fine-looking old *dagga* boy fell to her rifle the next day.

Ike always made me laugh. When it was Kate's turn to shoot after tracking an animal and if it was found to be inferior in any way, I would whisper to him that we should pass it up.

"Buzz," he would whisper back. "It's big enough for the lady."

With that, he'd tell Kate to go ahead and shoot. Immediately after Kate's bullet hit the animal, Ike would start firing at it like a madman with his Blazer .375. He did this when Kate shot a bull elephant, but when it was all over, he would compliment her.

"Well done, darling, you shot it perfectly," he would say.

No matter what either of them shot, they were always over the moon with their trophies.

On one of their safaris, I was able to offer Ike a lion that we still had on quota. Ike was eager, and we soon identified a suitable one for him to shoot.

As luck would have it, the animal would not feed on any of the baits that we'd hung. To make matters even more frustrating, the very same lion had the audacity to roar right next to our camp just before dark.

We were on his tracks at first light the following morning, and several hours of arduous tracking followed. By that stage of their lives, both Ike and Kate had bad knees that necessitated the use of walking sticks when following spoor. The lion took us on a marathon walk, up and down hills in some really rugged country.

Just how Ike and Kate managed this with their defective knees and walking sticks was testimony to their clenched-jaw determination. I still have a picture in my mind of my two friends. As the lion's tracks led us up yet another hill, I glanced back to see how they were faring only to be confronted with a hilarious sight: There they were, hobbling along side by side with their walking sticks and wearing face masks that they had camouflaged by scribbling on the masks with a child's green wax crayon!

Eventually we caught up to the lion, but he was too fast for us, and before we had a chance to shoot, he took off down the side of the hill. Upon seeing the vanishing lion, Ike dropped his walking stick and took off after it like a sprightly teenager. We thought the lion had made good his escape when all of a sudden one of the trackers spotted him about three hundred metres away slowly climbing up the opposite hill. Ike was carrying his Blazer .375. The lion was a long way off, so I asked if he thought he could take the shot.

"Nothing to lose, let's try," he replied confidently.

Ike's first shot was a little too low because he had not compensated for the distance, and the bullet dropped short. Amazingly, the lion just stood there, long enough for Ike to take a second shot. This time he had adjusted for the distance, and down the lion went.

It took us an hour to clamber down the hill and up the next one where the lion lay dead. There was no way to get a vehicle into such a remote and rocky place, so our only option was to skin the lion in situ. This we did, but it was still a two-kilometre hike, carrying the lion's heavy head and skin to the closest road.

Without a doubt this was one of my most memorable hunts. The Makuti Safari Area is not for sissies. Tracking a lion or leopard in that rugged area, with its many rocks and patches of long grass is a nightmare. To successfully follow a lion's tracks for seven hours in that harsh environment and then get the opportunity to shoot was testimony to the amazing ability of my two trackers and the tenacity of my elderly and tiny Asian clients.

It was late when we arrived back in camp. Alan, one of our other professional hunters, was there with a client named Jim. Jim was a retired New York firefighter and one of Ike's good friends. The opportunity to hunt in Africa had long been one of Jim's dreams, but on a fireman's salary, this was something that was likely to remain a dream. Even in retirement he was desperate to hunt in Africa, and as a result, Ike surprised him with a fully paid safari, an example Ike's generosity.

The success of the lion hunt resulted in much merriment round the campfire that evening, with Ike repeating the story of how we caught up to the lion. He also recalled saying "nothing to lose" after I asked him if he thought he could hit the lion. To which Allan casually remarked, "Yes, Ike, nothing serious to lose . . . only a professional hunter and a few trackers!"

The last day of our Makuti safari happened to coincide with my business partner, Myles, and I conducting the final stages of a bidding war for the concession rights to the Dande Safari Area. As a result, I excused myself from the fire that evening to call Myles on the satellite phone so that I could be updated with the latest news regarding the bidding process.

Myles broke the bad news. We were a substantial amount short of the highest bid. Having begged and borrowed from every conceivable source, we were still short of the amount, so I told Myles there was nothing further we could do. We had reached the end of the road in our quest for the Dande area. There was no chance we could find the required amount before the final bidding would take place.

In all honesty I thought we were out of the race that evening, and it was impossible for me to hide my disappointment when I returned to the fireside. Utterly dejected, I had dinner and went to bed. The following morning found Ike and me doing paperwork at the dining room table. When we had finished, he apologized for having overheard my discussion with Myles the previous evening. He then calmly informed me that he would like to loan us the required amount. I was at a loss for words. Eventually, when reality

Here Ike and Kate are fishing in the Ruese River, Makuti.

set in, I insisted we write out a proper contract with calculated loan repayments and interest rates. To this Ike agreed. He then leaned over, grabbed a paper serviette from the table, and upon it wrote.

"I, Ike, loan Buzz "X amount," which he will pay back as and when he can. It is a matter of HONOUR"!

As a result of Ike's generosity, we were able to secure the Dande concession. Within the first year we were able to pay Ike back all that was owed to him. His serviette note summed him up perfectly. He was a true gentleman, an honorable man, and a good friend.

Unfortunately cancer and old age have caught up with both Ike and Kate. I always call them whenever I'm in the States on my yearly marketing trips, just to see how they're doing. Inevitably, Ike says to me, "Not bad for an old guy. Maybe one more elephant, Buzz!"

Unfortunately, this will never happen, but age and sickness can't stop us dreaming! I count Ike and Kate as good friends, and we shared many wonderful safaris together.

Mike Jines

Chapter Twenty-Eight

Mike Jines is a retired corporate lawyer with an energy company in Houston. Prior to our meeting, he'd only been on one safari in Tanzania, a trip that was relatively successful despite a wheels-up landing on a bush airstrip that resulted in a few felled mopane trees. When I first met Mike, it was his intention to hunt only one elephant. We went on that hunt, and now, a dozen elephant hunts later, along with several buffalo, lion, and leopard hunts, we are now planning where to go for our next elephant. This is sure proof of just how addictive elephant hunting can be.

Mike's addiction began in the Makuti Safari Area, which is situated on the Zambezi Escarpment. While its location makes it one of the more picturesque parts of Zimbabwe, in hunting terms it also makes it one of the most demanding due to its undulating and mountainous country. Hunting elephants in Makuti is very different from hunting them in the adjacent Zambezi Valley. In the valley one has to rely on good trackers because the elephants seek refuge during the heat of the day in vast blocks of *jesse* bush where visibility can often be measured in feet. Hunting elephants in Makuti, on the other hand, entails climbing one of the numerous kopjes (hills) and viewing the area below with a high-powered binocular. If nothing is seen, the same process is repeated, again and again, until eventually you find what you're looking for.

In addition to the standard end-of-safari tip, Mike would offer the trackers an incentive of a hundred dollars for the first person to spot the bull elephant he would eventually kill. As a result, whenever we decided which kopje to climb, the trackers would enthusiastically bolt to the top, like mountain goats, each one hell-bent on being the first to spot the hundred-dollar bull. Mike and I would follow leisurely behind the stampede to avoid stumbling and possibly twisting an ankle on the rocky

Two beautiful old dagga *boys from the Dande and Makuti.*

surfaces of the mountains in the area. We obviously were nowhere near as fit or agile as the trackers.

During that initial fourteen-day Makuti hunt, we must have looked over at least a hundred and twenty bulls. It was extremely hard going, and, as a result of the difficult terrain, Mike's toes were bruised black and blue. Under the persistent excessive pressure, his toenails began to fall off. So it continued, day after day, climbing one kopje after another, only to descend without success after rejecting yet another "rat," a term I often use to describe a nontrophy elephant. After a while and as one elephant after another was rejected, Mike began to hate the term.

On the thirteenth day, having lost six of his toenails and shedding more than a few pounds—despite Crispen's good cooking—Mike declared that the kopje we were about to climb would definitely be his last. It so happened that we were looking for a particular old bull that we had turned down earlier in the safari. This bull had a hole in one ear, and we estimated his tusks would average around forty pounds a side. The elephant lived in one of several valleys that ultimately linked up to my favourite one, which I had christened the "Secret Valley."

In such vast areas trying to locate a specific elephant was like trying to find a needle in a haystack. As luck would have it, when we finally got to the top of a kopje, we saw a group of bulls in the valley below. None of them resembled the tusker we were looking for, but, nonetheless, they warranted a closer look. We never did find the bull with a hole in its ear, but eventually Ike, another client of mine, would shoot it.

One of the problems with locating an elephant in mountainous terrain like Makuti is the false impression one gets of distance. From an elevated position, what looks relatively close is actually deceivingly far away, and once you've descended, it is also difficult to get one's bearings at ground level, even after having pinpointed the location from the top of a prominent feature. This difficulty is compounded by thick and tall grass, a common feature in the escarpment.

We finally arrived at the point we had assumed the elephant to be, only to be confronted with the unusual sight of a huge warthog devouring the remains of a duiker. We watched the warthog eat his dinner for a while and

A picture of the Secret Valley.

were on the point of giving up the chase and returning to camp when in the distance we heard an elephant's communication rumble! Originally, these sounds were thought to come from an elephant's stomach, but they actually originate in its head. Elephants communicate with each other from as far as two miles apart by producing ultralow frequency sound waves.

Very cautiously we approached the bull by using an anthill as cover, and two shots later Mike had a fine trophy elephant that carried forty-two-pound tusks on each side. Since that time we have hunted annually together, sometimes twice a year, taking many stunning trophies.

******

One of those stunning trophies included a monster leopard that we hunted with dogs in our Nyamuswa concession. On that occasion we placed several baits around an area and soon had the leopard feeding. The following morning we arrived at first light to find that it had eaten the entire impala carcass. The fresh scent of the leopard had the dogs howling and barking

Mike's beautiful leopard.

in anticipation. Thinking the leopard wouldn't travel too far on such a full stomach, we figured the hunt would be easy. How wrong we were.

From kopje to kopje we chased after the baying dogs, and on numerous occasions when we caught up with them, it was only to find the pack milling about on another lost trail. It was then up to my trackers to find the spoor before setting off again. In the end after a long and hard chase, we finally lost the spoor for good. We repeated the same exercise daily as the leopard dutifully returned to feed on yet another carcass every night.

The chase was so demanding in the difficult terrain that the dog handlers had my trackers carrying twenty-litre containers of water up and down the kopjes in order to quench the dogs' thirst. Criton, my main tracker, is a Shona, and people who know him are aware of how proud he is. In Shona culture, a dog is considered a lowly creature and one that is not shown affection. With this in mind, I can only imagine how Criton felt, lugging heavy twenty-litre cans of water up and down kopjes for the benefit of a dog!

We repeated the same exercise over and over again for four long and arduous days. At the end of day four, when my trackers were once again called to action, this time to track a lost dog, Criton lost his patience. In no uncertain terms he asked me why we were messing around with a bunch of useless dogs when all we had to do was build a blind, set up the bait, and shoot the leopard when it came in to feed! In all honesty, I could find no fault with this reasoning, so we hung an impala in a selected tree on one side of a small river and built our blind on the other.

That evening saw us sitting comfortably in our blind watching the sun setting behind a hazy horizon. Around dusk we heard elephants coming down to drink, and moments later they appeared through the bush like prehistoric giants in the twilight. There were fifteen of them in total, with one being a monster. He was a single tusker, but what a tusk it was, looking at least four feet long from the lip. He was a truly magnificent animal, and we could barely control our excitement. Right there and then we decided to mark him as an animal worth hunting.

Watching the elephants at close quarters drinking and splashing themselves with water was a gratifying and rewarding experience, but as the light began to fade, Mike became concerned when the herd gradually started moving in our direction. We could hear branches being pulled off the trees and the swishing sound their bodies make when they rub against the undergrowth as they plodded slowly toward us. When darkness finally descended, we could quite clearly hear the herd moving in the bush barely feet away from our hide. They must have got a whiff of us, for moments later we heard them moving off through the undergrowth. Seconds later they were gone.

Shortly after the elephants had departed, we heard the leopard at the bait. Suddenly and much to my annoyance, a bush baby began to scream at us from a branch above the blind! I was sure the leopard had fled. Because we had used the dogs to hunt the leopard, I had not brought my spotlight. Since we needed light in order to see if the leopard was still there, I came up with an alternate plan. I removed one of the headlights from the Land Cruiser and attached it to the vehicle's twelve-volt battery. This proved highly successful, and when I turned the light on, much to our delight, there happily chewing at the bait was our leopard. One shot later and Mike had a fine-looking leopard skin in the salt.

Mike Jines's stunning one tusker, Nyamuswa.

Not only was the leopard hunt successful, but our good fortune on seeing the herd of elephant bulls at the waterhole earlier that night was proof of their presence in the area. It wasn't until some three years later that Mike and I were to find that very same bull. He was as magnificent then as I remembered him from three years previously. Mike's trophy bull carried a single, four-foot visible tusk, with a circumference of eighteen inches at the lip and a weight of just shy of seventy pounds.

On one particular safari I made a monumental mess-up by choosing the wrong elephant for Mike to shoot. There were two bulls in thick riverine bush in the Sengwa Research Area. The one was a shooter and we decided to take him. As we made our final approach on the chosen bull, he disappeared behind a large Combretum bush. Mike and I quickly walked around the other side of the bush in order to confront him and administer a frontal brain shot. Our plan appeared to have worked perfectly, but unknown to us, the chosen bull had met up with the younger animal behind the bush, and it was the latter who emerged in the front. Mike's perfectly placed frontal brain shot skewered the younger bull. Obviously Mike was disappointed, but he did not blame me. I did feel the mistake was somewhat ameliorated due to the circumstances.

One of Mike's hunts took place in 2008 during the country's run-off elections. The ruling party claimed the vote to be undecided after the original results were tallied, and the president then called for a second round of voting. This gave him enough time to cajole and intimidate the people into voting for him. Indirectly, this was somewhat of a gift for Mike, as we were asked to shoot seven elephants to distribute to the people prior to the elections.

I wanted nothing to do with this at first because I felt the elephants did not deserve to pay the ultimate price for an illegal election. Credit must go to Mike, for as much as he would liked to have shot seven elephants for free, he agreed with me, and we decided to not participate. It was only the following morning that we changed our minds and decided to assist.

We did this for a good reason, too. That morning we had seen National Parks scouts getting dropped off along the road, a kilometre or two apart. They were armed with AK-47 rifles, which are totally ineffective for killing elephants. The Parks staff had been instructed to shoot any elephants they came across. We knew that for every elephant they shot, several others would be wounded. Not only were their rifles ineffective for the job, their directive was to shoot at any elephant that moved. This would have been a disaster. At least if we shot the animals, it would be done properly. Accordingly, I offered our services, and Mike ended his hunt with an eight-elephant bag and a buffalo.

******

The following year we hunted lion. We tracked lions daily for a total of twenty-four days without sighting a good trophy. Mike was very disappointed, for a lion hunt is a huge financial investment, and I could under-

One of the eight brain-shot cows.

stand his feelings. The bottom line is simply this: In fair-chase hunting, there are no guarantees.

All was made up however, when the following year I offered Mike a late-season buffalo hunt with the opportunity of trying for a leftover lion. If we were lucky enough to track and shoot one, only then would he have to pay the trophy fee, which is a reasonable way of selling leftover lions.

One day we decided to walk down the Mkanga Gorge as it would take us past two of our lion baits that we had hung the previous afternoon. It's a beautiful walk but not for the faint-hearted. When you're not walking in loose sand, you have to climb over boulders and wade through water. On the walk we saw a lot of game, including a klipspringer, which we decided to pass up. At one spot a hyena that was sleeping under a rock scampered away right in front of us, but the sides of the gorge were too steep for him to escape, leaving him vulnerable. We were about to take a shot, but he was too quick for us. In a panic, he slipped, scrambled, and clawed his way up the steep embankment to safety. We had a good laugh.

On all our hunts together, we never saw a single bushpig, so one can imagine our excitement when we came around a bend in the river to find a group of them burrowing in the sand. Before Mike could get off a shot, the pigs bolted, but they made the mistake of trying to climb up the steep sides of the gorge and then onto a path that went parallel to where we were standing. It became open season for Mike, and he managed to bag three of them.

Our excitement in shooting the pigs was somewhat dampened when we realized we had to carry them out of the gorge. The GPS told us it was only three kilometres to the closest pick-up point, but this was a straight-line measurement. I knew only too well that the river was anything but straight and that it often curled back on itself. We gutted the pigs and cut their heads off. Criton carried the two smaller ones by skewering them on a pole. His effort in carrying the load out was an amazing feat when one considers the rocks and boulders we had to scamper over. I carried the third pig after we'd chopped off its limbs and put them in a satchel.

I decided to call Eddy and Nyati on the radio to ask for help. I asked them to drive up the riverbed to where we had put our first bait. From there, as it was the start of the rocky gorge, they were to continue

Mike's trio of bushpigs made the mistake of trying to climb up the steep sides of the gorge.

on foot until they lined up with us. They would then be able to help us carry out the pigs.

Half an hour later the radio crackled with an excited Nyati on the line. They had been charged by a lion when they got near the bait. I asked him if the lion was worth shooting, and, Nyati replied by saying it wasn't only a 100-percent shooter, it was more like 110 percent. So the game was on. Fortunately, they had the good sense to keep away from the bait in the hope that the lion would give us an opportunity when we eventually reached the spot.

With enthusiasm and renewed vigour, we carried on down the riverbed to a bend that was close to the bait. There we dumped the pigs and climbed a ridge that was directly overlooking the bait. This would give us an elevated view of the lion and should offer a perfect shot.

The approach was ideal, and as we peeped over the ledge, there under the bait, and not thirty yards away, was a fine-looking lion that was totally unaware of our presence. A perfectly placed shot with Mike's .375 H&H secured him the trophy of a lifetime!

As the boom of the rifle echoed down the gorge, two lionesses exploded from a ledge just below us and ran across the riverbed. The trail camera we had set up at the bait would later reveal that the lions had found the bait a few hours after we had placed it there. What's more, the lion Mike shot had selfishly refused to let the females feed on the carcass for ten hours straight.

******

My last safari with Mike was an eighteen-day, double-bull-elephant hunt in our Dande East concession, an area that borders Mozambique. It was an early season hunt that started in April when the bush is at its most beautiful. The pans are full of water, the trees are green, and the Combretum *jesse* bush is still in full leaf. The hunt was to be the basis for the creation of my fourth elephant hunting DVD, entitled "*Giants of the Jesse.*" The DVD was planned to show how stunning, yet challenging, an early season hunt can be when the rainy season is almost over and the Zambezi Valley bush is at its thickest.

Mike and a fantastic Zambezi Valley lion.

As the hunt progressed, we collected some amazing footage, but for several reasons getting an actual kill on tape was eluding us. We tracked and looked at quite a few bulls, but they simply were not big enough. In desperation we ended up following elephants deeper and deeper into unknown territory. Relations in camp were slightly strained as we had by then spent more than two weeks of hard tracking and pussy-footing around the *jesse* that was full of irate elephants.

On the seventeenth day we picked up a twenty-inch track, ten kilometres inside Zimbabwe. The bull was heading due east, and three hours later I figured that the bull was somewhere near the border between Zimbabwe and Mozambique. The border cutline had been made in the 1960s, and as one can imagine, with regrowth from nearly six decades, the cutline is barely recognizable today. To make a long story short, several hours later I called a stop to the hunt and told Mike that if the bull continued in an easterly direction, we would have no option but to turn round and abandon the search. As luck would have it, the bull did a semicircle and started back toward known territory! Several hours later and in fading light, we

Mike and his hard-earned elephant bull.

finally caught up with the bull. After an exciting and concentrated stalk, we managed to shoot him. He was a beautiful forty-eight-pound tusker.

With darkness descending, our picture session was quick. We were in "unfamiliar country," so we set off at a rapid pace. Even so, we still had to walk the last five kilometres in the dark. Trying to navigate through thick flame thornbush *(Acacia ataxacantha)* with the aid of a light from a nonfunctional GPS and then running into a herd of irate elephant cows at close quarters was an experience not recommended for the faint-hearted.

On returning to camp, I instructed Bongi, our camp manager, to recover the elephant carcass the next day. I explained to him that the bull was possibly in "hostile territory" and that I wanted a rapid and quiet recovery. Cell phones had only recently appeared in the valley, and someone from the camp sent a message to a villager telling him that if he followed the tractor the next morning, he was sure to get some leftover meat after the recovery.

Bush telegraph is an amazing and well-known method of African communication, and by the end of the next day what we thought had been a hushed-up recovery turned out to be a free-for-all, with about two hundred Zimbabwean villagers marching behind the tractor deep into the unknown.

As for Mike and me, it was day eighteen, the last day of our hunt. We picked up a large elephant track on the border and followed it, amazingly, along the same route that we'd taken the previous day. When we were only two kilometres from where Mike had shot his elephant the previous day, we received a garbled and distorted message from Bongi on the radio: "Elephant and poachers!" were the only discernible words we heard.

Alarmed by the turn of events, I told Mike we had no option but to abandon the tracks we were following and hightail it to the carcass to see what was going on. Thirty minutes of fast walking got us to the dead elephant where Bongi and his entourage were patiently waiting. Evidently a group of poachers had found the carcass and were in the process of removing the ivory when they were disturbed by Bongi's arrival. The sight of two hundred excited villagers must have put the fear of God into them, and they abandoned their devious operation and fled the scene.

Another ten minutes was all they would have needed to remove the precious tusks. Had the poachers been successful, I would have been in an awkward position as I would have had to report the stolen ivory to the police, and they would have wanted to come to see the site of the robbery! Since then everyone now has a GPS and the boundary is quite clear!

From my perspective, it has been nothing but a pleasure and an honour to have shared the many campfires and cigars I have had with Mike. I look forward to many more such occasions!

KELLY GILL

CHAPTER TWENTY-NINE

Kelly Gill is another client who became a good friend and business associate; in fact, Kelly helped me redefine the method I use to hunt elephants. We started hunting together about twelve years ago when he booked a hunt that included two tuskless elephants. The hunt took place in the rugged but beautiful Chete Safari Area.

Kelly, a lawyer by profession, had hunted a lot with Mark Sullivan. Mark is a contentious character and well known for the aggressive and controversial style of hunting he portrays in his DVDs. Having met but not hunted with Mark, I can honestly say he's an amiable and very nice person and quite different from the arrogant character he portrays in his videos.

That Mark and Kelly had often hunted together was clearly evident by Mark's aggressive influence upon Kelly. When I chatted to him about our forthcoming Chete hunt, I asked him what his expectations were. His reply was simple and to the point: He wanted close and personal experiences with as many elephants as possible.

Luckily, this is what he got. On our first hunt together, he killed two tuskless cows with frontal-brain shots, taken from a distance of no less than fifteen yards. To add to the drama of the occasion, another tuskless elephant charged us, and Kelly successfully dropped her a few feet from where we were standing. That's three tuskless cows at one go.

Our cameraman, Ryan, was filming the hunt, and at the precise moment the third cow attacked, he suddenly felt a sharp pain on his ankle. Too busy to look, he subconsciously imagined he had been bitten by a snake. After the excitement was over and the elephant confirmed dead, Ryan looked down and saw a set of puncture marks on his ankle.

This confirmed his worst suspicion: He had, indeed, been bitten by a snake. With visions of a slow and painful death, he lay down on the

Kelly and myself with a tuskless elephant that charged, Chete.

Kelly and I tracking after an elephant.

Kelly and a problem elephant bull from the Omay Reserve.

ground as pale as a sheet, waiting for the worst to happen. Half an hour later and with none of the symptoms of snake venom apparent, we got Ryan back on his feet and slowly traced his footsteps back to a "wait-a-bit" thorn tree. There, much to our amusement and to Ryan's great relief, we found traces of his blood on the tips of two thorns!

******

Kelly returned annually after that, and together we have successfully hunted and shot over twenty elephants, all of which were taken with frontal-brain shots at close range. We have faced several charges together, so I can honestly say that under stressful circumstances, there is no one I would rather have at my side than Kelly Gill. He is as calm as any man I've ever known in a dangerous situation, yet he clearly loves every second of the hunt!

I have also yet to meet a man with Kelly's tolerance to pain. Kelly played college football, and being a brutal sport, he suffered numerous injuries. Apart from having severe arthritis, he's had his spine fused in several places and on one occasion had therapy on his forefinger to help him pull a trigger! Before one of our hunts, Kelly fell off a horse and broke the head off his femur. Three months later, after a successful hip transplant, the two of us were back hunting elephants together.

In spite of his determined approach to hunting, Kelly is very laid-back and never puts me under undue pressure. Our efforts always seemed to fall in place, and we have shared many an elephant adventure together with only a single thought in mind: to get ever closer to our target. It is a practice I continue to this day.

Kelly introduced Lori, his girlfriend, to elephant hunting. She is now his wife. No exception was ever made to our hunting technique simply because we had a woman in our midst. Lori loved every minute of the hunt, and in due course brought her daughter, Eastern, on safari as well. They are two wonderful human beings who love life to the full and it is only a pleasure to have been in their company.

On our last safari, Kelly booked two elephants and a first buffalo for Lori. We were successful with the elephants, and that left ample time to find Lori's buffalo. I was confident there wouldn't be a problem.

Lori and Eastern with Lori's birthday impala.

The following seven days saw us from sunup to sundown chasing *dagga* boys in and out the *jesse* bush, sometimes without even stopping to eat. Blisters, cuts, and stings did not stop their smiles or determination, but in the end through no lack of effort on anyone's part, we failed to bag a buffalo. It was and still is my only failed buffalo hunt, and I felt dreadful about it.

As I said to Lori when the hunt was over, the only thing she did differently from any of the other successful hunters we'd had was that she had "walked farther, tried harder, and smiled more"! To top it off, she looked a great deal more beautiful than any of our other clients while doing so! Lori did get a "birthday impala," though, as a consolation!

I always look forward to seeing Kelly, Lori, and Eastern in Dallas at the hunting convention every year, and I know for sure that Kelly and I have still a few more elephants to take and that somewhere out in the *jesse* bush there's an old *dagga* boy just waiting for Lori. Let's hope all this happens in the not-too-distant future.

MARTY AND SUE VICK

CHAPTER THIRTY

Marty Vick is an anesthetist from North Dakota and, like me, is addicted to elephant hunting. Indeed, he is so addicted that in spite of his age, he says he has to keep working just to feed the addiction! Marty has an understanding wife named Sue who accompanies him on his adventures in Darkest Africa. Although Sue does not participate in the actual hunt, she has, nevertheless, become an important part of our team and is a close confidant of Eddy, my driver.

I have hunted with hundreds of clients over the years, and I can honestly say there is only a handful with whom I feel socially inadequate. Marty is one of those few. He would be horrified to hear me talking like this, for he is one of those people who go out of his way to communicate with everyone, no matter his or her social standing. Nor would he intentionally make anyone feel inadequate. The thing is that there are times when Marty is simply on a different level intellectually from the rest of us. Added to these attributes is his wonderful sense of humour; Marty has kept us entertained for many years.

Marty and Sue's first safari with me was in the Makuti area where he had booked a double tuskless elephant hunt. The hunt proved successful in that he shot two of the oldest tuskless elephants I have come across in my career. It is customary for us to give an age for each elephant that is shot, and in this case, one of them we estimated to be sixty-two years old. So great was the influence of this hunt upon Marty that he became hooked, and his passion for elephant hunting now supersedes the hunting of any other species.

Over the years I have shared many hunting adventures with Marty and Sue, but three hunts stand out above all. Having completed several tuskless elephant hunts, Marty's natural progression was to shoot the ultimate trophy animal, a bull elephant. As a result, he booked a hunt in our Dande East area, which borders Mozambique. It so happened we had recently sighted

Marty and his first elephant bull, Dande East.

several particularly fine-looking bulls. However, it should be mentioned here that this was a few years before poachers literally annihilated every bull elephant east of our border.

We tracked several bulls, all of which we passed on because they were either too young or they possessed inferior ivory. One morning we decided to walk through a massive block of *jesse* bush that was along the Mozambique border. As I said earlier, the border had been demarcated during the Rhodesian days, but in the ensuing years encroachment by ever-spreading bush had eliminated the demarcation line totally. By the time of our hunt, it was impossible to make out the old cut line boundary; added to this, I had an unreliable GPS tracking system at the time.

We meandered our way through unusually thick *jesse* bush, which, in this case, included the terrible ataxacantha bush. Ataxacantha can best be compared to a rose bush on steroids. Its huge black thorns rip through skin and cloth with equal ease, so the only way to progress through the impenetrable jungle is along the numerous elephant paths that meander back and forth through the thicket. Deviate off these paths at your peril! Amazingly enough, elephants love ataxacantha, and they feed on these bushes by ripping off the thorn-laden branches and stuffing them, with no obvious discomfort, in their mouths.

After a few hours of meandering along the paths, we heard sounds that indicated there were two elephants ahead of us. The wind was in our favour, so very cautiously we progressed toward them. The fact that it sounded like two animals suggested they were bulls. This boosted our adrenaline levels by a notch or two because it is in areas like these huge blocks of *jesse* that there is always an off-chance the elephants within may not have been hunted commercially for many years. I'm somewhat of a romantic, and it has always been my secret hope that hidden somewhere within these secluded strongholds is an elusive one-hundred-pound tusker that has managed to escape persecution from hunter and poacher alike.

It was early in the season, so the *jesse* bush was unbelievably thick, and visibility was down to a few metres on the narrow path we were on. As luck would have it, there suddenly appeared in front of us what could only have been an old logging road. Although the road was overgrown with shrub, it was certainly a great deal more open than the track we'd been on, making it much easier to approach the feeding elephants. However, at the back of my mind was the distinct possibility the logging road was, in fact, north of our border. Be that as it may, there were bull elephants in front of us, and for me there was no looking back.

Edging our way down the overgrown road, we suddenly saw an elephant tail full of hairs sticking out of the bush. My first impression was one of disappointment because the hairs meant the animal was mature but not the old chap we were expecting. This is exactly as it turned out, for when he turned, we got a brief glimpse of a tusk that looked to be in the thirty-pound category. Our focus quickly turned to the second bull. We could hear him feeding a few metres on the right side of the first one, but try as we might, we simply could not see his ivory, so thick was the *jesse* bush.

Suddenly, we felt a cool wind tickling the back of our necks. The feeding stopped immediately as the two bulls picked up the dreaded smell of their human adversary. A few seconds and an eternity later, the inevitable happened and the bulls turned and stampeded away. Not knowing exactly where we were standing, both bulls crossed the logging road scarcely several metres in front of us. The sight of them will remain imprinted in my mind forever. Barely metres away was a massive bull elephant with long, thick, dark tusks that looked in the eighty-pound category, something unheard of in today's Zambezi Valley. Here was the animal of every elephant hunter's dreams.

After the shock of seeing such a huge elephant so close, we were galvanized into action. Suddenly, there was a renewed energy and excitement in the team, and we quickly picked up the tracks and set off after the fleeing animals. Tracking was initially difficult as the ground was littered with a layer of thick leaves, but after a while we cut across a narrow, dry riverbed, and I was dismayed to see in the sand that the track we were following was not more than eighteen inches across. I was certain that this could not be from the huge elephant we were chasing.

I immediately halted the trackers, thinking they must have deviated onto the spoor of the young bull. Much to their obvious disgust, I had them backtrack to the original spot where we had commenced the follow-up. Yet, there it was, the very same track, imprinted quite clearly on the ground. How on earth could a bull of those massive proportions have such a mundane little track? Was this the reason previous hunters had let him slip by? Whatever their reasons, we knew this was most definitely a bull elephant worth shooting. A hurried team talk ensued. So desperate was I to bag this animal that I promised both trackers a motorcycle each if we were successful.

Unfortunately, the bull continued to flee farther and farther north, ever deeper into hostile territory, crossing the paths of several other bull elephants and a few family herds on the way. His unimpressive tracks were our ultimate demise, for they continually mingled with those of other elephants in the area, and try as we might, we eventually lost him. Downhearted and exhausted from the long chase, we now faced a several-hour "death march" all the way back to the vehicle.

At first light the next morning we made our way back to the place we had lost the spoor, hoping the hunting gods would give us a break and get us back on the tracks of this grand old bull once again. It was not to be. We did, however, come across several other elephants, and as time was not on our side, we decided to shoot a fair-size bull that we had spotted in some very thick cover.

In actual fact, we had very little choice anyway, for the bull broke out of the undergrowth and came charging toward us. I gave Marty the go-ahead, and a frontal-brain shot brought the elephant down about seven yards from where we were standing. Although this was certainly not the bull of our dreams, he was still a fine animal. . . and one that would also always remind us of the exciting adventure we had had with a monster bull that got the better of us in the end.

Two years later found us on another bull-elephant hunt, this time in the Dande North area. In the interim, the U.S. Fish and Wildlife Service had imposed a total ban on the importation of ivory into the United States. This ruling directly affected our antipoaching efforts and, as a result, has increased the overall poaching of elephants. That, however, is another story. Since Marty had already booked his hunt before the ban was imposed, he was in somewhat of a dilemma as to whether he should continue, knowing full well he would be unable to import his trophies back into the States.

For Marty there was a lot of soul searching to be done, but in the end he came to the conclusion that the experience of the hunt was more important to him than the trophy itself. As a result, he did not cancel but continued as planned. To me this proved that Marty was, indeed, a true hunter, and over subsequent years he has been handsomely repaid with some amazing elephant experiences.

The hunt proved to be action packed. One morning as we approached a herd of elephants with a few bulls amongst them, we noticed a tuskless cow that kept looking back at us, an action I associate with trouble. So I told Marty to keep an eye on her because I really didn't like what I was seeing. Sure enough, moments later she suddenly turned and came at us in a headlong charge. True to form, Marty calmly raised his rifle and dropped her, not five yards from where we were standing.

The next day we followed three bulls that were close to some villages. One of the bulls had an amazing twenty-two-inch spoor, a monster track for a Zambezi Valley elephant. Several hours later we caught up to them, but, unfortunately, luck was against us, for just as we started our final approach, the bulls caught our wind and ran off. We did, however, get a good sighting.

Marty was calm and collected when facing a cow charge at close quarters.

The result of a well-placed 500-grain solid.

Two of them were quite young and the other was our bull with the huge spoor. Just as he turned to go, we got a glimpse of a single, long, thick, beautiful tusk . . . but nothing on the other side. At that, we called for a water break and a team talk ensued. Marty said he would be over the moon with this huge old elephant despite it only having one tusk. So the hunt was back on. We continued tracking for a couple of hours, but with darkness approaching, we had no option but to call a halt and begin the long trek back to the Land Cruiser.

That evening we got together with the trackers and asked them where they thought the bulls were going. They unanimously agreed that the elephants would be raiding crops in a nearby village that evening. First light saw us driving slowly down a dirt track parallel to the village, and, sure enough, it wasn't long before we spotted the spoor crossing the road just ahead of us. I was keen to follow the spoor, but the trackers, being as good as they are, recommended we continue in our vehicle a few kilometres farther down the road to see if, after their crop raiding, the bulls hadn't recrossed the road on their way back into the *jesse* bush. Sure enough that is exactly what they had done.

Tracking commenced immediately. It was clear the bulls were moving fast, putting distance between themselves and their destructive handiwork of the previous night. Eventually they slackened their pace and began to meander through the thicket. That's when we knew they were close.

In the interim they had been spending a lot of time gorging on the yellow fruit of the marula trees, and as we made our way slowly forward, we heard an unusual and confusing sound. As the wind was in our favour, we slowly approached the noise . . . and were confronted with the most amazing sight: There, right in front of us, lying flat on the ground were all three elephants fast asleep. Our chosen bull was snoring away, oblivious to our presence. It would appear the marula plums had had a soporific effect, for all three were down for the count.

We were in a quandary. It is against all principles of fairness to shoot any sleeping animal, let alone an elephant. So what we decided was to try to get closer. The bush was very thick, so we managed to get within ten yards of them. It seemed like ages while we sat there waiting for something to happen, but eventually the bulls sensed our presence. Up they jumped at the same time. It is incredible how such a massive animal can stand up so quickly and without making a sound.

It was the moment of truth. After two solid days of tracking the same bull, here he was, offering Marty a perfect side-brain shot. Marty raised his rifle and pulled off the shot to perfection. Thus ended the life of a magnificent old elephant bull, a bull that we had hunted ethically on foot and killed humanely with a perfect brain shot. This remains one of my all-time favourite elephant hunts.

******

The following year saw Marty seeking a hunt in which Sue would be more involved. As I previously said, Sue does not herself hunt, but she does support Marty's addiction without complaint; consequently, she has spent countless hours sitting in the Land Cruiser while we were out tracking.

As a result, we decided on an unusual hunt that would incorporate Sue's passion for fishing. To that end, we booked a tuskless elephant and dry-land hippo hunt in our new Charara area on the banks of Lake Kariba. The hunt was to be divided into two parts: The first part would be from a basic fly camp in the hills where we would pursue the tuskless elephant. In the second part of the hunt we would use a houseboat, thus making our camp mobile. The houseboat would allow us to hunt the hippo and, we hoped, have some great fishing as well.

I always enjoyed the fly camp very much as it was remote and wild. Each tent had an en suite flush toilet and pull-up shower. Unfortunately, it was winter, which is our dry season, so countless bees and other insects were attracted to the moisture in the toilets. On arriving in camp, I showed Marty and Sue their quarters, and I left them to settle in.

A short while later Marty appeared, and he had a problem. Now, Marty is certainly not one to complain, but this time he certainly had grounds, for when he went into the bathroom, he had been greeted to a toilet full of bees. A problem indeed! The mere thought of sitting on a toilet seat with a hive of bees buzzing beneath is enough reason to give anyone constipation. Eventually we found a solution. We wrapped the

Marty and his big single tusker after two days of tracking.

toilets in black plastic during the day and we removed the covering in the evening after the bees had returned to their hives. Relative safety for ablution purposes was finally restored.

The tuskless elephant hunt proved successful. We tracked and looked at well over a hundred elephants before finding an old tuskless cow that Marty brain shot perfectly. After that, it was on to the hippo hunt. Marty really was looking forward to this part of the safari. He had specified that he wanted to hunt a hippo on dry land, which is considerably more challenging and exciting than shooting them in water. Earlier in the season I had seen an old bull in a pan about two kilometres from the lake, so that seemed the obvious place to start searching.

We arrived early in the morning to find the pan deserted. A careful search around the pan's perimeter revealed a hippo's tracks heading away from the pan. We determined that if we could hold to the tracks, we would

We tracked and shot Marty's big hippo bull in the jesse.

catch up to him in another pan or, better still, somewhere in the belt of *jesse* bush we could see in the distance.

The follow-up was very slow since there were countless tracks from the many hippos that had left the lake to feed inland during the night. My trackers, Nyati and Criton, established that the hippo we were tracking had a distinct scar on his left back foot. That enabled these highly skilled trackers to identify him from the multitude of other tracks. It was an amazing exhibition of tracking from two experts in the field.

A few hours later Nyati spotted the old bull asleep in the *jesse* just ahead of us. Very cautiously we crept forward and got within fifty yards of the hippo before it realized we were there. With a loud grunt it got up and began to move off, and Marty dropped the huge beast with a perfect brain shot. This was the ultimate dry-land hippo hunt, thanks mainly to the skill of Nyati and Criton, both trackers supreme.

The remainder of the hunt we dedicated to Sue. We explored the wonderful eastern basin of Lake Kariba, moving every other night to a new and exciting location in and around the Matusadona National Park. The game viewing and fishing were amazing. Sue managed to catch several huge catfish called vundu, and one evening in the Sanyati Gorge she lost a vundu of mega proportions that could well have been a new national record! Like Marty, Sue now has an addiction, albeit a lot more affordable one than Marty's . . . an addiction to vundu fishing!

Marty and Sue and I have had lots of adventures together, including taking a magnificent leopard that Marty shot on the last day of a combined elephant and leopard hunt. In discussing future adventures and where we would go next, Marty proclaimed that I was now his "elephant consultant." So, I have proposed a new elephant area for our next hunt, and we will dedicate the back end of the hunt to Sue in her quest to catch a monster vundu.

Sue and one of her vundus from Lake Kariba, 2016.

Marty and his last-day leopard.

Being a professional hunter has its disadvantages as well as its advantages. Marty and Sue are definitely one of the benefits I have found in my life as a professional hunter, for not only are they fine clients, but they are also great friends. I look forward to our continued safaris together.

ROB JOLLY

CHAPTER THIRTY-ONE

Joker, hunter, and storyteller extraordinaire best describes Rob Jolly. Coming from the East End of London, Rob, with his Cockney accent, certainly gives the impression of being more at home in a Sussex pub rather than shooting, dining, and hobnobbing with the stiff-lipped English upper class. Thanks to his wit, character, and shooting ability, Rob has been able to infiltrate the normally closed-door society of snobbish bird shooters to become a much-sought-after guest.

Not only does Rob enjoy his bird shooting and fishing, but he also loves big-game hunting. He has been on several safaris with me, and together we have hunted buffalo, lion, leopard, and a number of elephants. For him it's about the experience rather than the killing. "Fair chase" is always a top priority for Rob, and his ethics makes him the most principled hunter I have ever had the pleasure to guide. No matter what the hunt or its outcome, Rob makes sure he enjoys the experience by having a lot of fun along the way.

On one of our hunts together we were looking for a bull elephant. We tracked several before picking up the tracks of a suitable bull. The spoor revealed the elephant was dragging one of his back legs. Deep gouge marks in the sand made tracking easy, and it was not long before we caught up with the bull. Close inspection revealed a broken rear leg. Unfortunately, the injured animal only had a single tusk that looked like it weighed around fifty pounds.

We watched the bull for quite a while, fascinated at his ability to feed without putting undue pressure on his injured hind leg. What a sad plight this was for such a magnificent beast. With several days still to go and a good chance of finding a more suitable animal, we turned him down and walked back to the truck.

Rob said his conscience would bother him if he didn't shoot the one-tusk bull so as to prevent a slow and painful death, Dande.

Rob was silent on the way back, and I could see that the experience of watching an injured bull in so much pain was bothering him. I was, therefore, not in the least surprised when, upon arriving back at the Land Cruiser, Rob said it was only right that we should return and take the elephant as his trophy. He said his conscience would bother him for the rest of the hunt if he didn't. He knew the right thing to do was to shoot the bull so as to prevent a slow and painful death.

We turned around, went back to where we had left the bull, and Rob shot the injured animal. His tusk weighed fifty pounds, and his back leg was, indeed, broken, the result of several AK-47 bullets. This incident sums up Rob to perfection. We still had several days to hunt and could have tracked many more bulls with the possibility of finding a better trophy, but Rob's moral compass and ethics would not allow him to do so. For this he gained my utmost respect.

Besides being a great hunter, Rob is also a fun-loving person and the ultimate practical joker. Having been on the receiving end of many of his jokes means I'm always on high alert. Thus, what someone would normally view with complete innocence, I, more often than not, view with suspicion! Despite this, the last place I expected to be on the receiving end of Rob's wicked sense of humour occurred on a different continent.

We were attending one of our annual hunting conventions in Las Vegas. These shows always keep us busy, for we spend endless hours chatting and giving advice to a number of potential clients every day. Whilst there are those who can be called potential clients, there are others who visit our booth out of curiosity. At the risk of being called snobbish, where business is involved, one has to make decisions between those who are genuinely interested and those who are not. We refer to the latter as "tire kickers"!

Invariably this type of show attracts a conglomeration of weird and wonderful people, and it was there that I saw the astonishing sight of a bizarre-looking man hobbling down the alley toward us with the aid of a walking stick. I secretly hoped he wasn't headed for our booth as he looked a most unlikely customer. Grossly overweight, balding, and shockingly dressed, the apparition wore the thickest glasses I had ever seen, so much so that they exaggerated the size of his eyes, making them look like silver-dollar coins. As if that wasn't enough, he had badly stained buckteeth and at least three days of hairy stubble on his cheeks. Sure enough, as I stood mesmerized at the sight, he walked straight toward our booth. When Myles saw him coming, he conveniently wandered off, leaving me to contend with the apparition.

The first thing this weird-looking character did was to invade my private space by standing no less than a foot away from me. He said he wanted to hunt elephants, but, unfortunately, Ivan Carter, a well-known elephant hunter, was fully booked, so he had come to see "Baas Charlton." (This is the way most Africans refer to me.) I couldn't believe my eyes, and suspected a joke, but he appeared to be dead serious.

By this time, a crowd had gathered around our booth, drawn by the amusing and fascinating spectacle. Whenever I took a step backward to get to a more comfortable talking distance, the apparition would take a step forward! Trying to persuade the fat fellow that he wouldn't be up to

Rob, the ultimate practical joker, in disguise.

chasing elephants in the *jesse* bush would be a waste of my time. It was only after several minutes of haggling that I noticed a badly positioned microphone on his oversized waistcoat, and I realized then that I'd been well and truly tricked.

Once he realized the game was up, Rob took out the false teeth and removed the glasses and the pillow stuffed under his waistcoat. Much to the hilarity of all the clients who knew me, Rob had filmed the entire episode for their entertainment. The fact that Rob was prepared to travel halfway across the world not only to attend Safari Club International's convention but also to play a practical joke on me sums up Rob's wicked sense of humour perfectly.

There were two beautiful girls situated in our aisle who were selling calendars with pictures of themselves in scantily dressed outfits. The girls normally targeted older men, but when Rob in his convincing disguise approached them showing an interest in their product, both girls had turned tail and fled!

My team, including Justin the cameraman, and I had often been on the receiving end of Rob's pranks, and after several safaris we finally figured out a plan to get even with him. The plan involved Boris, as we affectionately called a fully mounted shabby old hyena. We hatched a plan to have our camp manager secretly put Boris in the riverbed close to one of the crossings, and when the following morning we conveniently went that way, we would have Rob "shoot" Boris. The fact that Rob genuinely wanted a hyena trophy only added to the fun.

Everyone except Rob was in on the plan, and next morning we duly set off in the Land Cruiser with the trackers and Justin, who was filming the hunt, seated on the back of the vehicle while Rob rode up front with me in the Land Cruiser's cab. As we crossed the chosen river, suddenly we heard great excitement and much banging on the roof.

"Bere! Bere!" yelled the trackers.

I slammed on the brakes, and Rob, who was fully aware that *bere* is the Shona word for hyena, leapt out the vehicle and grabbed his rifle that one of the trackers had conveniently removed from its case. Rob dashed around to the side of the Land Cruiser, and there before him, in the soft, early morning light, standing in the middle of the dry riverbed, was the trophy he so desperately wanted.

The rifle came into his shoulder and he fired. Much to his surprise the hyena just stood there, looking blankly at him. Thinking he had missed, Rob cranked another round into the chamber and whacked it again. For yet another moment, Boris and Rob stood staring at each other until the penny finally dropped. Turning around, Rob looked at us for a moment.

"You buggers!" he said with a sheepish smile on his face

We had finally got one back on Rob, but I'm sorry to say the stakes are still heavily stacked in his favour.

******

"Boris" has since been the object of many hilarious and practical jokes played on a number of my clients. Ike, my great Japanese client, shot him several times. "It's not running away, and it still has a bone in its mouth!"

It was pay-back time for Rob, who is shown here with "Boris."

Ike shouted in amazement. At that point he handed the rifle to his wife and told her to have a go.

Boris also beautifully entrapped Hilly, a huge, burly Australian client who worked in the mines and whose every second word was a curse. At the time Hilly was sharing our camp with a few other clients. We were all sitting at the breakfast table at first light when Hilly arrived looking a little under the weather. This was not surprising since he had consumed a dozen beers, several glasses of wine, and the entire contents of a bottle of Crown Royal the previous evening! Just as he was about to sit down, Pete, his professional hunter, jumped up and pointed down the river.

"Hyena, hyena," he thundered excitedly.

Like a madman, Hilly bolted to his room, grabbed his rifle, and sprinted back to the dining area. Amazed to see the hyena still standing there, he then proceeded to let fly with three rounds. Having missed all three times, he cursed all the way back to his room where he quickly grabbed more ammunition and then, returning, let fly another two rounds. One of the shots "scoped" him badly in the eye, which left him with blood pouring down his face. The language that ensued was unbelievable. My own client, Mike, told Hilly that he thought the hyena must have died leaning against the tree. Hilly's response was to proceed to shoot it again amidst a further bout of cursing.

At this point all those present were beside themselves with laughter, but at the same time, they were keeping a respectable distance from Hilly! At the end of the day, the only one who didn't see the humorous side of things was poor Boris. With a leg blown off, he certainly looked bedraggled and very much the worse for wear. As a result, he has since been retired.

******

Another amusing incident with Rob occurred when we were tracking a lion and using microphones for the first time. Our intention was to use these microphones to improve the audio and, thus, enhance the quality of the film. Previously the quality of the audio system had been poor, making dialogue between professional hunter and client almost inaudible. The new system has proved most effective.

Rob with a stunning Zambezi Valley elephant bull.

On that occasion we were tracking several lions and eventually caught up with them in thick cover. This resulted in getting charged a few times by an irate lioness. Unfortunately, there was not a shootable lion amongst the pride, so we left them and returned to the road. When we arrived there, nature called, so I grabbed a toilet roll, excused myself, and went out of sight behind a bush.

Having completed the task, I returned to the road to see Rob and Justin, my cameraman, looking at me with smug grins on their faces. I realized straightaway that I had forgotten to turn off the microphone before taking the "veltie," as it is called. So now they had an audio of the grunting and groaning such activity entails, and to make matters worse they took great pleasure in playing it to Kirsty when we got back to the office.

While on the subject of lavatory humor, another embarrassing incident happened to me on a previous elephant hunt with Rob and his charming wife, Theresa. On that occasion we had been tracking an elephant bull for several hours, and having lost its tracks, I asked Rob, Theresa, and Justin to wait in the shade of a baobab tree until the trackers had picked up the spoor. Nature called again, so with the loo roll in hand, I found a convenient anthill in the opposite direction from where the elephant bull had been heading.

I assumed that when tracking was resumed, my choice of a suitable toilet would be safely left behind. Ten minutes later the trackers returned to say that they had found the spoor, so off we set once more. To my horror the bull had done a U-turn and was slowly heading back from whence he had come. His tracks were angling straight toward the anthill! I was praying that the tracks would turn, but instead they continued on the same path. Then, very much to my embarrassment and alarm, Theresa stopped when we were a few metres away from the spot where I had taken my "veltie"!

"Oh, darling, look at those beautiful white flowers on the anthill," she called out to Rob.

It was at that point when both Justin and Rob realized the white flowers were pieces of toilet paper, and for the next hour they could not stop sniggering at me and passing sarcastic remarks my way.

******

Like so many of his countrymen, Rob had pale, sensitive skin, and tsetse flies were a particular torment for him. Whenever they bit him, he developed huge welts. As a result, we always drove with the Land Cruiser's air conditioning unit turned on and the windows rolled up. One time we were hunting leopard, which involves a lot of driving to check on baits. The combination of vehicle movement, carbon monoxide from the exhaust pipe, and the odour of rotten meat in the back of the Land Cruiser acts like a magnet to tsetse flies.

On that day, Rob and I were comfortably seated in the front, and much to our amusement we saw clouds of tsetse flies following us and unrelentingly biting the trackers and Justin, who were all in the back. After several

Rob in action in Chewore South.

days of enduring the tsetse flies and Rob's sarcastic comments, Eddy, my driver, decided enough was enough. He wanted to get even. Unbeknown to us, Eddy found a particularly rotten piece of impala stomach in the gut bucket, rolled it up in toilet paper, and placed it under Rob's seat before we set off to check baits that morning.

We got into the Land Cruiser, wound up the windows, and put on the air conditioner. That's all it took. After several minutes of breathing noxious air, I asked Rob if he had passed gas as there was a bad smell floating around the cab. Rob denied it and blamed me! Well, the day proved to be long and smelly! At the end of it, I was convinced that Rob had a bowel issue. When we got back to camp, Eddy, with much glee, revealed his little parcel under Rob's seat! The great thing about Rob was that he could take as much as he handed out when it came to practical jokes.

Rob is also generous to the extreme. On one of his hunts for an elephant bull and a buffalo, he invited Des to hunt the buffalo at his expense. Des was a charming old guy and a deerstalker in Scotland, and Rob employed him as a loader during the grouse season. It goes without saying that Des could never afford the trip to Africa let alone the price of a buffalo hunt.

At the end of a long hard day, Des finally got his buffalo, and I instructed them to wait at the kill while I went to collect the Cruiser. As I walked away, Rob looked up at the sky and asked if I thought it would rain. It being the middle of the dry season, I laughed and said that if it rained, I would give him a free lion. An hour later I arrived back at the carcass, and as I did so some very large raindrops began to fall. As I got closer, I could hear Rob and Des and the trackers singing, "It's raining lions; it's raining lions."

Hunting with Rob and Theresa has been a pleasure and an honor. Rob is a principled hunter and gentleman who never once has put me under pressure with regards to collecting trophies. He would say to me: "Stop stressing, Buzz. It will happen when it's supposed to, and if it doesn't, well, that's hunting, but I've still had an awesome time." Another of his sayings was, "Over a black bush whiskey and a beer chaser," which he said so often that it became a tradition of ours whenever we returned to camp.

What a pleasure it has been to hunt with such a fun, ethical character.

FAMILY HUNTS

CHAPTER THIRTY-TWO

MELANIE'S HUNT

I've always enjoyed guiding father-and-youngster-combination hunts, regardless if the youngster is a son or daughter. It's a great pleasure to see a father sharing unique and personal moments with his kids, special moments that a safari in a remote area can offer. Such unique and often dangerous situations elicit a protective aspect and an increased awareness of the responsibility that a father should feel for his child. Without pressure from the outside world, a child and the father tend to bond strongly, a relationship that is both honest and pure. As an outsider, to observe this bonding process has been a rare privilege, and there have often been times when I've been privileged to participate and share in such unique experiences. As a father of Zoe and Jess, my two young daughters, it is my sincere hope that I, too, will one day get to share such special moments with them.

After I became a qualified professional hunter, I guided Udo and his daughter Melanie on a leopard and buffalo hunt in the Dande North Safari Area. Udo must have been in his early fifties at the time and Melanie in her late twenties. Nicer people you could not have wished to meet.

Udo had chosen to hunt a leopard while Melanie was to shoot her first buffalo. She would also shoot whatever plains-game animals were needed to use as bait for the leopard. Udo was more than content with his part of the bag, preferring instead to accompany his daughter and share the special moments the hunt would create for her.

The hunt had its ups and downs. It started very well for Melanie, who proved to be an above-average shot. By the end of the first day we had several baits hung in a few of my favourite spots. The following morning we decided to hunt buffalo while checking the baits at the same time. Priority was given to the baits as there was no shortage of buffaloes in the area, and time was on our side.

It is important to check leopard and lion baits daily. Should a big cat be feeding on bait that hasn't been checked regularly, only a pile of gnawed bones will be found without any sign of the cat when it is finally checked. In Udo's case it was evident a good-size tom had hit the third bait, an impala carcass that we'd suspended from the lower branch of a fig tree. The tree was situated on the bank of a sandy riverbed that skirted a combination of low hills and rocky outcrops.

The rocky outcrops in the area were inhabited by klipspringers and a large population of rock rabbits, more commonly known as dassies, a favourite food of the leopard. This particular spot had become one of my most productive leopard locations. Indeed, the tree from which the impala carcass was hung had already yielded several fine trophies over the years, so much so that the trunk was heavily scarred from the numerous leopards that had clawed their way up to feed upon the free meals that we'd offered.

Udo and his leopard.

Having erected the blind, we left the area and found a shady spot several miles from the bait where we settled down to enjoy a picnic lunch. After the break, we returned to the blind around 3 P.M. that afternoon. We had only just settled in when suddenly a large leopard appeared as if from nowhere. In what can only be described as the epitome of feline grace, the big tom climbed effortlessly up the tree where it proceeded to carefully survey the area beneath him before commencing its meal.

It is difficult to explain to the uninitiated what an incredible and magnificent sight it is to behold a leopard taking the bait under such circumstances. They are visions of awe-inspiring raw nature as its best. Nothing compares to the breathtaking beauty of a leopard in its natural environment, especially when viewed from less than thirty yards away.

Udo's breathing became a series of short stabbing bursts as a thousand possibilities raced through his mind. This sort of reaction is not uncommon when a client views a leopard under these situations for the first time. The silence becomes deafening as adrenaline pumps through the veins, while fully aware that the slightest miscalculation, be it movement or unwanted sound, could result in the immediate disappearance of the trophy, never to be seen again.

Udo's rifle was carefully positioned in front of him, pointing directly at the bait. I laid my hand on his arm to restrain him from the natural temptation of leaning forward and grabbing it. I do this out of habit.

On most occasions there is no rush. When a leopard is already feeding on the bait, he is content, and with a fine meal in front of him, he becomes overconfident. This gives my client enough time to absorb the situation, get his breathing and emotions back to normal, and appreciate the amazing sight. In such situations, the actual shot at a leopard is the easiest a client will make on the whole safari.

A steady rest for both rifle and elbows, at a known shooting distance, and on a perfectly placed broadside target should contribute to a quick killing, yet despite this, there are a high percentage of woundings on leopard hunts. I believe there are two reasons for this. The first factor is the adrenaline coursing through the hunter's body that leads to an unsteady and rushed shot. The second reason is poor light. On most occasions a

Melanie and her "killer" buffalo.

leopard will approach the bait at last light when the visibility is so poor that a client struggles to locate his target in the telescopic sight. Against better judgement, many risk a shot, and this often results in a wounded leopard.

In Udo's situation, however, neither of these factors occurred. The late afternoon light was good, and, having been calmed by my influence, he was able to observe his leopard for a full five minutes before executing a perfect shot. A very happy and well-rewarded Udo secured one of Africa's most prized trophies, a fine male leopard.

The following few days were spent hunting buffalo. Over this time we looked at a number of bulls without finding anything worth taking. To my shame I'm guilty of prolonging the moment. I was getting great pleasure from guiding Melanie and Udo up to a number of buffaloes every day. On the tenth day I decided to get serious about finding a nice *dagga* boy and putting him "in the salt." This saying is derived from the conclusion of a successful hunt where the skins of a trophy are salted so as to preserve them for future taxidermy work.

Our hunt that day took us to some villages in the extreme north of the country near the Zambezi River. Crispen, who is from there, had told me of several old bulls that lived in the thickets along the Manzamtanda River, a watercourse that flowed through the villages. Old buffalo bulls often "retire" to such locations as there is ample food in the old maize fields and vegetable gardens that the womenfolk tend along the riverbank. Life becomes easy for the old *dagga* boys, and they generally coexist with the villagers without making too much of a nuisance of themselves.

In an old maize field we found fresh tracks of four bulls. We followed their spoor into a thicket not far from a collection of motley huts, and to my surprise we unexpectedly bumped into the buffaloes very close to the village. Caught with our trousers well and truly down, we were unable to get into a decent shooting position before they thundered off. They then entered the next patch of thicket, which turned out to be infested with the infamous buffalo-bean creeper.

This creeper is widespread throughout the valley and among thick patches of bush in the escarpment. The buffalo-bean pods are covered by millions of tiny hairs that become airborne when the beans are disturbed. The tiny hairs attach themselves to clothing and naked skin where they cause intense itching and excruciating pain. Buffaloes are tolerant to the beans as their hides are too thick to be affected, which is why they choose to live in such places. Obviously humans do their utmost to avoid areas where the dreaded bean occurs, and this, in turn, gives the buffalo an opportunity to live in comparative peace, away from their much-feared enemy.

We were soon to find out why buffalo beans have such a fearsome reputation. The *dagga* boys we were following had played the game before, so every time we caught up with them, they deliberately led us through yet another clump of the menace. Soon we were scratching, cursing, and rubbing wood ash onto the affected areas. This appeared to be the only way to relieve the pain and itching.

And so the hunt progressed. It was late afternoon when we finally caught up to the bulls. They were standing in the open looking back at us. This time of day is known as the "stupid hour" as buffaloes that have bolted at the sound of a leaf dropping throughout the day seem to lose their paranoia in the evening and placidly present themselves for a decent shot. In our case, this is exactly what happened.

The best of the four bulls stood facing us head on, presenting a frontal chest shot. I have come to dislike this particular shot as it often leads to a wounding. The target area is relatively small, and the shot must penetrate the chest square-on, neither too high nor too low. If the shot is too high, it will result in the bullet passing over the lungs, and, should it miss the spine, the bullet will end up in the guts. Too low a shot, and the bullet passes through the brisket, causing a lot of initial blood loss, but which eventually dries up. Frontal chest shots are often placed a little to the side, and when this happens, the bullet does not enter the chest cavity but travels under the armpit and along the ribcage. These shots are not fatal, and this is where Melanie placed her bullet.

The blast of Melanie's .375 H&H was the signal the protein-starved villagers had been waiting for. They came running from all directions, armed with an assortment of knives and axes in order to be first in the queue for the superior bits of meat. Pandemonium ensued. I shouted at them to get back as we had not even had time to look for blood; I needed to see what we were dealing with.

An overenthusiastic villager came running toward us from about forty yards away when, suddenly, an enraged buffalo emerged from the thicket. In the blink of an eye, the bull was on the man before he even saw it and before I had managed to get off a shot. I can clearly remember seeing the buffalo bowling the villager over, and then retreating a step back before lowering its massive head and crushing the villager with its boss. The crunching sound was audible to everyone as the buffalo's boss smashed into the villager's chest.

Fortunately, the huge animal only charged once before I put in a good shoulder shot. The buffalo hunched up and was slowly trotting away when I fired at it again. This time the old bull keeled over and lay twitching on the ground as the last moments of its life drained away.

We rushed up to the villager who lay moaning on the ground. Amazingly, there were no visible injuries nor was there any blood to be seen, but I suspected, and as time proved me correct, he had sustained massive internal injuries. We made him as comfortable as possible and having radioed Royal, my driver, we drove the wounded man to the local clinic before returning to camp. Understandably, both Melanie and her father were distraught.

There was no doctor at the clinic, and despite me voicing concerns of the possibility of internal injuries, the nurse, who examined the villager, claimed he was all right and only in shock. In retrospect I should have insisted that I drive him to hospital, but being young and inexperienced in medical conditions, I left the clinic and went back to camp. I was later to learn that the villager died during the night from internal hemorrhaging. I never told Melanie or her father, it was a bad enough experience for them. As they had left a generous amount of cash to aid his "recovery," I left it at that.

Melanie and Udo stayed in camp next day while I returned to the scene to carry out the necessary police reports. When the paperwork was completed, I received a request from the family to drop the buffalo carcass off at their village where it would be eaten at the funeral. Strange are the ways of the African. The dead villager had been taking care of his aged mother, so I happily continued to support her for the remaining five years of her life.

Fernando and Fernanditto

In the early days of my professional hunting career, I entertained a number of Spanish clients. I found them a very social and family-orientated people. Unlike Americans, the Spanish prefer hunting with friends or family. Seldom do they hunt alone. I once had a Spanish client by the name of Fernando Leon who came out with his wife and eleven-year-old son Fernanditto.

The plan was for Fernando to hunt a lion, elephant, and buffalo while Fernanditto would try for a leopard and a buffalo. While I enjoy guiding young hunters, I do not agree that they should be hunting dangerous game until they have several safaris under their belts. I believe the professional hunter should have the final say as to whether a juvenile is capable or old enough to hunt a dangerous animal. In this case Fernanditto should have been encouraged to shoot a couple of impalas to be used as bait for his father's lion and leopard. I have found that kids as young as Fernanditto are too young

Fernanditto and his leopard.

to appreciate the enormity of hunting dangerous animals; furthermore, if at eleven you have already shot two of the Big Four, what is there left to aspire to in your hunting career?

Fernanditto's first trophy was a buffalo bull, and to his credit he was remarkably calm and collected. The young boy shot very well with his Blazer .375 H&H, and two days later he shot a beautiful leopard. This was after a failed attempt when his father had snored so loudly that we banned him from the blind the following night.

We had placed lion bait at one of my favourite places called Buffalo Bend, on the Mkanga River. As the name implies, Buffalo Bend is a huge draw for large herds of buffaloes that come down to drink at two permanent springs that feed into the otherwise dry river. While driving toward Buffalo Bend at midday to check the bait, we were surprised to see a pride of lionesses already there. This was unusual, as lions normally rest up during the heat of the day and only come to feed on the bait in the evening. Having seen the tracks of a large lion two kilometres from the bait, we were obviously on high alert.

Suddenly there he was, a magnificent lion standing at the base of a small hill barely one hundred yards from the Land Cruiser. We jumped out of the vehicle and got Fernando onto the tripod, but he was shaking so badly that in spite of the easy shot, I knew no good would come of it, so I made him wait. Casually the lion walked over the crest of the hill and down into a belt of thick riverine bush. We assumed the pride had already been feeding on the bait, so we hurriedly built a makeshift blind on the opposite side of the Mkanga and settled in to wait.

The distance between the bait and blind was approximately sixty yards, a comfortable distance for Fernando to take a shot. By that stage it was early evening. In the distance, we could see my driver, Royal, heading up the hill when the first lioness arrived. Nonchalantly she settled down in the middle of the dry riverbed between the bait and us. Over the next half an hour we were given a grandstand view watching a pride of lions relaxing in the fading light, barely thirty metres away. As the sun began to set, it became obvious that time was quickly running out if we were to get our lion before dark. In that area it is illegal to shoot animals after dark.

The Leon family and my team with their huge lion from Dande.

Suddenly a more alert lioness sensed that there was more to the wall of grass on the opposite side of the river. She locked her large, yellow penetrating eyes upon the blind and stared intently at us. Then, keeping low to the ground and flicking her tail from side to side, she quietly and stealthily began to stalk the blind. When she was only ten paces away from the blind, the lioness veered off to the left and vanished from the limited vision of my shooting hole. The next moment I heard her breathing on my right side no less than a hairsbreadth from the blind.

I was sitting in the middle of the group, with Fernando on the left and his young son on the right. Understandably, the lad's eyes widened with fear and he edged closer to me. The lioness heard the movement and emitted a low rumbling growl, at which point Fernanditto began to cry. It was an extremely tense situation. I was reaching for my radio to call Royal back because I felt the situation was becoming very dangerous when I noticed the other lionesses in the riverbed were also staring at our blind.

Just as I was about to call Royal, there in the last light of day stood the king of the jungle himself, a magnificent lion. It was as though the fading daylight was concentrated on the king himself. He was immense with a beautiful mane, a picture of power and beauty in the last few moments of shooting light. With urgency I whispered to Fernando to shoot, which he did, and well. As the gunshot exploded, the lioness that was still next to us, roared out. This was too much for Fernanditto, and he leapt up from his seat and onto my lap. Thankfully the lioness appeared to get as much of a fright as Fernanditto, and much to my relief she ran away.

As Fernando's bullet ploughed into the lion, it leapt into the air and somersaulted over the bank. Letting out the most reverberating roars, it landed on its back while biting at its hind leg—something lions often do when wounded. After several guttural growls, the king suddenly lay still and it did not move again.

This was the first time I experienced real regret at what we had just done. He had been such a magnificent animal only seconds before, but now he was no longer. For me, most lions lose their magnitude and beauty upon death. The upside was that Fernando had bagged an extraordinarily good-looking specimen. To make the situation better, Fernanditto had stopped crying. When Royal arrived, we loaded the lion onto the Land Cruiser and headed back to camp. To end off what could only be described as an eventful day, Fernando was lucky enough to shoot a hyena on the way back to camp.

A few days later we picked up the spoor of a good elephant bull in the *jesse* bush. We followed the tracks into a narrow gully that continued for some distance before opening out into an area of flat ground. As we emerged from the gully, we saw the bull. He had long, symmetrical tusks, but they were thin. Fernando, who was very overweight and a diabetic to boot, was also not a great walker, but in any case he decided to take the elephant. We were about twenty yards from the bull when it turned and faced us. Fernando went for a frontal brain shot, but he shot too high.

As the bullet ploughed into the elephant's head, it came straight toward us. Whether this was an intentional charge or whether the bull was disorientated and just ran in our direction, I cannot say, but the sight of this huge animal bearing down upon us had its desired effect, for both Fernando and Crispen decided it was time to depart, and with haste the two of them began scampering away up the gully behind us. Before I could lift my rifle to drop the bull, little Fernanditto placed a perfect brain shot into the elephant's head with his .375 Blazer.

Fernando and Fernanditto with their elephant bull.

As soon as the bull collapsed, I turned quickly to see what had happened to Fernando and Crispen. I was presented with a hilarious sight. There they were, in a frantic race between the old and the fat. Unfortunately, both arrived simultaneously at the narrowest part of the gully where they subsequently became jammed together between the two banks, all the while wrestling each other in an attempt to be the first one to get ahead.

We regrouped and were admiring the elephant barely moments after it had straightened its legs (a sure sign of final departure) when Fernanditto turned to me and said impatiently, "We must hurry. I want to shoot sandgrouse."

It was then that I realized the young lad had no concept of what he had just done. He was far too young to appreciate the enormity of the hunt or his actions. It was, indeed, a sad moment for me as there should always be time to reflect and honour the elephant that has just been killed. Such a special and humble moment was lost on the boy, simply because he was far too young to appreciate his actions.

Fernanditto ended up shooting two more buffaloes that we had on license, and one of them caused a second bout of tears from the poor little lad. While rolling the *dagga* boy over to get a few pictures, Fernanditto was on the receiving end of the dreaded buffalo beans that were attached to the animal's hide. The bean hairs had become attached to the *dagga* boy's hide earlier on when it had enjoyed its daily siesta deep in the infected bush.

The irritating hairs got all over Fernanditto, and I cannot blame the lad for crying. Indeed, I have seen grown men close to tears when infected by the dreadful scourge. At the end of the day, his tears were probably worth the effort because he managed to bag three buffaloes, a leopard, and a charging bull elephant as well as a few sandgrouse. Not bad for an eleven-year-old.

Marius and Franco

Marius is a long-standing client of ours. Hunting with him has always been a pleasure. Marius is a South African, a neighbour from the other side of the Limpopo River. South Africans have a lot in common with us, for they appreciate our warped sense of humour much better than folks from other countries.

Marius has shot several buffaloes, a leopard, and an elephant with me. When his son Franco turned sixteen, Marius brought him down to the valley to hunt a buffalo and a tuskless elephant as a birthday present. He wanted an authentic African experience for his son's first-game hunting safari, so he asked me to set up a "fly camp" in a remote part of the valley.

These camps are comfortable but rather basic. They are tented with en suite pull-up showers and long drop toilets. To add to the rudimentary atmosphere of such places, the lower jaw of an elephant is conveniently used as a toilet seat. I love hunting from these simple camps, for they emphasize the very essence of wild Africa where the sounds of the bush at night are brought right into your camp. There is no noisy interference from manmade conveniences such as a generator in these camps.

Marius and his son, Franco, with Franco's first tuskless elephant, Dande.

Indeed, the silence has the same effect upon the animals that wander or seek food in the dark. Hyenas scrap for titbits in the bone yard. The yapping and cackling comes to a head when a leopard interferes with their meal. Attracted to the smell of raw meat, lions prowl around the perimeter, grunting and roaring their presence. An elephant may pluck fruit or pull branches from the huge tree under which you have made camp, so don't be surprised if on hearing a branch snap you look outside the tent to see a goliath hovering. Such is the beauty of Africa at night when fly camping.

In these camps we use solar power, and one of the drawbacks is the low-power light that the panel supplies. One morning soon after our 4 A.M. wake-up call, Franco complained of a painful eye. Scratching through his case in the poor light, Marius found the eye drops and put them into his son's eye. Instantly Franco screamed out that his eye was burning. On closer inspection Marius was horrified to find that instead of eye drops, he had put

Marius's ugly buffalo.

water purifying drops into his son's eye. To be fair to Marius, the purifying drops were in the same sort of bottle as the eye drops.

Unfortunately we had to call an end to the safari and hastily fly Marius and Franco to Harare where Kirsty was waiting. She rushed them both to an eye specialist who thoroughly irrigated Franco's eye. The specialist informed Marius that we had made the correct decision and that any further delay in treatment would have resulted in permanent eye damage. Thankfully, the eye incident happened during the second half of the hunt, and by that time Franco had already shot his tuskless cow. This meant he lost out on the buffalo.

Marius has a wonderful and endearing quality of understating his qualifications and capabilities. He always plays himself down. When he first came to hunt with me, I asked him what he did for a living. He told me he was "a chicken gynecologist"! It turned out that Marius is one of the leading poultry researchers in South Africa. He is also one of the best double-rifle shots I have ever had the pleasure of guiding!

Over the years I have enjoyed watching Marius progress as a hunter. When he first arrived on the scene, he primarily focused on trophy quality, but these days he places more emphasis on the enjoyable aspects and the quality of each hunt. The age of animals being hunted is foremost in his mind nowadays, which in my opinion is the way it should be.

One of our highlight hunts was the bagging of an old *dagga* boy that we basically ran into the ground. We tracked the bull for ten solid hours, and during this time we caught up with him several times. Marius shot him at one hundred and twenty paces using his open-sighted, double-barrel rifle.

The buffalo turned out to be a very old *dagga* boy that was blind in one eye. His horns were narrow and very worn down, and he barely had a hair on his old face. To Marius this was indeed a magnificent trophy. Had we taken the old guy on one of our earlier hunts, Marius would have been absolutely furious.

Our first hunt together was in the Makuti Safari Area. Marius came with the intention to hunt the Big Four—a lion, a leopard, a buffalo, and an elephant—all on the same hunt. Amazingly, we got the leopard on the

Marius and his "first-morning" leopard.

The great beast came at us like a steam train, and Marius shot him at fifty yards, Makuti.

first day, right in front of the camp! He was a magnificent animal and a thief. We knew he was coming into the skinning shed to steal bits of meat at night, so we left the remains of a bushbuck about a hundred metres from camp the day before Marius arrived.

Sure enough, the next morning we found the leopard had fed on the bait. We built the blind and first thing the following morning as we walked in to the hide, there he was, feeding on the bait. So Marius shot his leopard within the first five minutes of "shooting light" on the first day of the safari! When we walked back to camp to collect our cameras, our coffee was still warm! How I wish most leopard hunts were that easy!

Marius also shot a great buffalo and a charging elephant bull that we relentlessly tracked for six hours, bumping into him on several occasions in the process. Unlike the dense thicket of the Zambezi Valley, Makuti is largely open country, and we were unable to get close enough for a shot. On the sixth stalking attempt to get within shooting distance, the bull decided he had had enough. The great beast came at us like a steam train from all of a hundred yards away.

Marius waited patiently, and as the beast got close, he dropped him with his .458. The elephant was charging so fast that it cartwheeled head over heels before coming to a stop only several feet away from where we were standing.

Despite seeing and tracking several lions, we so far have failed to get one. I hope for Marius' fiftieth birthday we can remedy that! The only time I was ever annoyed with him was on his first hunt. At that time we were having super inflation in Zimbabwe. Store shelves were empty, it was nearly impossible to get basic supplies, and we were forced to make plans wherever we could. One such plan was to ask the drivers of heavy-duty trucks that passed Makuti, bound for Zambia, to buy us essential supplies and smuggle them back. This service came at a huge cost. It was in this manner that we managed to get Marius his favourite drink, gin and tonic.

In frustration together with a little anger, I had to bite my tongue when he complained there were no lemons for his G&T's! Several years later, without thinking, I told Marius the story about the "idiot client" who had complained about the lack of lemons for his evening drink especially after I had busted my butt and moved mountains to get him everything else. Much to my embarrassment, Marius replied with a laugh, "That idiot client was me, Buzz!"

We have often laughed about that incident.

Marius has been a pleasure to hunt with, and I hope to hunt many more times with him! I have often said to Steph, my wife, that if we can bring up our kids half as well as Marius and Annalees have brought up Franco, then I will be happy.

Duggi and one of her buffalo bulls.

The Lippmanns

When it comes to buffalo hunting, there was no family that enjoyed it more than the Lippmanns. Fritz, his wife, Dagmar, together with son, Felix, and daughter, Mia, came out every year for three-week hunts that included a bag of up to twelve buffalo bulls. They did this for ten consecutive years. One can imagine that their trophy room in Germany was very impressive with well over one hundred European mounts of *dagga* boys, all taken in the Dande.

Fritz shot the majority of the buffaloes, while Dagmar and Felix shot a few. Mia, being young, would shoot a few plains-game animals, and I will never forget taking her on her first hunt when she was very young. Her victim was an Egyptian goose on the Zambezi River. I spotted the goose on the riverbank, and to make things as exciting and memorable as possible, I decided to make a great stalk for the goose.

Carefully getting her into position, she shot the goose with a .22 Hornet and hit it perfectly! The goose started flopping around, accompanied by excited yells from Mia. As she proudly rushed forward to admire her first trophy, her cheers turned to tears when a small crocodile slid out the water, snapped up the goose, and swam away with it.

I thought the Lippmanns were the perfect family, close-knit and very happy. I was fortunate to spend six weeks with them in the beautiful little town of Michelstadt in Germany where Fritz owned a brewery. They made

Fritz and Mia with a buffalo bull.

Felix with his first buffalo bull.

a wonderful beer called Schmucker. This was to my detriment as the town had six pubs, all of which Fritz supplied with his beer. He told the pub owners that should I ever come in, I was to have as many free beers as I could drink. Six weeks of free beer complemented with awesome German sausages saw my weight increase by six kilos.

I became very close to the Lippmann family, so one can understand my surprise when Fritz arrived one year accompanied by a strange lady and no Felix and Mia. At an opportune time I asked Fritz what happened to his lovely wife. He simply said he was now divorced. He told me that he had lost half of what he owned, so now he could only afford to shoot six buffaloes that year!

I have to admit I was saddened that my "perfect family" was no more. It just goes to show that one never knows what goes on behind closed doors.

TRIBUTE TO MY TRACKERS

CHAPTER THIRTY-THREE

It's been my privilege to have been able to hunt throughout the vast expanses of the Zambezi Valley. The Selous Game Reserve in Tanzania is reputed to be the largest game park in the world, but this is not technically correct. If the hunting areas and national parks located along both sides of the Zambezi River are combined, then the Selous Game Reserve is most definitely smaller. In the Zambezi Valley there are no major roads, fences, or borders to restrict the movement of game.

The Zambezi Valley has been my playing field over the years, and its vast expanses are a far cry from the small, fenced-hunting operations of South Africa with their immaculately graded roads and five-star camps. So vast is the Zambezi Valley that it would be impossible to attain great trophies in this huge wildness without the assistance of expert trackers. "A professional hunter is only as good as his trackers," is a well-known saying and one in which I firmly believe.

I have been fortunate when it comes to trackers. Over the years, most of my trackers have proved skillful and efficient, some occasionally were flops, and then there were the rare ones who few could match. This essay is dedicated to these peerless few.

Crispen and Morgan, my faithful duo, hunted with me for the first twelve years of my career. Then there are Criton and Nyati, with whom I am hunting today. These fine and loyal men have been an intricate part of my hunting career, and, without a doubt, most of my professional hunting successes can be attributed to their uncanny ability to follow an animal through difficult terrain under extreme conditions. Their determination, humour, and ability in the bush made my job easier; it is a marvel to watch them work.

I have forgotten how many times my clients have inquired if we were still on the tracks when it appeared, in every practical sense, that the animal

Crispen was an exceptional tracker who loved a practical joke.

had disappeared. More often than not, my trackers would find the animal, and the situation would be saved. These men are not only experts in tracking, they are also brave.

They are on the front line of any charge, be it a lion, elephant, leopard, or buffalo, and the one undeniable truth in such a situation is that all these great game animals are intent on causing bodily harm. Both Criton and Morgan have sustained a number of wounds that can attest to this. Their faith and absolute trust in me and in my shooting ability is astonishing, but I must admit there have been times when I had to question that trust, as the next story shows!

Crispen

In the year 2000 I was hunting in Chewore North with an American by the name of Mike McKinney. Mike, who hailed from Dallas, was after a buffalo and a leopard. On the second day of the hunt we followed tracks of a lone *dagga* boy for roughly two hours over relatively easy ground. Mike had requested I back him up after his initial shot. We eventually caught up to the old bull in open mopane country where I was able to get a good look at him. The old fellow was certainly worth taking.

Mike immediately got onto the tripod and took a shot at the bull the moment it turned broadside-on, the shooting distance about sixty yards. Immediately after his shot, I backed Mike up as requested with a 400-grain bullet through the bull's shoulders. Unfortunately my shot placement was

Crispen lectured me whenever I did something wrong!

poor and the bullet hit the bull in the guts. Mike's shot was also off target, his bullet hitting the bull a shade too high through the muscles of its shoulder hump, most definitely a nonfatal shot. A tracking marathon ensued.

Our dismal efforts did, however, produce a decent blood trail that made tracking fairly easy for the first three hours of the follow-up, and although we made rapid progress on the spoor, we did not catch up to the wounded bull. This was cause for concern. Another worry was that the bull had been wounded not far from the Chewore River, which provides a common boundary with the Sapi Safari Area, and, it looked as though this was where the bull was heading. Numerous buffalo herds water at the Chewore River every evening, and if our bull made it to the river, there was a good chance we would lose his trail among all the other tracks.

At this stage, the blood spoor was beginning to dry, and two hours later there was no sign at all. All we had to go on now were his tracks, and, unfortunately, he had entered an area that was popular with other lone *dagga* boys. His spoor was now mingling with theirs, making our tracking efforts considerably more difficult. I knew our situation would become worse if our bull joined up with, or if his spoor had crossed, other buffaloes near Chewore River. Should this happen, it would be nigh impossible to sort out the tracks in the sandy riverbed.

Relentlessly, we followed the bull we had nicknamed "Big Foot." Our pursuit was aided by the fact that the buffalo had extremely large front hoofs, and this greatly assisted my trackers in identifying his spoor from all the other old *dagga* boys that lived in the area. By late evening his tracks were heading directly toward the Chewore River. We were now a great distance from the Land Cruiser, so we decided to call it quits. Our only option was to take up the spoor again the following morning.

Walking back to a vehicle in pitch dark is not a pleasant experience, what with all the animals of the night now up and about, including small breeding herds of elephants of which there were a great number. All this took place before the days of satellite tracking systems, so to make sure we would be able to find the spot where we had left off tracking the bull, we dragged a stick along the ground all the way back to the vehicle. This enabled us to find the exact spot first thing the following morning.

Mike McKinney with his old dagga *boy we tracked for four days.*

I endured a troubled night, worrying that the old bull might cross the river and go into Sapi or, worse still, join up with a big herd of buffaloes. At the crack of dawn the next morning, we set off, and over the next few days, Crispen and Morgan accomplished the impossible.

On that first day, we arrived a little after sunup at the same place we had abandoned the spoor the previous evening. We had only been on tracks for about ten minutes when, much to our surprise, we caught up with the wounded bull. He was hidden in a thick patch of *jesse* bush, but before we could see him, let alone get off a shot, we heard him crashing through the bushes not far from where we were standing.

We then proceeded to track that old bull the whole day, from sunup to sundown, his tracks leading us in a huge figure eight. Thankfully, the bull kept turning back on his path whenever he came to the Chewore River. I assumed he was reluctant to cross the open, sandy riverbed, knowing that we were close behind. At sundown, having followed him without a break for over ten hours, we again were forced to tramp wearily back to the Land Cruiser, once more dragging a stick to mark our return path the next morning.

For four solid days this became our modus operandi. Like a pointer following a winged francolin, we followed the old *dagga* boy's tracks that sometimes mingled with the spoor of big buffalo herds and other times with those of old *dagga* boys. We followed him over hills and through valleys, across small, dry, sandy riverbeds, and never once did we lose his tracks. It was a remarkable feat of tracking. Even so, by the evening of day four, there was a genuine element of doubt as to whether we would ever get close enough to get in a shot at the bull.

In the end, persistence paid off. We had just come around a small hill when we were suddenly confronted with the old fellow. Despite being almost dead on his feet, the valiant, old bull made a last stand. It was obvious he knew he could go no farther. He dropped to a couple of well-placed shots, and Mike finally got his old *dagga* boy. This was thanks to Crispen and Morgan's fantastic tracking skills and sheer determination never to give up.

******

Crispen was a remarkable tracker, but he was also a womanizer and a practical joker. Like most good trackers, he certainly wasn't a saint and had his faults, women being one of them. He just couldn't help himself when it came to the fairer sex, and, be they sixteen or sixty, he would attempt to smooth talk them into his bed.

How this man managed to cheat the dreaded AIDS virus is a miracle. When I warned him of the dangers of the dreaded disease, he explained that being the ripe old age of eighty, should he get *chiwere*, as AIDS is known locally, it would take him a good ten years to die, and by then he would rather be dead anyway!

Crispen had two wives, the youngest in her twenties, which is the reason, he told me, that he was still so young and fit! He had numerous children and outlived a number of them.

Crispen's hunting career started at a very young age when he accompanied his father into the bush on hunting-and-gathering missions. This was in the Chewore area before it was turned into a hunting zone under the Parks & Wildlife Management Authority. When this occurred, Crispen and the rest of his family were moved to the Dande area where they have remained ever since.

Crispen was of the Vadoma tribe, a shy and harmless people who live in harmony with nature and unlike poachers, only kill enough animals to feed themselves and their families. Some might describe the Vadomas as backward; in reality, they are bush people who live a very simple life, shunning any form of civilization. Even in this modern day, it is amazing that there are still a number of Vadomas who wander the Zambezi Valley, living off wild fruits, honey, and whatever game they can trap. As a result, their bushcraft skills are second to none.

The Vadoma are known as the "two-toed tribe," the moniker a result of a genetic defect. Some Vadomas are born with feet that resemble those of

Mbarane, the two-toed Vadoma.

an ostrich, with a huge big toe and only a single small one. As a Vadoma seldomly marries outside his own tribe, I am sure the defect is due to inbreeding. Luckily, Crispen was not born with this problem.

By the end of his life, Crispen no longer roamed the valley like the rest of his clan. He had a permanent home in the northern part of Dande where he was regarded as an accomplished herbalist, who specialized in *"vuka-vuka,"* the bush equivalent of Viagra. The direct translation of the Shona term *vuka-vuka* is "get up, get up," and from a male's perspective, this is self-explanatory. Such is Crispen's reputation in this field that he would get visits from patients seeking his help from as far afield as Tete in Mozambique.

On one of my trips to Harare, Crispen persuaded me to try some of his latest, strongest, and most-improved *vuka-vuka*. He instructed me to put the concoction in my beer while I was en route to Harare. He assured me that on arrival, my latest girlfriend was sure to be impressed. I duly downed the concoction, and two hours later a reaction set in, and for three miserable days and nights I had painful diarrhea! That was the last time I tried Crispen's *vuka-vuka* muti (medicine).

If there was a weakness to Crispen's tracking ability, I would have to say that it was on account of his passion for finding traditional medicines. Even though we happened to be hot on the tracks of a wounded animal, Crispen would suddenly stop, abandon the spoor, and quickly dig up a root or pluck the leaves off some bush. Hardly ever did we arrive back at the hunting vehicle after a tracking session without the back pocket of Crispen's overalls overflowing with a variety of leaves, roots, and bits of tree bark.

At the age of about twenty, Crispen joined the Tsetse Control Division in what was then Rhodesia. The department was responsible for eradicating the dreaded tsetse fly, which transmits the disease known as *ngana* to all domestic animals. Research at the time revealed that tsetse flies do not move great distances and cannot survive for longer than twenty-four hours without feeding on a host. With this in mind, the department created corridors between wildlife and the country's cattle ranching and farming areas. These corridors were to be two miles wide, and every living animal within the corridor was to be killed. Crispen began his career as a tracker to

Crispen.

the various hunters the department employed to kill off all the dangerous-game species within these corridors.

After demonstrating his competency in the bush and his ability to handle a rifle, Crispen was allocated an old .303 Lee Enfield rifle and a bag of ammunition. He had become a *magocha*, the local name for a "fryer of meat." Crispen's new job entailed shooting the remainder of the nondangerous game animals within the corridors. For this he did not receive a salary; instead, as an incentive, he was allowed to keep or sell all the meat he obtained from his hunting forays. In this way Crispen gained invaluable hunting experience. Having to make important decisions by himself over and above the perimeters of tracking was certainly a great help to me throughout my hunting career.

Even in areas that were declared "dangerous-game free" and in which the *magochas* were operating, there was often the odd elephant or buffalo that had managed to evade the hunters of dangerous game. Within these corridors was also the occasional elephant that had broken through the fence from the nearby Zambezi Valley. During one of his hunting expeditions in a corridor that ran parallel to the valley, Crispen wounded a kudu, which he followed into a patch of thick bush.

Pushing his way through the thicket with his eyes glued to the ground while following the kudu's spoor, Crispen walked straight into a lone cow elephant. Now this cow was not in a good mood. Hearing her scream of rage from a few metres away, Crispen turned and hightailed it out of the bush. Right on his heels was the irate elephant hell-bent on ending his career, which, in fact, she very nearly accomplished.

As Crispen fled for his life, the tip of the cow's outstretched trunk managed to grab the collar of his old and tatty T-shirt, which she ripped right off his body. Shirtless and in panic, Crispen continued running as fast as his legs would carry him, and never once did he look back over his shoulder, lest the cow was still in pursuit, until at last he arrived safely back at his camp.

As a consequence, it should come as no surprise that Crispen developed a healthy respect for elephant cows. He would happily track them, but as soon as they were found, he would hastily position himself at the back of the line so as to give himself a head start should the situation take a turn for the worse and a rapid withdrawal be necessary.

Once the tsetse-corridor programme came to an end, Crispen returned to his village in Dande where he started tracking for Zambezi Hunters, which at the time was one of the first registered hunting operators in Zimbabwe. I served my apprenticeship with Zambezi Hunters, and when I went out on my own, I asked Crispen to track for me. I hired him in 1997 and hunted with him until 2005. I am deeply indebted to him not only for his incredible knowledge of tracking but also for his understanding of bushcraft that, I am happy to say, he proudly took the time to teach a young white city boy.

Crispen's greatest asset was his marvelous sense of humour. Despite being over eighty, he was the first to appreciate a practical joke, and in many instances it was I who bore the brunt of his humour, jokes initiated by the old devil himself! Nothing tickled Crispen's sense of humour more than his success in tripping up the "bwana" with one of his carefully laid schemes. When they worked, his wrinkled old face would light up and tears of delight would run down his old cheeks.

Eventually after nearly ten years of hunting together, Crispen's sight deteriorated so badly that, despite the body being willing, he simply could not see well enough to track. Crispen had severe cataracts, yet when I told him all it required was a simple operation in which the eye surgeon would remove the milky lenses and replace them with new ones, he took one look at me and said that there was no way he would allow anyone to touch his eyes. Considering the only medical consultations Crispen had ever known were from the local "medicine men" in the middle of the bush, I can only imagine he had an image of someone using a rusty old knife to attack his eyes! Little wonder he refused.

Sadly, truth be told, with his poor eyesight, he became a liability in the bush. In the end it was a very sad day when I had no option but to retire the old fellow. Crispen died two years ago. He must have been close to ninety years old at the time.

Morgan

Morgan was also an incredible tracker, but he lacked Crispen's sense of humour. Crispen's strength lay in his amazing aerial tracking skills, which

Morgan poses in his favourite hat from Michigan.

can be defined as any sign that is above ground like broken leaves and bent grass, while Morgan was phenomenal on spoor. In this way both trackers complemented each other and made an unbeatable team. To put it bluntly, Morgan was a "no bulls--- tracker."

Whenever we were on the tracks of an animal, Morgan would roll his homegrown tobacco into pieces of old newspaper, light the foul-smelling cigarette, put his head down, and doggedly track the animal until I could stand the smell no longer, and told him, "Enough." He was possessed with a grim determination and a remarkable stamina, but unlike Crispen, he preferred to be out of the limelight.

Morgan is now about fifty years old. He has two wives, one of whom is Crispen's daughter. He has fathered seven children, all of them boys! In Shona culture, to father a son is something to be very proud of. To accomplish this feat seven times out of seven has elevated Morgan to an almost godlike status in the Kanyemba area!

Morgan lives about an hour's walk from where Crispen used to live. He, too, was forced to relocate from the Chewore area as a child. Unfortu-

Morgan and I next to a buff we hunted in my younger years.

nately, Morgan's father was bitten and killed by a black mamba while he was clearing a field in preparations for the maize planting season, and being the eldest son, it became Morgan's responsibility to take care of the family.

Before he joined me as a tracker in 1996, Morgan was a known poacher in the area. He killed many buffaloes by running the herd down and spearing any young or old animal lagging behind. After hurling his spear at the unfortunate beast, he would wait an hour or so before following it up. If he found lung blood, he would continue on the tracks until he found the dead animal. If, however, he found stomach or gut content, he would abandon the tracks, go home, make another spear, and repeat the performance the following day. His bushcraft was second to none.

Morgan was on a hunting safari with me one year when he received news that his brother had been mauled by a lion. Evidently the brother had attempted to chase the lion off its kill in order to steal the meat and was mauled for his efforts. As if this was not enough, the same hapless brother was later killed by an elephant when he tried to chase it out of his field one night.

Unfortunately, Morgan turned to drink and became unreliable. He let me down on numerous occasions, once disappearing in the middle of a safari because he had heard of a beer drink close-by. Even so, I am pleased to say that Morgan still plays a part with our company as he now tracks for my partner Myles.

Criton

While Crispen, Morgan, and I would follow the first elephant track we found, I had Royal, my driver, and Criton continue looking for other tracks. If the result was positive, Criton, armed only with a radio, would follow the elephant's tracks. He was so good at tracking that he never once failed to find the elephant he was following. As a result, when I retired Crispen, Criton stepped into the vacant spot and capably took over. Having now hunted with Criton for fourteen years, I can honestly say that not only is he as good as Crispen, but he also might even be better.

Criton hails from a family of trackers. His grandfather was a real old character by the name of Danger who tracked for my first boss, Ian Piercy. Danger's son was Bashop, who was Criton's father. Bashop hunted with me for a while before joining Allan, another professional hunter who hunts for our company. He hunted with Allan for many years but finally ended up tracking for Ivan Carter. This was a family that produced excellent trackers, but unfortunately, they all possessed, to a greater or lesser extent, an unpleasant trait, namely the "sulks."

Whenever Bashop got the sulks, he would not talk or engage with anyone for sometimes a week at a time. It got to the point that at lunchtime when the trackers communally cook their traditional maize meal porridge called *sadza*, Bashop would sulk off and cook by himself. In the end it got so bad that Allan ended up firing him because his behaviour not only left bad vibes with the team but was also noticed by the clients as well.

Criton does not have this trait quite as badly as his father. On average he gets the sulks about once a year, and when he does, I feel like putting a solid-nose, 500-grain bullet in the back of his skull. I'm thankful that such occasions are rare and they do pass quickly, so I put up with them because he is arguably the best tracker in Zimbabwe today.

Criton.

Apart from the odd-sulking attack, Criton is an amazing worker who willingly takes on any task with zest and enthusiasm. He is a natural-born tracker and hunter at heart, and many professional hunters who have borrowed him over the years will confirm he is a "game changer." Skillfully tracking a lion or an elephant through the roughest, most difficult terrain can make the difference between a successful hunt or a failure! When assisted by Nyati, my additional tracker, these two are an unstoppable force, boosted by an adept ability to read each other's mind. Given time and a bit of space to perform together, both trackers invariably end up with a positive result.

Criton has matured tremendously over the past fifteen years. He was a boy when he started with me all those years ago, and it has been a rewarding experience to watch him mature and fine-tune his skills. Criton is now in his prime, and I hope to share many more tracking sessions with him. In my opinion a successful hunt is in the tracking and catching up of the animal, rather than the shooting, and it is in this role that Criton is the master!

Over the years we have shared many close calls. His uncanny ability to read an animal's behaviour combined with his athletic ability has so far kept him a whisker away from death from claw, horn, and tusk. Like many other facets in life, big-game hunting is a "numbers game," a dangerous activity that will surely end when one's luck runs out. This is what happened to Criton in the Save when he got his pelvis squashed by an elephant bull. (I related this story in chapter 13.) That only three months later Criton was standing without flinching in front of another charging elephant sums up his character!

There is a saying that everything has a "silver lining." Criton also found silver lining in having his pelvis crushed by an elephant bull, and in his case it was to be a major change in his life. Once he had recovered from the ordeal, he subsequently managed to get both his wives pregnant within two weeks—something he had been unable to accomplish in the previous five years!

Criton with a nice elephant bull.

Nyati (left) and crew with the buffalo that gored Allan.

Nyati, "the Professor"

Nyati came into my employment thanks to Allan. One of his clients had wounded a buffalo, with the result that the buffalo's horn ended up in Allan's backside. He was lucky to survive the incident, and he spent three months in the hospital recovering. The old *dagga* boy had one worn-down horn and the other had a fine, sharp tip. Luckily for Allan, it was the worn-down horn that found its way between Allan's legs.

Still, this horn did a nasty job of opening up Allan's exhaust pipe. Had it been the longer, sharper horn, it more than likely would have killed him! The buffalo attack left Allan's rear-end black and blue, about which Rosie, Allan's wonderful and witty wife commented, "I never thought I'd ever sleep with a man with a black willy!" Only Rosie could get away with a comment like that.

After recovering from the incident, Allan decided to hang up his hunting boots and go mining. He asked me if I could look after Nyati. At the time I was hunting with Criton and Morgan, but Morgan was by that time drinking excessively and had become unreliable. Myles, who was not hunting as much as I, took on Morgan, and I hired Nyati. I'm fortunate that I did.

At the time I had no idea what an asset I was inheriting from Allan. Nyati is a fine gentleman! He is always polite, kind, and charming! Initially, he was a schoolteacher, earning a grand total of U.S. $100 per month. On this miserly salary, he could barely make ends meet, so he found a job on a game farm as a game guard. This was where Nyati, whose real name is Nkulanjani, got his nickname. Evidently the game-farm owner could never pronounce the name Nkulanjani, so in true colonial style, he renamed his game guard "Nyati." Allan, who hunted on the game farm, met Nyati and, realizing his potential, offered him a job. This lasted for several years until the buffalo incident.

Nyati's nickname, "the professor" is well founded. Not only had he been a schoolteacher, but he also absorbed every bit of information that he gleaned from Allan who, in his own right, is an accomplished "bush person." As a result, Nyati can name every tree in the country and tell you the English, Latin, Shona, and Ndebele names for them as well!

Nyati is not only intelligent; he also has a strong moral compass. In other words and as the following story illustrates, he has character. Our client at the time was a well-to-do oilman named Dave. Initially, Dave hunted with Allan, and because it turned out to be a pressure hunt, I let Nyati go with Allan, who had returned to hunting after realizing that mining was not for him.

They had a great hunt. Dave's son James bagged a fine leopard and an elephant while Dave himself shot an elephant, a buffalo, and a few extras. Dave said that he wanted to return the following year for a big jumbo, so he booked a Kazuma hunt with me. Kazuma is a forestry area bordering Botswana where the elephant hunting is as good as any area available today. He subsequently shot a great fifty-five-pound tusker, and after the hunt he said he really liked Nyati and wanted to do something special over and above the amazing tips that he gave everyone.

I spoke to Nyati on the side about this, and he said he would sleep on the suggestion and let me know what he would like in the morning. Had

Nyati, "the professor."

such an offer been made to Criton, there's no doubt in my mind that he'd have asked for something that would have benefitted himself directly, like a car or motorbike. I expected a little more from Nyati and was not disappointed. The following morning he told me his six-year-old son was gifted (something every father thinks of his son!) and that he would like Shelton, the boy's name, to go to a better school as the school he was attending was not challenging enough.

I then spoke to Dave and passed on Nyati's wish. I also pointed out that if Dave did decide to pay for Shelton's schooling, he should realize that it could not only be for the junior school but he would have to pay senior school fees as well. I told Dave that it would not be fair to Shelton to give him a good junior education and then set him back by sending him to a poor secondary school, which would be all that Nyati could afford.

Dave is one of the most generous men I have met, and to his credit he insisted on financing Shelton's entire education. So we organized for the lad to attend a good school in Karoi, the town where Nyati lives. Rydings School is a multiracial school where the teaching is of a very high quality. Right from his first term at Rydings, Shelton has come first in class in every subject, and I firmly believe the little guy is going to do something very special with his life. In fact, I often joke with Nyati that Shelton will be president of Zimbabwe one day.

Eddy

A hunting team is never complete without a driver, and it is Eddy who fills this spot. Eddy is small in stature but huge in character! He is the glue that holds us all together. I have never seen Eddy in a bad mood. When things get tough and tempers become strained, he is always there to lighten the mood and help keep us focused.

Eddy, "the joker."

Eddy's strength belies his size.

No one has a larger, more natural smile than Eddy, and his job is essential. He keeps my Land Cruiser in tiptop condition; he is also in charge of the radio. This means regularly collecting us after long tracking sorties, thus saving us from trudging many miles back to the vehicle. He is never idle, and while we are out tracking, he drives around searching for additional tracks in case we should need a plan B.

Eddy is an entrepreneur par excellence. He owns a successful grocery store in Kanyemba, the little town on the Zambezi in Dande, and trades in Mozambique and Zambia. He also owns the "Two Sisters Hair Salon," which his capable wife runs. As if these were not enough, Eddy also has a bootleg liquor operation and does very well in this endeavour! Eddy bought two canoes that he uses, under cover of darkness, to ferry his contraband across the Zambezi into Zambia en route to the Congo.

Eddy is, regrettably, on the receiving end of many practical jokes. This is partly his own fault because he never bears a grudge. Often these pranks revolve around snakes. So great is his fear of snakes that he is even terrorized by the harmless ones, so, of course, this leaves him open to shenanigans by the others in the crew.

We once caught a small python, which Justin and Blake concealed in front of themselves just as Eddy arrived on the scene. The two were standing shoulder to shoulder bent over while pretending to look at some object on the ground. Eddy, who secretly wishes to be a tracker, asked about the spoor they were looking at. As he went up to investigate, Justin and Blake stood up and tossed the python at him. Screaming like a terrified teenager, Eddy took off, and in his haste to escape, tripped over an exposed root, fell flat on his face, and in the process wet his pants.

Eddy is the only person I know who can claim to have run himself over. On that occasion we were tracking a hyena, and time was not on our side. So I asked Eddy to take the old company Land Cruiser to retrieve a smelly lion bait that was no longer needed and bring it to a designated spot so that we could build a blind. The site chosen was at the dead end of a road and at the bottom of a steep hill. While building the blind, we heard Eddy arriving.

My own Land Cruiser was at the bottom of the hill, and as Eddy approached, he realized the handbrake on his vehicle wasn't working. So,

Eddy's trademark smile.

still on the slope looking down, he stopped the vehicle, left it in gear, and got out to place a rock under the front wheel to prevent it from rolling forward. As he did so, the old Land Cruiser jumped out of gear and began to roll forward . . . straight toward my brand-new vehicle.

Eddy panicked and tried to stop the old vehicle by putting his one-hundred-and-thirty-pound body in front of it. Of course, the Land Cruiser knocked him down and proceeded to run him over, breaking a few ribs in the process, before coming to a stop only inches from my new vehicle. Eddy's ankle was the reason the vehicle stopped. The old Cruiser's back wheel had landed bang on top of Eddy's ankle. Ouch! In spite of two broken ribs and a broken ankle, Eddy still had a smile on his face as we dragged him out from under the vehicle and rushed him to the hospital.

Regardless of his earning a good living with the other enterprises, Eddy absolutely loves his job and loves being part of the team. I am sure he, as well as Nyati and Criton, will be with me until the day I decide to hang up my rifle! Our motto, the one that has long held us in good stead is simply this: "Hunt hard, have lots of fun, and let the hunting Gods decide our fate!"

CONCLUSION

CHAPTER THIRTY-FOUR

In 1967 my father gave up professional hunting in Kenya because he felt the end was in sight for traditional big-game hunting as he knew it in that part of Africa. He was correct in his assumption. In 1977 Kenya made the disastrous decision to ban all forms of consumptive wildlife utilization. This resulted in not only the decimation of much of its wildlife, but worse still it destroyed vast tracks of land. Once a rich countryside that supported a prolific wildlife population, now the land is barren and overgrazed. Turned into communal lands, the Kenyan countryside has deteriorated to the point that it will be unable to support any form of wildlife in the future, even if indigenous animals are reintroduced.

Dad in traditional East African camp, Kenya, 1965.

Dad with a big elephant, Kenya, 1965.

Here I am with an elephant from the Dande in 2014.

This was a bull I took in Kazuma in 2016.

Elephant bulls eating albida pods.

Fortunately, countries like Zimbabwe realized the importance of hunting and the value it brought, not only to the future of wildlife, but also to the people who live in these fragile ecosystems. It is in wild and beautiful concessions like the Dande Safari Area in the Zambezi Valley, which is demarcated as a hunting area, that some sixty years later I am still able to guide clients and friends on new adventures.

Hunting has been the common ground for forging many wonderful friendships between me and my clients and between me and other professionals in the hunting industry. I would never have met any of these delightful people had it not been for hunting. Surely my life would have been the much poorer for it. Hunting has given me an identity I love and thrive in. The past twenty-five years in the field has been a wonderful adventure. I can only hope that Zimbabwe, its national parks, and its private initiatives like DAPU, our antipoaching team, will continue the good work to preserve and protect our national heritage so that our rich resources can be enjoyed for future generations.

SAFARI PRESS